BICENTENNIAL
1807
⊕ **WILEY**
2007
BICENTENNIAL

THE WILEY BICENTENNIAL—KNOWLEDGE FOR GENERATIONS

*E*ach generation has its unique needs and aspirations. When Charles Wiley first opened his small printing shop in lower Manhattan in 1807, it was a generation of boundless potential searching for an identity. And we were there, helping to define a new American literary tradition. Over half a century later, in the midst of the Second Industrial Revolution, it was a generation focused on building the future. Once again, we were there, supplying the critical scientific, technical, and engineering knowledge that helped frame the world. Throughout the 20th Century, and into the new millennium, nations began to reach out beyond their own borders and a new international community was born. Wiley was there, expanding its operations around the world to enable a global exchange of ideas, opinions, and know-how.

For 200 years, Wiley has been an integral part of each generation's journey, enabling the flow of information and understanding necessary to meet their needs and fulfill their aspirations. Today, bold new technologies are changing the way we live and learn. Wiley will be there, providing you the must-have knowledge you need to imagine new worlds, new possibilities, and new opportunities.

Generations come and go, but you can always count on Wiley to provide you the knowledge you need, when and where you need it!

WILLIAM J. PESCE
PRESIDENT AND CHIEF EXECUTIVE OFFICER

PETER BOOTH WILEY
CHAIRMAN OF THE BOARD

Supervision

Bob Nelson, Peter Economy, Kerry L. Sommerville,
Sullivan University

with Laura Town

Credits

PUBLISHER
Anne Smith

PROJECT EDITOR
Beth Tripmacher

MARKETING MANAGER
Jennifer Slomack

SENIOR EDITORIAL ASSISTANT
Tiara Kelly

PRODUCTION MANAGER
Kelly Tavares

PRODUCTION ASSISTANT
Courtney Leshko

PROJECT MANAGER
Tenea Johnson

CREATIVE DIRECTOR
Harry Nolan

COVER DESIGNER
Hope Miller

COVER PHOTO
Romilly Lockyea/The Image Bank/Getty Images

Wiley 200th Anniversary Logo designed by: Richard J. Pacifico

This book was set in Times New Roman by Techbooks, printed and bound by R.R. Donnelley. The cover was printed by R.R. Donnelley.

This book is printed on acid free paper. ∞

To order books or for customer service please, call 1-800-CALL WILEY (225-5945).

ISBN-13 978-0-470-11127-7

Printed in the United States of America

10 9 8 7 6 5 4 3 2 1

PREFACE

College classrooms bring together learners from many backgrounds with a variety of aspirations. Although the students are in the same course, they are not necessarily on the same path. This diversity, coupled with the reality that these learners often have jobs, families, and other commitments, requires a flexibility that our nation's higher education system is addressing. Distance learning, shorter course terms, chunked curriculum, new disciplines, evening courses, and certification programs are some of the approaches that colleges employ to reach as many students as possible and help them clarify and achieve their goals.

Wiley Pathways books, a new line of texts from John Wiley & Sons, Inc., are designed to help you address this diversity and the need for flexibility. These books focus on the fundamentals, identify core competencies and skills, and promote independent learning. The focus on the fundamentals helps students grasp the subject, bringing them all to the same basic understanding. These books use clear, everyday language, presented in an uncluttered format, making the content more accessible and the reading experience more pleasurable. The core competencies and practical skills focus help students succeed in the classroom and beyond, whether in another course or in a professional setting. A variety of built-in learning resources promote independent learning and help instructors and students gauge students' understanding of the content. These resources enable students to think critically about their new knowledge, and apply their skills in any situation.

Our goal with *Wiley Pathways* books—with its brief, inviting format, clear language, and core competencies and skills focus—is to celebrate the many students in your courses, respect their needs, and help you guide them on their way.

Wiley Pathways Pedagogy

To meet the needs of working college students, all *Wiley Pathways* texts explicitly use an outcomes and assessment-based pedagogy for the books: students will review what they have learned, acquire new information and skills, and apply their new knowledge and skills to real-life situations. Based on the recently updated categories of Bloom's Taxonomy of Learning, *Wiley Pathways Supervision* presents key topics in supervision (the content) in easy-to-follow chapters. The text then prompts analysis, synthesis, and evaluation with a variety of learning aids and assessment tools. Students move efficiently from reviewing what they have learned, to acquiring new information and skills, to applying their new knowledge and skills to real-life scenarios:

With *Wiley Pathways,* students not only achieve academic mastery of Supervision *topics,* but they master real-world *skills* related to that content. The books help students become independent learners, giving them a distinct advantage in the field, whether they are starting out or seek to advance in their careers.

Organization, Depth and Breadth of the Text

▲ **Modular format.** Research on college students shows that they access information from textbooks in a non-linear way. Instructors also often wish to reorder textbook content to suit the needs of a particular class. Therefore, although *Wiley Pathways Supervision* proceeds logically from the basics to increasingly more challenging material, chapters are further organized into sections that are self-contained for maximum teaching and learning flexibility.

▲ **Numeric system of headings.** *Wiley Pathways Supervision* uses a numeric system for headings (for example, 2.3.4 identifies the fourth sub-section of section 3 of chapter 2). With this system, students and teachers can quickly and easily pinpoint topics in the table of contents and the text, keeping class time and study sessions focused.

▲ **Core content.** Topics in the text are organized into sixteen chapters.

Chapter 1, Supervision, examines the basics of the supervisory role, including the different styles of management, the challenges of management, and new functions that managers must carry out in today's workplace. An overview of the various laws that supervisors should be aware of, including those related to discrimination, harassment, and equal pay, is also provided.

Chapter 2, Leadership, explores the differences between management and leadership. Students learn what leaders do and what traits are characteristic of effective leaders, as well as steps that can be taken to create an environment of collaborative leadership.

Chapter 3, Goal Setting, takes a look at the similarities and differences between supervisory goals and supervisory vision. Steps for identifying goals using the SMART system are also discussed. In addition, students learn methods for communicating goals, juggling priorities, and helping see their goals to fruition.

Chapter 4, Effective Communication, introduces readers to the various methods of communication employed in the workplace, both formal and informal. Students discover situations in which written communication is preferable to verbal communication, and vice versa, as well as to how to overcome common obstacles to getting their message across. Finally, the value of listening is examined.

Chapter 5, Employee Discipline, tackles the often difficult task of reprimanding staff members. The importance of focusing on an employee's actions rather than his or her personality is emphasized, and students learn the difference between dealing with misconduct and dealing with poor employee performance. The chapter then examines the five steps in an effective disciplinary program, as well as how to make and implement plans for employee improvement.

Chapter 6, Building a Team, explores best practices for locating and hiring new employees. Students learn how to create accurate job descriptions, recruit suitable candidates, review résumés and applications, and conduct effective and legal interviews. The value of further candidate evaluation and making objective hiring decisions is also discussed.

Chapter 7, Training a Team, focuses on the steps that a supervisor should take once he or she has located and hired the right person for the job. Concepts covered in this chapter include how to set up and support teams, how to empower employees, and how to conduct effective meetings. Students also learn methods and guidelines for coaching the individuals that they supervise.

Chapter 8, Inspiring Employees to Better Performance, continues some of the concepts introduced in Chapter 7 by illustrating the importance of employee development. Steps for creating career development plans and helping staff members put these plans into action are examined. The concept of mentoring is explored in depth, as is the importance of determining what employees want from their jobs and helping them achieve these ends.

Chapter 9, Evaluating the Team Members, illustrates the importance of measuring employee performance. Students learn how to develop a performance appraisal system, chart staff members' progress toward their performance goals, and deliver an employee evaluation. The chapter concludes with a review of some of the common mistakes that supervisors make during the appraisal process.

Chapter 10, Leading Change, looks at steps supervisors can take to maintain control in crises and other situations characterized by change. The four stages of change, the ways in which change affects all individuals in an organization, and the importance of encouraging employee initiative in the face of change are examined. Finally, the chapter introduces students to some recommended actions for dealing with the difficulties associated with mergers and layoffs.

Chapter 11, Managing Diversity, investigates the increasingly important topic of workplace diversity. Students explore common differences in national cultures as well as various diversity trends in the American workplace. Students also learn ten steps for maximizing the advantages that differences among staff members can provide.

Chapter 12, Ethics and Office Politics, begins by defining the concept of ethics and illustrating the importance of codes of ethics in the work environment. Steps for evaluating one's political environment, uncovering written workplace rules, scrutinizing organizational communication, and protecting oneself from unscrupulous coworkers are also introduced.

Chapter 13, Working with Unions, explores supervisors' responsibilities in relation to organized labor. Students learn about the laws that govern unions, including the National Labor Relations Act and the Taft-Hartley Act. Various actions that supervisors can take to work both legally and effectively with unionized employees round out the chapter.

Chapter 14, Budgeting and Accounting, illustrates the different types of budgets supervisors must deal with, as well as steps for creating and working with such budgets. Students are also provided the opportunity to practice some of the basics of accounting and interpreting financial statements, including balance sheets, income statements, and cash-flow statements.

Chapter 15, Using Technology, teaches students how to harness the power of workplace technology to their advantage. The benefits and potential detriments of technology are explored, as are steps for improving employee productivity and efficiency through the use of technology. In addition, the increasing prevalence of "virtual" employees is examined, and students learn how to best supervise these employees who may not be part of a traditional bricks-and-mortar work environment.

Finally, Chapter 16, Common Management Trends and Management Mistakes, introduces some of latest developments in the field of supervision, including the use of learning organizations, flat organizations, open-book management, and Six Sigma. The book concludes with a look at common errors supervisors make, including failure to delegate, failure to recognize employee achievement, and failure to embrace change, to name a few.

Pre-reading Learning Aids

Each chapter of *Wiley Pathways Supervision* features the following learning and study aids to activate students' prior knowledge of the topics and orient them to the material.

▲ **Pre-test.** This pre-reading assessment tool in multiple-choice format not only introduces chapter material, but it also helps students anticipate the chapter's learning outcomes. By focusing students' attention on what they do not know, the self-test provides students with a benchmark against which they can measure their own progress. The pre-test is available online at www.wiley.com/college/nelson.

▲ **What You'll Learn in This Chapter.** This bulleted list focuses on *subject matter* that will be taught. It tells students what they will be learning in this chapter and why it is significant for their careers. It will also help students understand why the chapter is important and how it relates to other chapters in the text.

▲ **After Studying this Chapter, You'll Be Able To.** This list emphasizes *capabilities and skills* students will learn as a result of reading the chapter. It focuses on *execution* of subject matter that show the relationship between what students will learn in the chapter and how the information learned will be applied in an on-the-job situation.

Within-text Learning Aids

The following learning aids are designed to encourage analysis and synthesis of the material, support the learning process, and ensure success during the evaluation phase:

▲ **Introduction.** This section orients the student by introducing the chapter and explaining its practical value and relevance to the book as a whole. Short summaries of chapter sections preview the topics to follow.

▲ **"For Example" Boxes.** Found within each chapter, these boxes tie section content to real-world examples, scenarios, and applications.

▲ **Figures and tables.** Line art and photos have been carefully chosen to be truly instructional rather than filler. Tables distill and present information in a way that is easy to identify, access, and understand, enhancing the focus of the text on essential ideas.

▲ **Self-Check.** Related to the "What You'll Learn" bullets and found at the end of each section, this battery of short answer questions emphasizes student understanding of concepts and mastery of section content. Though the questions may either be discussed in class or studied by students outside of class, students should not go on before they can answer all questions correctly.

▲ **Key Terms and Glossary.** To help students develop a professional vocabulary, key terms are bolded in the introduction, summary, and when they first appear in the chapter. A complete list of key terms with brief definitions appears at the end of each chapter and again in a glossary at the end of the book. Knowledge of key terms is assessed by all assessment tools (see below).

▲ **Summary.** Each chapter concludes with a summary paragraph that reviews the major concepts in the chapter and links back to the "What You'll Learn" list.

Evaluation and Assessment Tools

Each *Wiley Pathways* text consists of a variety of within-chapter and end-of-chapter assessment tools that test how well students have learned the material. These tools also encourage students to extend their learning into different scenarios and higher levels of understanding and thinking. The following assessment tools appear in every chapter of *Wiley Pathways Supervision*:

▲ *Summary Questions* help students summarize the chapter's main points by asking a series of multiple choice and true/false questions that emphasize student understanding of concepts and mastery of chapter content. Students should be able to answer all of the Summary Questions correctly before moving on.

▲ *Applying this Chapter Questions* drive home key ideas by asking students to synthesize and apply chapter concepts to new, real-life situations and scenarios. Asks student to practice using the material they have learned in contrived situations that help reinforce their understanding, and may throw light on important considerations, advantages, or drawbacks to a specific methodology.

▲ *You Try It Questions* are designed to extend students' thinking, and so are ideal for discussion, writing assignments, or for use as case studies. Using an open-ended format and sometimes based on Web sources, they encourage students to draw conclusions using chapter material applied to real-world situations, which fosters both mastery and independent learning.

▲ *Post-test* should be taken after students have completed the chapter. It includes all of the questions in the pre-test, so that students can see how their learning has progressed and improved.

Instructor and Student Package

Wiley Pathways Supervision is available with the following teaching and learning supplements. All supplements are available online at the text's Book Companion Website, located at www.wiley.com/college/nelson.

▲ **Instructor's Resource Guide.** Provides the following aids and supplements for teaching an Introduction to Supervision course:

• *Sample syllabus.* A convenient template that instructors may use for creating their own course syllabi.

• *Teaching suggestions.* For each chapter, these include a chapter summary, learning objectives, definitions of key terms, lecture notes, answers to select text question sets, and at least 3 suggestions for classroom activities, such as ideas for speakers to invite, videos to show, and other projects.

▲ **PowerPoints.** Key information is summarized in 15 to 20 PowerPoints per chapter. Instructors may use these in class or choose to share them with students for class presentations or to provide additional study support.

▲ **Test Bank.** One test per chapter, as well as a mid-term, and two finals: one cumulative, one non-cumulative. Each includes true/false, multiple choice, and open-ended questions. Answers and page references are provided for the true/false and multiple choice questions, and page references for the open-ended questions. Available in Microsoft Word and computerized formats.

BRIEF CONTENTS

CONTENTS

1

SUPERVISION
Meeting Challenges and Obeying Laws

Starting Point

Go to www.wiley.com/college/nelson to assess your knowledge of supervision.
Determine where you need to concentrate your effort.

What You'll Learn in This Chapter

▲ Different theories and styles of management
▲ Current management challenges
▲ How to manage employees so they perform at their best
▲ State and federal laws that affect supervisors

After Studying This Chapter, You'll Be Able To

▲ Construct a management style that works for you and your employees
▲ Design ways to meet current challenges that face managers
▲ Build a good team by empowering, supporting, and listening to employees
▲ Create a work environment that is in compliance with all state and federal laws

INTRODUCTION

One definition describes management as getting things done through others. Another definition more specifically defines management as making something planned happen within a specific area through the use of available resources. Seems simple enough. But why do so many bright, industrious people have trouble managing well?

Unfortunately, good management is a scarce commodity—at once precious and fleeting. Many managers were good workers and promoted to management positions but do not have people skills or the necessary management skills to be as equally successful as a manager. For example, an accountant can be terrific with numbers but not know how to manage people. Despite years of management theory's evolution and the comings and goings of countless management fads, many workers and managers have developed a distorted view of management and its practice, with managers often not knowing the right approach to take, or exactly what to do.

Believe it or not, many managers are never formally trained to be managers. For many, management is just something that's added to your job description. One day you may be a computer programmer working on a hot new web browser, and the next day you may be in charge of the new development team. Before, you were expected only to show up to work and create a product. Now, you're expected to lead and motivate a group of workers toward a common goal. Sure, you may get paid more to do the job, but the only training you may get for the task is in the school of hard knocks.

1.1 Identifying the Different Styles of Management

The earliest theories of management primarily consisted of three different views: (1) the traditional model, (2) the human relations model, and (3) the human resources model. Basically, the only thing these three theories have in common is that each one attempts to construct a single model of motivation that would apply to every employee in every situation. Aside from that, each one provides a very different way of viewing and explaining human behavior in the workplace.

1.1.1 The Traditional Model

The traditional model was the brainchild of Frederick W. Taylor (1856–1915). Taylor and other early scholars are credited with an approach to management known as the scientific management theory. This theory arose in part due to a need to increase worker productivity in the United States at the beginning of the twentieth century, when skilled labor was in short supply. Based on Taylor's research, he believed, among other things, that more efficient workers should be paid higher wages than less-efficient workers. In other words, managers should determine the most efficient way to perform repetitive, on-the-job tasks and then "motivate" workers with a system of wage incentives: the more they produce, the more they earn. The traditional model of motivational theory makes the following assumptions about workers:

▲ Most people do not like to work.
▲ Most people will avoid work if at all possible.
▲ What people do is less important than what they earn for doing it.
▲ Few people want or can handle work that requires creativity or self-direction.

As you might imagine, this model began to fail as productivity in the United States increased and it took fewer workers to get the job done. As more workers were laid off and as companies began to reduce the size of wage incentives, workers started to demand job security over short-term, minor wage increases.

1.1.2 The Human Relations Model

The human relations model of employee management proposes that the boredom and repetitiveness of many tasks actually reduce employee motivation, whereas social contact helps create and sustain motivation. In other words, managers can motivate their employees by making them feel useful and important. This theory of motivation is attributed to Elton Mayo (1880–1949) and some other associates from Harvard, who developed theories of management that would later be known as the behavior school of management. Mayo was interested in helping managers deal with the "people side" of their organizations. The human relations model of employee motivation assumes the following about workers:

▲ Workers want to feel important, valued, and useful.
▲ Workers want to belong and to be recognized as individuals.
▲ These social needs are more important than money in motivating people to work.

According to the human relations model, workers are expected to accept management's authority because supervisors treat them with consideration and allow them to influence how tasks should be accomplished to a certain extent.

1.1.3 The Human Resources Model

The human resources model is attributed to Douglas McGregor and other theorists, who basically criticized both of the earlier models as being oversimplified and flawed because they focused on just one or two factors of motivation, either money or social relations. McGregor determined that managers have essentially two different sets of assumptions about their employees:

▲ **Theory X:** The traditional view, which assumes that most people do not like to work and will avoid work whenever possible.

▲ **Theory Y:** A more optimistic view that assumes that people actually do want to work and that under the right circumstances, they derive a great deal of satisfaction from work.

Theory X Management

Here's the $64,000 question: What is the best way to make something planned happen? Everyone seems to have a different answer to this question. Some people see management as something you do *to* people—not *with* them. Does this type of manager sound familiar? "We're going to do it my way. Understand?" Or perhaps the ever-popular threat: "It had better be on my desk by the end of the day—or else!" If worse comes to worst, a manager can unveil the ultimate weapon, "Mess up one more time, and you're out of here!"

This type of management assumes that people are inherently lazy and need to be driven to perform. Managing by fear and intimidation is always guaranteed to get a response. The question is: Do you get the kind of response that you really want? When you closely monitor your employees' work, you usually end up with only short-term compliance. In other words, you never get the best from others by building a fire under them; you have to find a way to build a fire within them.

Sometimes managers have to take command of the situation. If a proposal has to be shipped out in an hour and your customer just sent you some important changes, take charge of the situation to ensure that the right people are on the task—that is, if you're serious about keeping your customer. When you have to act quickly with perhaps not as much discussion as you would like, however, it's important to apologize in advance and let people know why you're doing things the way you are.

Theory Y Management

At the other end of the spectrum, some people see management as a nice-guy or nice-gal kind of idea. This theory assumes that people basically want to do a good job. In the extreme interpretation of this theory, managers are supposed to be sensitive to their employees' feelings and be careful not to do anything that may disturb their employees' tranquility and sense of self-worth.

"Uh, there's this little problem with your report; none of the numbers are correct. Now, don't take this personally, but we need to consider our alternatives for taking a more careful look at these figures in the future."

Again, managers may get a response with this approach, but are they likely to get the best possible response? No, the employees are likely to take advantage of the managers.

The Ideal Compromise

Good managers realize that they don't have to be tough all the time—and that nice guys and gals often finish first. If your employees are diligently performing their assigned tasks and no business emergency requires your immediate intervention, you can step back and let them do their jobs. Not only do your employees learn to be responsible, but you also can concentrate your efforts on what is most important to the bottom-line success of your organization.

A manager's real job is to inspire employees to do their best and establish a working environment that allows them to reach their goals. The best managers make every possible effort to remove the organizational obstacles that prevent employees from doing their jobs and to obtain the resources and training that employees need to do their jobs effectively.

Bad systems, bad policies, bad procedures, and poor treatment of others are organizational weaknesses that managers must be talented at identifying and repairing or replacing. Build a strong organizational foundation for your employees. Support your people, and they will support you. Time and time again, when given the opportunity to achieve, workers in all kinds of businesses, from factories to venture capital firms, have proven this rule to be true. If you haven't seen it at your place of business, you may be mistaking your employees for problems. Quit squeezing them and start squeezing your organization. The result is employees who want to succeed and a business that flourishes right along with them. Who knows, your employees may even stop hiding when they see you coming their way!

Squeezing employees may be easier than fighting the convoluted systems and cutting through the bureaucratic barnacles that have grown on your organization. You may be tempted to yell, "It's your fault that our department didn't achieve its goals!" Yes, blaming your employees for the organization's problems may be tempting, but doing so isn't going to solve the problems. Sure, you may get a quick, short-lived response when you push your people, but ultimately, you're failing to deal with the organization's real problems.

We all want to "win." The challenge of management is to define winning in such a way that it feels like winning for everyone in the organization. This, of course, is extremely difficult. People are often competing with coworkers for a "piece of the pie" rather than trying to make the pie bigger. It's your job to help make a bigger pie.

Despite what many people want you to believe, management is not prone to simple solutions or quick fixes. Being a manager is not simple. Yes, the best management solutions tend to be common sense; however, turning common sense into common practice is sometimes difficult.

Management is an attitude—a way of life. Management is a very real desire to work with people and help them succeed, as well as a desire to help your organization succeed. Management is a lifelong learning process that doesn't end when you walk out of a one-hour seminar or finish viewing a twenty-five-minute video. Management is a people job. If you're not up to the task of working with people—helping them, listening to them, encouraging them, and guiding them—then you shouldn't be a manager.

SELF-CHECK

1. **Theory Y** suggests that people actually like to work and that they derive satisfaction from their jobs under proper conditions. True or false?

2. McGregor's later theories of motivation led to participative management. True or false?

3. The _____ _____ model of employee management proposes that the boredom and repetitiveness of many tasks actually reduce employee motivation.

4. Management is a _____ job.

1.2 Meeting the Management Challenge

When you're assigned a task in a nonmanagement position, completing it by yourself is fairly simple and straightforward. Your immediate results are in direct response to your effort. To accomplish your task, you first review the task, you decide how best to accomplish it, and then you set schedules and milestones for its successful completion. Assuming that you have access to the tools and resources necessary to accomplish your task, you can probably do it yourself quickly and easily. You're an expert doer—a bright, get-things-done type of person.

However, if you hold a management position, you were probably selected because you proved yourself to be very skilled in the areas that you're now responsible for managing.

When you want to get a task done through someone else, you employ a different set of skills than when you do the task yourself. All of a sudden, because of this simple decision to pass the responsibility for completion of a task on to someone else, you introduce an interpersonal element into your equation: "Oh, no! You mean I have to actually work with people?" Being good technically at your job is not enough—no matter how good your technical skills are. Now you must have good planning, organization, leadership, and follow-up skills. In other words, in addition to being a good doer, you have to be a good manager of doers.

If this challenge isn't already enough, managers today face yet another challenge—one that has shaken the foundations of modern business. The new reality is the partnership of managers and workers in the workplace.

Originally, management was about dividing the company's work into discrete tasks, assigning the work to individual workers, and then closely monitoring the workers' performance and steering them toward accomplishing their tasks on time and within budget. The old reality of management often relied on fear, intimidation, and power over people to accomplish goals. If things weren't going according to management's plan, then management commanded its way out of the problem: "I don't care what you have to do to get it done—just get it done. Now!" The line between managers and workers was drawn clearly and drawn often.

In the new business environment, what's going on inside the organization is a reflection of what's going on outside the organization. The following factors are creating rapid and constant change in today's new business environment:

▲ A surge of global competition.
▲ New technology and innovation.
▲ The flattening of organizational hierarchies.
▲ Widespread downsizing, reengineering, and layoffs.
▲ The rise of small business.
▲ The changing values of today's workers.
▲ The increasing demands for better customer service.

Sure, managers still have to divide and assign work, but workers are taking on more of that responsibility. Most important, managers are finding out that they can't command their employees' best work—they have to create an environment that fosters their employees' desire to do their best work. In short, the new reality is the partnership of managers and workers in the workplace.

The landscape of business worldwide has changed dramatically during the past couple of decades. If you don't change with it, you're going to be left far behind your competitors. You may think that you can get away with treating your employees like "human assets" or children, but you can't. You can't because your competitors are discovering how to unleash the hidden power of their employees. They're no longer just talking about it; they're doing it!

In business, times are changing. Now that employees have tasted the sweet nectar of empowerment, you can't turn back. Companies that stick with the old way of doing business—the hierarchical, highly centralized model—will lose employees and customers to those companies that use the new ways of doing business and make them a part of their corporate culture. The best employees will leave the old-model companies in droves, seeking employers who treat them with respect and who are willing to grant them greater autonomy and responsibility.

FOR EXAMPLE

Meetings

Meeting the management challenge doesn't necessitate meetings, although a lot of a manager's time is taken up with meetings. According to the experts, managers are attending more meetings than ever. Although meetings take up more than 25 percent of an average business person's time, the figure rises to 40 percent for middle managers and up to a staggering 80 percent for executives. What's even more shocking is that about half of every hour spent in meetings is wasted due to the inefficiency and ineffectiveness of the participants.

SELF-CHECK

1. Name two factors that force businesses to be in a flux of constant and rapid change.
2. The best employees will leave _____-model companies in droves in search for companies that empower them.
3. What's going on in an organization is a reflection of what is going on outside an organization. True or false?

1.3 Explaining the New Functions of Management

Remember the four "classic" functions of management—plan, organize, lead, and control—that you learned in school? These management functions form the foundation from which every manager works. Although these basic functions are fine for taking care of most of your day-to-day management duties, they fail to reflect the new reality of the workplace and the new partnership of managers and workers. What is needed is a new set of management functions that builds upon the four classic functions of management. You're in luck. The sections that follow describe the functions of the new manager in the twenty-first-century workplace.

1.3.1 Trusting Employees

Companies that provide exceptional customer service unleash their employees from the constraints of an overly controlling hierarchy and allow frontline workers to serve their customers directly and efficiently. For example, although many companies devote forests of paper to employee manuals, Nordstrom, Inc., devotes exactly one page to its manual (see Figure 1-1).

Figure 1-1

> **We're glad to have you with our Company. Our number one goal is to provide outstanding customer service.**
>
> **Set both your personal and professional goals high.**
>
> **Nordstrom Rules:**
>
> **Rule #1: Use your good judgement in all situations.**
>
> **There will be no additional rules. Please feel free to ask your department manager, store manager, or division general manager any question at any time.**

(Source: *Business and Society Review,* Spring 1993, n85)

Employee manual for Nordstrom, Inc., shows an exceptional amount of trust in employees.

You may think that a small company with five or ten employees can get away with a policy like that, but certainly not a big company like yours. However, Nordstrom is not a small business by any stretch of the imagination—with 50,000 or so employees and more than $5 billion in annual sales.

How does management at a large business like Nordstrom get away with such a policy? They do it through trust.

First, Nordstrom hires good people. Second, the company gives them the training and tools to do their jobs well. Then management gets out of the way and lets the employees do their work. Nordstrom knows that it can trust its employees to make the right decisions because the company knows that it has hired the right people for the job and has trained them well.

That's not saying Nordstrom doesn't have problems—every company does. But Nordstrom has taken a proactive stance in creating the environment that employees most need and want.

Can you say the same for your organization?

When you trust your employees, they respond by being trustworthy. When you recognize them for being independent and responsive to their customers, they continue to be independent and responsive to their customers. And when you give them the freedom to make their own decisions, they make their own decisions. With a little training and a lot of support, these decisions are in the best interest of the company because the right people at the right level of the organization make them.

1.3.2 Energizing Employees

Today's managers are masters of making things happen, starting with themselves. "If it's to be, it's to begin with me." Think of the best managers you know. What one quality sets them apart from the rest? Is it their organizational skills, their fairness, or their technical ability? Perhaps their ability to delegate or the long hours that they keep sets them apart.

Although all these traits may be important to a manager's success, we haven't yet discussed the unique quality that makes a good manager great. The most important management function is to get people excited and inspired, that is, to energize them.

You can be the best analyst in the world, the most highly organized executive on the planet, or fair beyond reproach, but if the level of excitement that you generate can be likened more to that of a dish rag than to that of a spark plug, then you're handicapped in your efforts to create a truly great organization.

Great managers create far more energy than they consume. The best managers are organizational catalysts. Instead of taking energy from an organization, they channel and amplify it to the organization. In every interaction, effective managers take the natural energy of their employees, add to it, and leave the employees in a higher energy state than when they started the interaction. Management becomes a process of transmitting the excitement that you feel about your organization and its goals to your employees in terms that they can understand and appreciate. Before you know it, your employees are as excited about the organization as you are, and you can simply allow their energy to carry you forward.

1.3.3 Empowering Employees

Have you ever worked for someone who didn't let you do your job without questioning your every decision? Maybe you spent all weekend working on a special project only to have it casually discarded by your boss. "What were you thinking when you did this, Elizabeth? Our customers will never buy into that approach!" Or maybe you went out of your way to help a customer, accepting a return shipment of an item against company policy. "Why do you think we have policies—because we enjoy killing trees? No! If we made exceptions for everyone, we'd go out of business!" How did it feel to have your sincere efforts at doing a great job disparaged? What was your reaction? Chances are, you didn't bother making the extra effort again.

Despite rumors to the contrary, when you empower your employees, you do not stop managing. What changes is the way you manage. Managers still provide vision, establish organizational goals, and determine shared values. However, managers must establish a corporate infrastructure—skills training, teams, and so on—that supports empowerment. And although all your employees may not want to be empowered, you still have to provide an environment that supports those employees who are eager for a taste of the freedom to apply their personal creativity and expertise to your organization.

Great managers allow their employees to do great work. This role is a vital function of management, for even the greatest managers in the world can't succeed all by themselves. To achieve the organizations' goals, managers depend on their employees' skills. Effective management is the leveraging of the efforts of every member of a work unit toward a common purpose. If you're constantly doing your employees' work for them, not only have you lost the advantage of the leverage that your employees can provide you, but you're also putting yourself on the path to stress, ulcers, and worse.

However, far worse than the personal loss that you suffer when you don't empower employees is that everyone in your organization loses. Your employees lose because you aren't allowing them to stretch themselves or to show creativity or initiative. Your organization loses the insights that its creative workforce brings with it. Finally, your customers lose because your employees are afraid to provide them with exceptional service. Why should they if they're constantly worried that you will punish them for taking initiative or for pushing the limits of the organization to better serve your customers?

As William McKnight, former CEO of manufacturing giant 3M put it, "The mistakes people make are of much less importance than the mistakes management makes if it tells people exactly what to do."

1.3.4 Supporting Employees

Increasingly, managers must be coaches, colleagues, and cheerleaders for the employees they support. The main concern of today's managers needs to be shaping a more supportive work environment that enables each employee to feel valued and be more productive.

When the going gets tough, managers support their employees. Now, this doesn't mean that you do everything for your employees or make their decisions for them. It does mean that you give your employees the training, resources, and authority to do their jobs, and then you get out of the way. You're always there for your employees to help pick up the pieces if they fall, but fall they must if they're going to learn. The idea is the same as learning to skate: If you're not falling, you're not learning.

The key to creating a supportive environment is establishing trust or openness throughout an organization. In an open environment, employees can bring up questions and concerns. In fact, they're encouraged to do so. When the environment is truly open, an individual can express concerns without fear of retribution. Hidden agendas do not exist, and people feel free to say the same things in business meetings that they'd say after work. When employees see that their managers are receptive to new ideas, they're more likely to feel invested in the organization, and to think of more and better ways to improve systems, to solve problems, to save money, and to better serve customers.

Managers also support each other. Personal fiefdoms, fighting between departments, and withholding information have no place in the modern organization;

companies cannot afford to support these dysfunctional behaviors. All members of the organization—from the top to the bottom—must realize that they play on the same team. To win, team members support each other and keep their coworkers apprised of the latest information.

1.3.5 Communicating with Employees

Without a doubt, communication is the lifeblood of any organization, and managers are the common element that connects different levels of employees with one another. We have seen firsthand the positive effects on a business and its employees of managers who communicate, and the negative effects on a business and its employees of managers who don't. Managers who don't communicate effectively are missing out on a vital role of management. Communication is a key function for managers today. Information is power, and as the speed of business accelerates, information must be communicated to employees faster than ever. Constant change and increasing turbulence in the business environment necessitate more communication, not less. Who's going to be around in five years? The manager who has mastered this function or the one who has not? With the proliferation of email, voice mail, and the other new means of communication in modern business, managers simply have no excuse not to communicate with their employees. You can even use the telephone or try a little old-fashioned face-to-face talk with your employees and coworkers.

To meet the expectations that you set for them, your employees have to be aware of your expectations. A goal is great on paper, but if you don't communicate it to employees and don't keep them up-to-date on their progress toward achieving that goal, how can you expect them to reach it? Simply, you can't. It would be like training for the Olympics but never being given feedback on how you're doing vs. the competition.

Employees often appreciate the little things: an invitation to an upcoming meeting, praise for a job well done, or an insight into the organization's finances. Not only does sharing this kind of information make a business run better, but it also creates tremendous goodwill and cements the trust that bonds your employees to the organization and to the successful completion of the organization's goals.

1.3.6 Learning from Employees

If you're fortunate enough to have had a skilled teacher or mentor during the course of your career, you're treated to an education in management that's equal to or better than any MBA program. You learn firsthand the right and wrong ways to manage people. You learn what it takes to get things done in your organization, and you learn that customer satisfaction involves more than simply giving your customers lip service.

Unfortunately, any organization with good management also has living, breathing examples of the wrong way to manage employees. You know whom we're talking about: the manager who refuses to make decisions, leaving employees and customers hanging. Or the boss who refuses to delegate even the simplest decision to employees. Or the supervisor who insists on managing every aspect of a department—no matter how small or inconsequential. Examples of the right way to manage employees are, regrettably, still few and far between.

You can benefit from the behaviors that poor managers model. When you find a manager who refuses to make decisions, for example, carefully note the impact that the management style has on workers, other managers, and customers. You feel your own frustration. Make a mental note: "I'll never, ever demotivate another person like that." Indecision at the top inevitably leads to indecision within all ranks of an organization, especially when employees are punished for filling the vacuum left by indecisive managers. Employees become confused, and customers become concerned as the organization drifts aimlessly.

Observe the manager who depends on fear and intimidation to get results. What are the real results of this style of management? Do employees look forward to coming to the office every day? Are they all pulling for a common vision and goal? Are they extending themselves to bring innovation to work processes and procedures? Or are they more concerned with just getting through the day without being yelled at? Think about what you would do differently to get the results that you want.

You can always learn something from other managers—whether they're good managers or bad ones.

1.3.7 Improving Your Skills

Perhaps you're familiar with this old saying (attributed to Lao Tze):

> *Give a man a fish, and he eats for a day,*
> *Teach a man to fish, and he eats for a lifetime.*

Such is the nature of managing employees. If you make all the decisions, do the work that your employees are able to do given the chance, and try to carry the entire organization on your own shoulders, you're harming your employees and your organization far more than you can imagine. Your employees never find out how to succeed on their own, and after a while, they quit trying. In your sincere efforts to bring success to your organization, you stunt the growth of your employees and make your organization less effective and vital.

To take advantage of the lessons that you learn, you have to put them into practice. Keep these key steps in mind.

1. **Take the time to assess your organization's problems.** Which parts of your organization work, and which don't? Why or why not? You can't focus on all your problems at one time. Concentrate on a few problems that are the most important, and solve them before you move on to the rest.

2. **Take a close look at yourself.** What do you do to help or hinder your employees when they try to do their jobs? Do you give them the authority to make decisions? Just as important, do you support them when they go out on a limb for the organization? Study your personal interactions throughout your business day. Do they result in positive or negative outcomes?

3. **Try out the techniques that you learn from your reading or from observing other managers at work.** Go ahead! Nothing changes if you don't change first. "If it's to be, it's to begin with me."

4. **Step back and watch what happens.** It's guaranteed that you will see a difference in the way you get tasks done and in the way your customers and employees respond to your organization's needs and goals.

FOR EXAMPLE

Managers Must Improvise

By many measures, Jack Welch is considered to be one of the United States' top business leaders. Welch, who until recently was chair of General Electric, radically transformed his company's culture while dramatically improving its performance—and in the process created some $57 billion in value.

Although Welch did many different things to make the transformation a reality, one of the most telling was his takeover of GE's training facility in Ossining, New York. As Welch realized, designing a new culture is one thing, but getting the word out to employees and making it stick is another thing altogether. By directing the class curricula for all levels of workers, and by personally dropping into the training center every two weeks or so to meet with students, Welch was able not only to determine what message would be communicated to GE employees, but also to ensure that the message was received loudly and clearly. If the employees were confused, they had ample opportunity to ask Welch for clarification.

In a gesture that was at once symbolic and real, Welch directed the ceremonial burning of the old-school GE "Blue Books." The Blue Books were a series of management training manuals that prescribed how GE managers were to get tasks done in the organization. Despite the fact that the use of these books for training had been mothballed for some fifteen years, they still exerted tremendous influence over the actions of GE managers. Citing the need for managers to write their own answers to day-to-day management challenges, Welch swept away the old order by removing the Blue Books from the organization's culture once and for all. Now, GE managers are taught to find their own solutions rather than to look them up in a dusty old book.

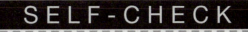

SELF-CHECK

1. What is the difference between energizing and empowering employ-ees?
2. When you empower your employees, you do not stop _____.
3. Great managers create far more energy than they consume. True or false?
4. There is nothing you can learn from the bad managers you work with. True or false?
5. To improve your own performance, you should study your personal _____ throughout the business day.
6. To meet the expectations that you set for them, your employees have to be _____ of your expectations.

1.4 Laws That Supervisors Should Be Aware Of

There are numerous federal and state employment laws that managers must obey as they go about the business of making daily, routine management decisions. One of the most important of these laws is **Title VII of the 1964 Civil Rights Act.** This law applies to businesses with fifteen or more employees, including state and local governments. Title VII prohibits employment discrimination based on an individual's sex, race, color, religion, and national origin. Whether writing a job description, placing a help-wanted advertisement in the local newspaper, or conducting a job interview, it is essential that managers have a thorough understanding of Title VII to ensure no employment discrimination of any sort occurs. The **Equal Employment Opportunity Commission (EEOC)** is the federal agency that provides oversight and coordination of Title VII as well as other federal equal employment opportunity (EEO) laws.

In addition to the guidelines the law imposes on the hiring process itself, managers must understand that all matters that are employment related are covered under Title VII. Determining whether to promote or not promote a specific employee, deciding who will and who will not receive a raise in pay, designing work schedules, training schedules, and even administering employee discipline are all management duties that in one way or another will fall under the broad spectrum of Title VII.

1.4.1 Illegal Discrimination

The word *discrimination* has typically gotten a bad rap. When we hear the word, we automatically think of it as something negative or ugly. Truthfully, we discriminate each and every day as we live our lives. For example, deciding which pair of socks to wear when we dress for work or school—or whether to wear any socks at all—is a form of discrimination. When we choose one pair of socks over the other, we are doing so based on some selection criteria that we somehow deem relevant. Will the blue socks look better with the khaki slacks or would black socks look best? Discrimination then is simply about making choices. Title VII does not necessarily prevent hospitality managers from making informed choices in matters of employment; it prevents managers from making *illegal* choices, or decisions that are based on some flawed or illegal selection criteria, such as race, religion, sex, and so forth.

There was a time in our nation's history—roughly thirty years ago—when society felt that certain types of people were best suited for certain types of jobs. A good example comes from our nation's airline industry, a relatively new industry in the grand scheme of things. Airline pilots had to be male, and what were then called stewardesses had to be female. It did not matter whether pilots and copilots were married or single, but stewardesses had to remain single—to get married meant losing one's job. When hiring stewardesses, the airlines were careful to select only those female applicants who were deemed the most attractive. There were strict height and weight requirements, and most airlines required that the stewardess applicant attach both a head-and-shoulders photo as well as a full-body photo to her application. It is not hard to imagine what probably happened to the applications of the less-attractive applicants.

In our more enlightened world today, these hiring practices seem ridiculous and unreasonable. Whereas the estimated 4000 female airline pilots flying today still account for only about 5 percent of all airline pilots, clearly, women are making inroads in the world of aviation. The term *stewardess* has been replaced with the more modern term flight attendant, and anyone who flies today will see that the modern flight attendant comes in all shapes, colors, ages, and sexes. A flight attendant's marital status is also no longer a job qualification.

Changes in employment practices such as these and many others were a result of the enactment of Title VII of the 1964 Civil Rights Act. According to Title VII, choosing one job applicant over another or making other employment decisions based on an individual's sex, race, color, religion, or national origin is illegal. The penalties for illegal discrimination can be severe as well as expensive, and the fallout from such acts can also be a public relations nightmare.

Bona Fide Occupational Qualification

When Title VII was enacted, Congress *did* realize that there would be legitimate occasions when management would need to choose a male applicant over a female applicant, or vice versa. Congress also knew that some positions might require that the job applicant be of specific religion or national origin. Based on these realizations, Congress created what one might call a legal loophole. This loophole is known as **bona fide occupational qualification (BFOQ).** Let's say that a manager of a resort hotel needs to hire a men's locker room attendant. Because of BFOQ, the manager could legally discriminate against any females who might apply for this job. It is important to note that the BFOQ defense is construed narrowly by the courts. Generally, two elements are necessary to qualify: (1) the job in issue must require a worker of a particular sex, religion, or national origin and (2) such requirement must be necessary to the essence of the business operation. BFOQ is not a defense against a claim of racial discrimination.

1.4.2 Sexual Harassment

Sexual harassment is a form of sex discrimination that violates Title VII of the 1964 Civil Rights Act. There are numerous documented incidents in which hotels and restaurants have been fined hundreds of thousands of dollars for engaging in sexual harassment. The EEOC defines sexual harassment as "unwelcome sexual advances, requests for sexual favors, or other verbal or physical conduct of a sexual nature when this conduct explicitly or implicitly affect's an individual's employment, unreasonably interferes with an individual's work performance, or creates an intimidating, hostile or offensive work environment."

Sexual harassment in the workplace generally occurs in one of two ways: A manager or a supervisor—someone in a position of power—sexually harasses an employee by virtue of the power held over that employee. This is known as **quid pro quo** or "this for that" type of harassment. Promising or withholding a raise or a promotion in return for sexual favors is an example of quid pro quo harassment. Another form of sexual harassment is known as creating a **hostile work environment.** This occurs when a manager allows employees to engage in telling dirty jokes or allows employees to circulate offensive pictures, Web sites, or email messages. Allowing employees to make crude or suggestive comments of a sexual nature could also lead to a charge of hostile work environment sexual harassment by another employee.

It is important to note that the harasser's conduct must be unwelcome. It is important for the victim to inform the harasser directly that the conduct is unwelcome and that it must stop. If the unwelcome harassment continues, the victim should use any employer complaint mechanism or grievance system that is available. It is also important that hospitality organizations have a system in place that allows the employee to bypass the supervisor in case the supervisor is also the harasser.

Clearly, supervisors must have well-established guidelines for preventing the sexual harassment of employees. Training is essential, and prevention is usually the best tool to eliminate this unlawful behavior. The EEOC recommends that managers clearly communicate to employees that sexual harassment will not be tolerated. It is important that managers train their employees and clearly define what constitutes sexual harassment.

FOR EXAMPLE

Sexual Harassment Laws

In January 2004, the EEOC settled bias suits with two Florida restaurants that were required to pay over $500,000 in fines for the sexual harassment of female employees. ABC Pizza, a Tampa Bay–area pizza chain, was found guilty of subjecting female employees to a sexually hostile working environment. The EEOC contended that the conduct was created by the restaurant's manager and was primarily directed toward two sisters who were ages sixteen and seventeen at the time they were employed with the company. The manager's conduct included inappropriate touching as well as crude sexual comments. The other Florida case involved a Longhorn Steakhouse where an assistant manager subjected female employees to conduct ranging from hip and lower back touches and breast grabbing to inappropriate verbal comments. The company was forced to pay the three victims $200,000.[1] Both of these companies are now required to conduct annual training on Title VII with emphasis on sexual harassment.

Employees should also be informed about an effective complaint or grievance system that allows victims to come forward and report harassment when it occurs. When an employee does complain, the manager must take immediate and appropriate action, including a fair investigation and disciplinary action when appropriate. As with all other areas of Title VII, managers are prohibited from retaliating against employees who may come forward and report illegal employment practices. Retaliation on the part of management could take various forms. Examples might include cutting an employee's work hours, demoting an employee, disciplining an employee for infractions that are normally overlooked, and transferring an employee to a less-desirable job or a less-desirable location.

1.4.3 The Americans with Disabilities Act

President George H. W. Bush signed the **Americans with Disabilities Act (ADA)** into law in 1990, and the law went into effect in July 1992. This sweeping legislation covers five areas: employment, public transportation, public accommodations, telecommunication services, and public services. Title I governs areas of employment discrimination and is overseen by the EEOC. Our discussion will be focused only on Title I of the ADA—employment issues. Under the provisions of Title I of the ADA, it is illegal to discriminate against people with disabilities in all employment and employment-related issues. The ADA defines a **disabled individual** as "any individual who has a physical or mental impairment that substantially limits one or more major life activities, has a record of such impairment, or is regarded as having such impairment." Protected groups under the ADA include individuals who use wheelchairs, walkers, and so on; individuals who are speech, vision, or hearing impaired; people with mental retardation or emotional illness; individuals with a disease such as cancer, heart disease, asthma, diabetes, or AIDS; and individuals with drug and alcohol problems who are in supervised rehabilitation programs. It is estimated that there are over fifty million Americans who qualify as being disabled under the ADA.

Under the guidelines of the ADA, it is illegal for employers to discriminate against disabled individuals who are otherwise qualified to perform the essential functions of the job, with or without reasonable accommodation, so long as the individual does not pose a threat to the health and safety of others. It is important for hospitality industry managers to understand the importance of clearly determining a position's essential functions.

Accommodating an individual's disability is generally less costly and less intrusive than many managers realize. The EEOC has suggested that most **reasonable accommodations** cost less than $50, and there are many examples of reasonable accommodation that cost absolutely nothing. Minor changes in work duties, procedures, or work schedules, or minor changes in the physical work environment are often all that is required to make a reasonable accommodation. The ADA stipulates that an employer must provide work areas and equipment that are wheelchair accessible unless this is not **readily achievable** (cannot be easily accomplished without great difficulty or expense) or unless it would cause **undue hardship** (this could refer to a financial hardship or a business hardship). Generally, whether something is readily achievable or whether something would cause undue financial hardship is left up to the EEOC to decide.

You are required to provide a reasonable accommodation not only to the disabled applicant for employment but also to employees already on staff who are or who become disabled and cannot perform their original jobs.

1.4.4 Age Discrimination in Employment

To prevent employment discrimination based on an individual's age, in 1967 the U.S. Congress passed the **Age Discrimination in Employment Act (ADEA) of 1967.** This law prohibits discrimination against individuals who are forty years of age and older. The ADEA was amended in 1986 to eliminate rules requiring mandatory retirement ages that were common in many industries. Enforcement of this law is handled by the EEOC, and violations can be time-consuming and costly. As with Title VII, exceptions based on BFOQ are permitted, but they are extremely limited.

1.4.5 Equal Pay Act

To prevent huge disparities in pay and wages between men and women, Congress passed the **Equal Pay Act** in 1963. This law requires businesses to pay equal wages for equal work. Jobs are considered equal when both sexes work at the same place and the job requires substantially the same skill, effort, responsibility, and working conditions. Pay differences based on a seniority or merit system or on a system that measures earnings by quantity or quality of production are permitted. The law is interpreted as applying to "wages" in the sense of all employment-related payments, including overtime, uniforms, travel, and other fringe benefits. The EEOC handles equal pay violations, and the penalties can be severe.

1.4.6 Immigration Reform and Control Act

The **Immigration Reform and Control Act (IRCA) of 1986** was passed to control illegal immigration to the United States. This federal law imposes civil and criminal penalties on employers who knowingly hire illegal aliens. The law is administered by the Department of Homeland Security's U.S. Citizenship and Immigration Service, and penalties against business that knowingly use illegal labor can include fines of up to $10,000 per worker as well as potential criminal charges against the business or its owner. The law requires employers to verify the identity and employment eligibility of all workers hired after November 6, 1986. Hospitality managers accomplish this by requiring all employees to complete Form I-9, Employee Eligibility Verification.

Form I-9 must be kept by the employer either for three years after the date of hire or for one year after employment is terminated, whichever is later. The form must be available for inspection by the authorized U.S. government officials. Currently, the debate in Washington, DC has heated up considerably over the "immigration issue" where some estimate that nearly four million immigrants are in the country illegally. Some members of Congress prefer a new law that would provide many of these immigrants a "pathway to citizenship," whereas others call this route "amnesty" and are calling for the criminalization and deportation of all illegal immigrants.

1.4.7 State and Local Employment Laws

Title VII of the 1964 Civil Rights Act is a federal law, but many states, cities, and towns have enacted their own civil rights and equal employment opportunity laws and have added additional protected classes. For example, some states' and cities' civil rights laws not only make it illegal to discriminate based on race, sex, color, religion, and national origin (Title VII), but they have also included such protected categories as marital status, disability, age, and sexual orientation. A state or local law must be at least as strict as the federal law, but it may also be stricter. It is important to note that the law that is deemed stricter is the one that must be followed. If ever in doubt, the prudent manager will always consult with an attorney who is well versed in federal as well as in any local laws that may apply to matters of employment.

SELF-CHECK

1. Choosing a white applicant over a black applicant because of customer preferences would be in violation of **Title VII of the 1964 Civil Rights Act.** True or false?

2. Title VII impacts only the manager's relationship with job applicants—not with current employees. True or false?

3. The **Americans with Disabilities Act (ADA)** requires that managers hire individuals who are disabled, regardless of the individual's ability to perform the essential functions of the job. True or false?

4. The **Equal Pay Act** prohibits sex discrimination as it relates to pay and salary issues and requires equal pay for equal work. True or false?

5. The **Age Discrimination in Employment Act (ADEA)** prohibits employment discrimination against those who are thirty years of age and over. True or false?

6. **Bona fide occupational qualification (BFOQ)** is a legal defense against discrimination in the areas of sex, religion, and national origin, but the courts _____ construe this defense.

SUMMARY

As a manager, it is important that you are good not only in the technical aspects of your field but also in dealing with others. Empowering, trusting, and supporting your employees are ways you can bring out the best in others and improve your organization.

As a manager, it is also important that you are familiar with employment laws. Employment laws affect virtually every aspect of the employee–employer relationship, so it is important to follow specific guidelines when asking job applicants to fill out applications and when interviewing prospective job candidates.

In this chapter, you assessed different management styles and how to get around management obstacles. You also examined techniques that you can use to build a great team. Finally, you briefly examined the main employment laws that affect you as a supervisor, your employees, and your employee applicants.

KEY TERMS

Age Discrimination in Employment Act of 1967	This law prohibits discrimination against individuals who are forty years of age and older.
Americans with Disabilities Act (ADA)	A federal law that makes it illegal to discriminate against a job applicant or a current employee who is disabled.
Bona fide occupational qualification (BFOQ)	A legal loophole, or a legal defense, to job discrimination based on sex, national origin, or religion. There is no BFOQ defense to racial discrimination.
Disabled individual	The ADA describes a disabled individual as "any individual who has a physical or mental impairment that substantially limits one or more major life activity, has a record of such impairment, or is regarded as having such impairment."
Equal Employment Commission (EEOC) Opportunity	The EEOC is the U.S. government agency charged with overseeing Title VII of the 1964 Civil Rights Act and Title I of the ADA.
Equal Pay Act	The law requires businesses to pay equal wages for equal work without regard to the sex of the employee.
Hostile work environment	An environment that is hostile can be created when management allows employees to tell off-color jokes, send off-color emails, or put up pictures or photos that someone could deem offensive.
Immigration Reform and Control Act	All workers hired after November 6, 1987, must provide proper documentation and complete the Form I-9 to prove that they have the legal right to work in the United States.
Quid pro quo	Latin for "this for that."
Readily achievable	This term is associated with the ADA and generally refers to the adjustment of a task or a physical adjustment to the facility that is easily accomplished without great difficulty or expense.
Reasonable accommodation	Under the ADA, an individual who is disabled but otherwise qualified to perform the essential functions of a job may require a reasonable accommodation. This could be a minor adjustment of the individual's work schedule, an

	adjustment of policy or procedure, or the purchase of a device that would allow the individual to perform the duties of the job.
Sexual harassment	A form of sex discrimination according to Title VII of the 1964 Civil Rights Act.
Theory X	A traditional view of motivation that assumes that employees do not want to work and need to be driven to perform.
Theory Y	A view of motivation that assumes that employees actually enjoy work and derive a great deal of satisfaction from work when the proper conditions are met.
Title VII of the 1964 Civil Rights Act	A federal law that makes it illegal to discriminate against job applicants as well as current employees on the basis of sex, race, color, religion, or national origin.
Undue hardship	A legal defense to the ADA that is generally left up to the interpretation of the courts. It could refer to a financial hardship or a business hardship.

ASSESS YOUR UNDERSTANDING

Go to www.wiley.com/college/nelson to evaluate your knowledge of supervision. *Measure your learning by comparing pre-test and post-test results.*

Summary Questions

1. Title VII of the 1964 Civil Rights Act prohibits job discrimination on the basis of age. True or false?
2. Those who subscribe to the human relations model believe that management can motivate employees by making them feel useful and important. True or false?
3. The rise of small business is one of the factors that creates constant change in the workforce. True or false?
4. Micromanaging employees stunts the growth of the organization. True or false?
5. The U.S. Department of Justice has legal jurisdiction over Title VII of the 1964 Civil Rights Act. True or false?
6. With respect to the I-9 form, acceptable documentation must include which of the following?
   (a) An item from List A, List B, and List C
   (b) An item from List B only
   (c) An item from List A only
   (d) An item from List C only
7. The following statement is true for which model? Managers should determine the most efficient way to perform repetitive, on-the-job tasks and then "motivate" workers with a system of wage incentives.
   (a) Traditional model
   (b) Human relations model
   (c) Theory X
   (d) Human resources model
8. Title VII of the 1964 Civil Rights Act prohibits discrimination based on all of the following *except:*
   (a) race.
   (b) color.
   (c) age.
   (d) national origin.
9. Refusing to hire a female applicant for the position of men's locker room attendant would be a legal defense of Title VII based on:
   (a) reasonable accommodation.
   (b) bona fide occupational qualification (BFOQ).

(c) essential duties.

(d) undue hardship.

10. Which of the following individuals would currently *not* be covered under the ADA?

(a) An individual who is HIV positive or who has AIDS

(b) An individual who illegally uses drugs

(c) An individual who is in supervised alcohol rehab

(d) None of the above

11. It is important to establish openness in an organization. True or false?

Applying This Chapter

1. Eric Holmes has applied for the position of a reservations clerk in your hotel. The individual has no experience, but he types quickly and accurately and has good listening skills as well as a pleasant speaking voice. Eric has very limited eyesight; he is considered to be "legally blind" and is covered under the ADA. Discuss ways in which management in your hotel could accommodate Eric's disability with or without a reasonable accommodation.

2. Review the traditional model of management, the human relations model of management, and the human resources model of management. Which one do you subscribe to and why?

3. How do technology and global competition affect managers and today's business environment?

4. You are the owner of a small accounting firm. You founded the firm without the help of a human resources assistant or a procedure manual. You hire ten employees. What steps can you take to create a supportive and empowering employee environment?

5. Provide examples for ways in which businesses could make a *reasonable accommodation* for each of the following job applicants:

(a) An applicant for the position of dishwasher who has a hearing disorder

(b) An applicant for the position of sales manager who is wheelchair bound

(c) An applicant for the position of server who lacks use of the left arm

Hiring Managers

You are the CEO of a large marketing firm. You are un-happy with your current management staff, and decide to replace five managers. What qualities do you look for in managers and why? Write a list of qualities you would want in your managers.

Sexual Harrassment Policy

Write a sexual harassment policy for a business. Be sure to define both quid pro quo and hostile environment ha-rassment. What steps and procedures should employees take if they feel that they are victims of sexual harass-ment? What steps should management take when an employee makes a claim of sexual harassment?

2

LEADERSHIP
Inspiring Others

Starting Point

Go to www.wiley.com/college/nelson to assess your knowledge of leadership. *Determine where you need to concentrate your effort.*

What You'll Learn in This Chapter

▲ The difference between leaders and managers
▲ How leaders interact with others
▲ Common leadership traits
▲ What collaborative leadership means

After Studying This Chapter, You'll Be Able To

▲ Critique employees' leadership skills
▲ Assess which employees will do well in leadership positions
▲ Foster collaborative leadership

INTRODUCTION

What makes a leader? Experts have written countless books, produced endless videos, and taught interminable seminars on the topic of leadership. Still, leadership is a quality that eludes many who seek it. Let's look at the difference in the definitions for managers and leaders.

▲ A **manager** is a person who supervises others in an effort to complete tasks or accomplish goals.

▲ A **leader** is a person who has commanding authority or influence over others and inspires them toward goals.

Studies show that the primary traits that all effective leaders have in common are (1) a positive outlook and (2) forward thinking. They have a positive outlook and are sure of themselves and their ability to influence others and impact the future. Although similar, leadership and management are different; leadership goes above and beyond management. A manager can be organized and efficient at getting tasks done without being a leader—someone who inspires others to achieve their best. In short, managers manage processes; they lead people. According to management visionary Peter Drucker, leadership is the most basic and scarcest resource in any business enterprise.

A leader is many things to many people. In this chapter, we discuss the key skills and attributes that make good managers into great leaders. As this chapter explains, leadership requires the application of a wide variety of skills. No single trait, when mastered, suddenly makes you an effective leader. "You mean that I can't become a great leader just from watching this video?" However, you may notice that some leadership skills that follow are also key functions of management—ones that we reviewed in Chapter 1. This similarity is no coincidence.

2.1 Understanding the Differences between Management and Leadership

Being a good manager is quite an accomplishment. Management is by no means an easy task, and mastering the wide range of varied skills that is required can take many years. The best managers get their jobs done efficiently and effectively—with a minimum of muss and fuss. Like the person behind the scenes of a great performance in sports or the theater, the best managers are often those employees whom you notice the least.

Great managers are experts at taking their current organizations and optimizing them to accomplish their goals and get their jobs done. By necessity, they focus on the here and now—not on the tremendous potential of what the future can bring. Managers are expected to make things happen now—not at some indefinite, fuzzy point in the future. "Don't tell me what you're going to do for me next year or the year after that! I want results, and I want them now!" Having good managers in an organization, however, isn't enough.

Great organizations need great management. However, great management doesn't necessarily make a great organization. For an organization to be great, it must also have great leadership.

Leaders have vision. They look beyond the here and now to see the vast potential of their organizations. And although great leaders are also effective at getting things done in their organizations, they accomplish their goals in a way different from managers.

How so? Managers use values, policies, procedures, schedules, milestones, incentives, discipline, and other mechanisms to push their employees to achieve the goals of the organization.

Leaders, on the other hand, challenge their employees to achieve the organization's goals by creating a compelling vision of the future and then unlocking their employees' potential. Think about some great leaders. President John F. Kennedy challenged the American people to land a man on the moon. We did. Lee Iacocca challenged the management and workers of the Chrysler Corporation to bring their company out of the clutches of financial disaster and to build a new corporation that would lead the way in product innovation and profitability. They did. Jack Welch of General Electric challenged his workers to help the company attain first or second place in every business that it owned. They did.

All these leaders share a common trait: They all painted compelling visions that grabbed the imagination of their followers and then challenged them to achieve these visions. Without the vision that leaders provide and without the contributions of their followers' hard work, energy, and innovation, the United States would never have landed a man on the moon, the name *Chrysler* would have slipped quietly into history, and GE wouldn't be the hugely successful firm that it is today.

FOR EXAMPLE

Jack Welch, Manager of the Century

Jack Welch, CEO of GE from 1981 to 2001, was named by *Fortune* magazine as the "Manager of the Century" in 1999. Welch began working for GE in 1960 as an engineer, making $10,500 per year. Because he had a vision, he was promoted several times within the organization and became CEO in 1981 with a reported salary of $94 million per year. Welch worked hard to dismantle the bureaucracy of GE. Employees resented him at first for making the changes, but many eventually grew to respect him.

SELF-CHECK

1. For an organization to be great, it only needs great **managers**. True or false?

2. _____ must have a vision for the organization that they are a part of.

2.2 Figuring Out What Leaders Do

The skills required to be a leader are no secret; some managers have figured out how to use the skills and others haven't. And although some people seem to be born leaders, anyone can discover what leaders do and how to apply these skills themselves.

2.2.1 Inspiring Action

Despite what some managers believe, most workers want to feel pride for their organization and, when given the chance, would give their all to a cause they believe in. A tremendous well of creativity and energy is just waiting to be tapped in every organization. Leaders use this knowledge to inspire their employees to take action and to achieve great things.

Leaders know the value of employees and their critical importance in achieving the company's goals. Do the managers in your company know the importance of their employees? Check out what these managers had to say in Bob Nelson's *1001 Ways to Reward Employees*[1]:

▲ The former chair and CEO of the Ford Motor Company Harold A. Poling said, "One of the stepping stones to a world-class operation is to tap into the creative and intellectual power of each and every employee."

▲ According to Paul M. Cook, founder and CEO of Raychem Corporation, "Most people, whether they're engineers, business managers, or machine operators, want to be creative. They want to identify with the success of their profession and their organization. They want to contribute to giving society more comfort, better health, [and] more excitement."

▲ Hewlett-Packard cofounder Bill Hewlett said, "Men and women want to do a good job, a creative job, and if they are provided the proper environment, they will do so."

Unfortunately, few managers reward their employees for being creative or for going beyond the boundaries set by their job descriptions. Too many managers search for workers who do exactly what they are told—and little else. This practice is a tremendous waste of worker creativity, ideas, and motivation.

Leaders are different. Instead of draining energy from their employees, leaders unleash the natural energy within all employees. They do so by clearing the roadblocks to creativity and pride from the paths of their workers and by creating a compelling vision for their employees to strive for. Leaders help employees tap into energy and initiative that the employees didn't know they had.

Create a compelling vision for your employees and then clear away the roadblocks to creativity and pride. Your vision must be a stretch to achieve, but not so much of a stretch that the vision is impossible to achieve.

2.2.2 Communicating with Others

Leaders make a commitment to communicate with their employees and to keep them informed about the organization. Employees want to be an integral part of their organizations and want their opinions and suggestions to be heard. Great leaders earn the commitment of their workers by building communication links throughout the organization—from the top to the bottom, from the bottom to the top, and from side to side.

So how do you build communication links in your organization? Consider the experiences of the following business leaders as listed in Bob Nelson's *1001 Ways to Reward Employees*[2]:

▲ Andrea Nieman, administrative assistant with the Rolm Corporation, summarized her company's commitment to communication like this: "Rolm recognizes that people are the greatest asset. There is no 'us' and 'them' attitude here; everyone is important. Upper management is visible and accessible. There is always time to talk, to find solutions, and to implement changes."

▲ Robert Hauptfuhrer, former chair and CEO of Oryx Energy, stated: "Give people a chance not just to do a job but to have some impact, and they'll really respond, get on their roller skates, and race around to make sure it happens."

Great leaders know that leadership isn't a one-way street. Leadership today is a two-way interchange of ideas where leaders create a vision and workers throughout an organization develop and communicate ideas of how best to reach the vision. The old one-way, command-and-control model of management doesn't work anymore. Commanding workers may have worked in the traditional U.S. Army, but as a daily means of managing a company, it doesn't work well at all. Most employees aren't willing to simply take orders and be directed all day long.

2.2.3 Supporting and Facilitating Achievement

Great leaders create environments in which employees can feel safe to speak up, to tell the truth, and to take risks. The numbers of managers who punish their employees for pointing out problems that they encounter, for disagreeing with

FOR EXAMPLE

Asking for Employees' Opinions Makes a Difference

According to Donald Petersen, former president and CEO of Ford Motor Company, "When I started visiting the plants and meeting with employees, what was reassuring was the tremendous, positive energy in our conversations. One man said he'd been with Ford for 25 years and hated every minute of it—until he was asked for his opinion. He said that question transformed his job."

the conventional wisdom of management, or for merely saying what is on their minds is incredible. Even more incredible, many managers punish their employees for taking risks and losing, instead of helping their employees win the next time around.

Great leaders support their employees and facilitate their ability to reach their goals. The heads of some companies do just the opposite: instead of leading their employees with vision and inspiration, they use fear and intimidation. The management team members then live in constant fear. When this approach is taken, some managers simply withdraw into their shells and say as little as possible in the leaders' presence. Consider these managers' statements in *1001 Ways to Reward Employees*[3]:

▲ Catherine Meek, president of a compensation consulting firm Meek and Associates, says, "In the 20 years I have been doing this and the thousands of employees I have interviewed in hundreds of companies, if I had to pick one thing that comes through loud and clear it is that organizations do a lousy job of recognizing people's contributions. That is the number one thing employees say to us. 'We don't even care about the money; if my boss would just acknowledge that I exist. The only time I ever hear anything is when I screw up. I never hear when I do a good job.'"

▲ According to Lonnie Blittle, an assembly-line worker for Nissan Motor Manufacturing Corporation U.S.A., "There was none of the hush-hush atmosphere with management behind closed doors and everybody else waiting until they drop the boom on us. They are right down pitching in, not standing around with their hands on their hips."

▲ James Berdahl, vice president of marketing for Business Incentives, says, "People want to feel empowered to find better ways to do things and to take responsibility for their own environment. Allowing them to do this has had a big impact on how they do their jobs, as well as on their satisfaction with the company."

Instead of abandoning their employees to the sharks, great leaders throw their followers life preservers when the going gets particularly rough. Although leaders allow their employees free rein in how they achieve their organizations' goals, leaders are always there in the background—ready to assist and support workers whenever necessary. With the added security of this safety net, employees are more willing to stretch themselves and to take chances that can create enormous payoffs for their organizations.

SELF-CHECK

1. Most employees are rewarded for creativity. True or false?
2. Leaders:
   (a) keep employees on a strict schedule regardless of the obstacles.
   (b) micromanage employees.
   (c) often ask for employees' opinions.
   (d) care only if employees do what they are asked.
3. Leaders:
   (a) make sure their employees never take risks.
   (b) make sure their employees do not say anything in meetings to embarrass them.
   (c) allow employees to take risks and help them to do well.
   (d) try to keep morale up by not discussing issues or obstacles.

2.3 Surveying Leading Leadership Traits

Today's new business environment is one of unrelenting change. Businesses will continue to transform in the foreseeable future. Although so many factors in business keep shifting, great leadership remains steadfast—like a sturdy rock standing up to the storms of change. Numerous traits of great leaders have remained the same over the years and are still highly valued today. The following sections discuss the leading leadership traits.

2.3.1 Maintaining an Optimistic Outlook

Great leaders always see the future as a wonderful place. Although they may find much adversity and hard work on the way to achieving their goals, leaders always look forward to the future with great promise and optimism. This optimism becomes a glow that radiates from all great leaders and touches all those employees who come into contact with them.

People want to feel good about themselves and their futures, and they want to work for winners. Workers are therefore naturally attracted to people who are optimistic rather than pessimistic. Who wants to work for someone who enjoys nothing more than spouting doom and gloom about the future of a business? Negative managers only demotivate their employees and coworkers and lead workers to spend more time polishing their résumés than they do concentrating on improving their organizations.

Optimism is infectious. Before long, a great leader can turn an organization full of naysayers into one that's overflowing with positive excitement for the future. This excitement results in greater worker productivity and an improved organizational environment. Morale increases, and so does the organization's bottom line.

2.3.2 Displaying Confidence

Great leaders have no doubt—at least not publicly—that they can accomplish any task they set their minds to. Confident leaders make for confident followers, which is why organizations led by confident leaders are unstoppable. An organization's employees mirror the behavior of their leaders. When leaders are tentative and unsure of themselves, so are workers (and the bottom-line results of the organization). When leaders display self-confidence, workers follow suit, and the results can be astounding. Confident leaders inspire the best performance from their employees at the same time as they help them become more confident in their abilities.

2.3.3 Maintaining Integrity

One trait that sets great leaders apart from the rest of the pack is integrity: ethical behavior, values, and a sense of fair play. Honest people want to follow honest leaders. People want their leaders to have integrity. **Integrity** is adherence to a moral code. In a recent survey, integrity was the most desired trait that employees wanted from their leaders. When an organization's leaders conduct themselves with integrity, the organization can make a very real and positive difference in the lives of its employees, its customers, and others who come in contact with it. This, in turn, results in positive feelings from employees about the organization.

Most working Americans devote a third (or more) of their waking hours to their jobs. Whether the organization makes light fixtures, disposes of radioactive waste, develops virtual reality software, or delivers pizzas, people want to be part of an organization that makes a positive difference in people's lives. Sure, money is important—people have to make car payments and clothe their children—but few would not count this *external* reward a secondary consideration to the *internal* rewards that they derive from their work.

> ### FOR EXAMPLE
>
> #### Enron and a Lack of Integrity
>
> A lack of integrity can cause organizations to lose more than just a few employees. Enron, an energy company that was based in Houston, Texas, is an example of a company that had charismatic leaders who did not have integrity. After a series of scandals that included improper accounting procedures and fraud, Enron went bankrupt in 2001. Enron's 21,000 employees lost their jobs. Enron stock went from $90.00 a share to $0.30 a share, which had a ripple effect throughout the economy. Thousands of employees lost their life savings as well in company stock.

2.3.4 Making Decisions

The best leaders are decisive. If employees make the same complaint again and again, they say that their bosses won't make decisions. Despite the fact that making decisions is one of the key reasons that people are hired to be managers, too few are willing to risk the possibility of making a wrong decision. Instead of making wrong decisions—and having to face the consequences—many so-called leaders prefer to indefinitely postpone making a decision, instead continually seeking more information, alternatives, and opinions from others. They hope that, eventually, events may overtake the need to make the decision, or perhaps that someone else may step up to the plate and make the decision for them.

Great leaders make decisions. Now, this statement doesn't mean that great leaders make decisions in a shoot-from-the-hip, cavalier, gotta-do-it-right-now fashion. No, great leaders take whatever time is necessary to gather whatever information, people, or resources they need to make an informed decision within a reasonable time frame. If the data are immediately available, so be it. If not, then a leader carefully weighs the available data vs. the relative need of the decision and acts accordingly.

SELF-CHECK

1. _____ is an adherence to a moral code.
2. Explain why optimism is an important quality in a leader.
3. An organization's employees mirror the behavior of their leaders. True or false?
4. Why are some managers afraid to make decisions?

2.4 Fostering Collaborative Leadership

A new kind of leadership is gaining traction in an increasing number of organizations: collaborative leadership. **Collaborative leadership** is a leadership style where everyone works together; the leader shares leadership with the employees of the organization. This leadership sharing occurs not just with other managers and supervisors, but with employees at *all* levels—from the shop floor to the front line and everywhere else.

So, what exactly does collaborative leadership look like in the workplace? Here are a few examples:

▲ W. L. Gore and Associates—manufacturer of a variety of products including GORE-TEX®—is famous for its unique lattice organizational structure that encourages collaborative leadership. W. L. Gore and Associates has no formal hierarchy: Ranks, titles, and layers of management don't exist. The company only has sponsors and associates. Sponsors must attract and engage a sufficient number of associates to get their projects off the ground.

▲ To achieve its ultimate goal of "the genuine care of and comfort of our guests," management of the Ritz-Carlton Hotel Company promotes lateral service—a philosophy that encourages every employee to handle whatever problem comes his or her way, without consulting higher-ups regardless of their place on the organizational chart.

▲ Aside from president Carol Sturman, employees of the Woodland Park, Colorado–based Sturman Industries don't have titles, the organization is flat, and all employees are encouraged to play an active role in decision making. Even high-level corporate policies—such as the company's drug-free workplace policy and the company's at-will employment policy—are subject to vigorous discussion, debate, and input by all employees before they're adopted.

In the book *Leadership Ensemble: Lessons in Collaborative Management from the World's Only Conductorless Orchestra*,[4] coauthored by Harvey Seifter, Peter Economy takes a close look at the unique brand of collaborative leadership practiced by New York City's Orpheus Chamber Orchestra. Orpheus is one of the world's truly great orchestras, and it is one of very few to perform without a conductor. The vast majority of orchestras are noted not because of the musicians who play the music, but because of their conductors, who are often visionary, charismatic (and autocratic) leaders. The conductor calls all the shots when it comes to the notes that an orchestra's musicians play, and how and when they play them.

By foregoing the traditional model of a conducted orchestra—with one leader and many followers—Orpheus fosters a culture of collaboration where every musician can be a leader and is expected to play an active role in the shaping of the group's final product: its music. Does this system work? Yes. Orpheus's performances have been acclaimed throughout the world, and the group has numerous Grammy-winning albums and other awards to its credit.

At the heart of the Orpheus Process—the system of collaborative leadership that has brought the group great success over its three-decade history—are eight principles. These principles include:

1. **Put power in the hands of the people doing the work.** Those employees closest to the customers are in the best position to know the customers' needs, and they're in the best position to make decisions that directly impact their customers.

2. **Encourage individual responsibility for product and quality.** The flip side of putting power in the hands of the people doing the work is requiring employees to take responsibility for the quality of their work. When employees are trusted to play an active role in their organization's leadership, they'll naturally respond by taking a personal interest in the quality of their work.

3. **Create clarity of roles.** Before employees can be comfortable and effectively share leadership duties with others, they first need clearly defined roles so that they know exactly what they are responsible for, as well as what others are responsible for.

4. **Foster horizontal teamwork.** Because no one person has all the answers to every question, effective organizations rely on horizontal teams—both formal and informal—that reach across department and other organizational boundaries. These teams obtain input, solve problems, act on opportunities, and make decisions.

5. **Share and rotate leadership.** By moving people in and out of positions of leadership—depending on the particular talents and interests of the individuals—organizations can tap the leadership potential that resides within every employee, even those employees who aren't part of the formal leadership hierarchy.

6. **Discover how to listen, discover how to talk.** Effective leaders don't just listen; effective leaders talk—and they know the right times (and the wrong times) to make their views known. Effective organizations encourage employees to speak their minds and to contribute their ideas and opinions, whether or not others agree with what they have to say.

7. **Seek consensus (and build creative systems that favor consensus).** One of the best ways to involve others in the leadership process is to invite them to play a real and important role in the discussions and debates that lead to making important organizational decisions. Seeking consensus requires a high level of participation and trust, and it results in more democratic organizations.

FOR EXAMPLE

Collaborative Leadership

To encourage collaborative leadership, banking powerhouse JPMorgan Chase maintains a flat organization with only four levels of employees worldwide: managing director, vice president, associate, and analyst. With fewer lines of reporting, every employee has the opportunity—and the responsibility—to play a much greater role in leading and in making decisions.

8. **Dedicate passionately to your mission.** When people feel passion for the organizations in which they work, they care more about them and about their performance. This caring is expressed in the form of increased employee participation and leadership.

Collaborative leadership is growing in popularity in all kinds of organizations in all kinds of places. Why? Collaborative leadership is growing because organizations today can't afford to limit leadership to just a few individuals at the top. To survive and prosper, today's organizations need to get the most out of every employee. Every employee needs to take a leadership role in his or her organization, to make decisions, to serve customers, to support colleagues, and to improve systems and procedures. Employees and leaders who can't meet this challenge may soon find that they will be left behind by others who can.

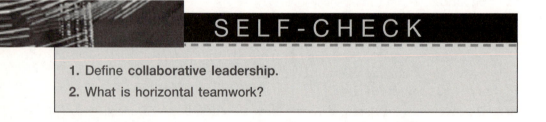

SELF-CHECK

1. Define **collaborative leadership**.
2. What is horizontal teamwork?

SUMMARY

Everyone in an organization wants to work with great leaders. A leader is someone who has influence, vision, confidence, and integrity. Leaders inspire others to action by communicating a vision for a better tomorrow, communicating that vision, and listening to input from others. A leader's vision becomes reality when employees are encouraged to take risks and be creative. One way to achieve the best for an organization is through collaborative leadership, a leadership style where everyone works together and shares the leadership role.

KEY TERMS

Collaborative leadership	A leadership style where everyone works together; the leader shares leadership with the employees of the organization.
Integrity	Adherence to a moral code.
Leader	A person who has commanding authority or influence over others and inspires them toward goals.
Manager	A person who supervises others in an effort to complete tasks or accomplish goals.

ASSESS YOUR UNDERSTANDING

Go to www.wiley.com/college/nelson to assess your knowledge of leadership. *Measure your learning by comparing pre-test and post-test results.*

Summary Questions

1. *Manager* and *leader* are interchangeable terms. True or false?
2. According to a recent survey, _____ was the most desired trait in leaders.
3. Collaborative leadership:
   (a) maintains a strict hierarchy.
   (b) is common in many U.S. companies.
   (c) seeks to put power in the hands of the people doing the work.
   (d) involves having a different leader every day.
4. Leaders make decisions based on:
   (a) their personal priorities.
   (b) what their employees want.
   (c) the available data.
   (d) how they think the boss will react to their decision.
5. Optimism increases employee _____.
6. Leaders encourage employees to take risks. True or false?
7. If people feel passionately about their organization, their _____ improves.
8. Leaders use values, policies, procedures, schedules, milestones, incentives, and discipline to push their employees to achieve the goals of the organization. True or false?

Applying This Chapter

1. What is the difference between a manager and a leader?
2. What are three things leaders can do to get better performance from their employees?
3. What qualities make a good manager?
4. Why is encouraging individual responsibility for the quality of their work important?
5. What is involved in building a consensus within an organization?

YOU TRY IT

What Makes a Leader

Think about a leader you either know personally or you know of. This person can be a leader in a company, in the community, or in a political position. Write a paper discussing how this person has demonstrated leadership characteristics. Include a discussion of this person's vision, communication style, confidence, optimism, and integrity.

Improve Your Organization

You were just named vice president of General Motors, an automobile manufacturer that has suffered several financial problems in recent years. Employee morale is low because of the company losing sales to the Japanese automakers as well as recent layoffs. What general steps do you take to improve morale?

3

GOAL SETTING
Improving Performance

Starting Point

Go to www.wiley.com/college/nelson to assess your knowledge of goal setting.
Determine where you need to concentrate your effort.

What You'll Learn in This Chapter

▲ The difference between goals and vision

▲ The characteristics of SMART goals

▲ Different methods used to communicate goals with employees

▲ The importance of having a few goals and prioritizing them

▲ The characteristics of different sources of power

After Studying This Chapter, You'll Be Able To

▲ Align an organization's goals to its vision

▲ Create SMART goals

▲ Communicate goals effectively

▲ Select a few vital goals and prioritize them

▲ Use different sources of power to achieve your goals

INTRODUCTION

In most companies, top management sets the overall purpose—the vision—of the organization. Middle managers then have the job of developing goals and plans for achieving the vision set by top management. Managers and employees work together to set goals and develop schedules for attaining them.

Goals provide direction and purpose. Goals help you see where you're going and how you can get there. And the way that you set goals can impact how motivating they are to others. Studies have shown that those who achieve the most in life have personal and professional goals. Managers are usually immersed in personal goals and goals for employees, their department, and their organization.

In this chapter, you will examine the difference between a company's goals and a company's vision. You will assess the characteristics of effective goals and how to achieve them. Even the best goals, however, are not useful when they are not communicated to others. You will learn how to communicate goals effectively. Finally, you will compare and contrast the different sources of power that employees have.

3.1 Setting a Direction

The first step in setting goals is knowing what you want the end result to be. For example, suppose that you have a vision of starting up a new sales office in Prague so that you can better service your Eastern European accounts. How do you go about achieving this vision? You have two choices:

▲ An unplanned, non-goal-oriented approach
▲ A planned, goal-oriented approach

You are much more likely to be able to set up a new sales office in Prague when you take a planned, goal-oriented approach, communicate this approach, and have the support of other employees.

3.1.1 The Difference between Goals and Vision

Managers and supervisors are expected to lead their department in achieving their organization's vision and follow-through on goals. The difference between an organization's vision and goals is as follows:

▲ A **vision** is the overall purpose of the organization. A vision is a long-term, broad, strategic direction that will take several years to achieve. The vision is usually set by the CEO, president, or another top-level executive.
▲ A **goal** is the specific result of an effort to improve an organization in some way. Goals can be short-term or long-term and should also align with the vision of the organization.

An organization's vision is usually to be at the top of its industry. For example, Kimberly-Clark, the company that makes Kleenex®, has the vision to become the best in the world at paper-based consumer products.[1] This vision was set by Darwin Smith, the former CEO of the company, back in 1971. When Procter & Gamble entered the paper-based business in the 1960s, other companies were resigned that P&G would take some of their market share. However, Smith was not deterred from his vision. One day he asked his managers to meet; he then asked them to observe a moment of silence. The managers were confused. After the pause, Smith said, "That was a moment of silence for P&G." This approach excited employees and everyone worked hard to beat P&G for market share; Kimberly-Clark was able to beat P&G for market share as well.[2]

Taking the example of Kimberly-Clark, its goals may resemble the following:

▲ To increase domestic market share by 5 percent over the next year.
▲ To reduce expenses by 8 percent over the next year.
▲ To increase international presence, by selling into select Japanese markets.

When it comes to goals, the best ones:

▲ Are few in number, specific in purpose.
▲ Are stretch goals—not too easy, not too hard.
▲ Involve people: when you involve others, you get buy-in so it becomes *their* goal, not just yours.

3.1.2 The Link between Goals and Vision

Following are the main reasons to set goals whenever you want to accomplish something significant:

▲ **Goals provide direction.** For our first example (starting up a new sales office in Prague), you can probably find a million different ways to better service your Eastern European business accounts. However, to get something done, you have to set a definite vision—a target to aim for and to guide the efforts of you and your organization. You can then translate this vision into goals that take you where you want to go. Without goals, you may waste countless hours going nowhere. With goals, you can focus your efforts and your staff's efforts on only the activities that move you toward where you're going—in this case, opening a new sales office.

▲ **Goals tell you how far you've traveled.** Goals provide milestones along the road to accomplishing your vision. If you determine that you must accomplish several specific milestones to reach your final destination and you complete a few of them, you know exactly how many remain. That is, you know exactly where you stand and how far you have yet to go.

▲ **Goals help make your overall vision attainable.** You can't reach your vision in one big step—you need to take many small steps to get there. Again, if your vision is to open a new sales office in Prague, you can't expect to proclaim your vision on Friday and walk into a fully staffed, functioning office on Monday. You must accomplish many goals—from shopping for office space, to hiring and relocating staff, to printing stationery and business cards—before you can attain your vision. Goals enable you to achieve your overall vision by dividing your efforts into smaller pieces that, when accomplished individually, add up to big results.

▲ **Goals clarify everyone's role.** When you discuss your vision with your employees, they may have some idea of where you want to go but no idea of how to get there. As your well-intentioned employees work to help you achieve your vision, some employees may duplicate the efforts of others, some employees may ignore certain tasks, and some employees may simply do something else altogether (and hope that you don't notice the difference). Setting goals with employees clarifies what the tasks are, who does which tasks, and what is expected from each employee.

▲ **Goals give people something to strive for.** People are typically more motivated when challenged to attain a goal that's beyond their normal level of performance; this is what's known as a **stretch goal.** Not only do goals give people a sense of purpose, but they also relieve the boredom that can come from performing a routine job day after day. Be sure to discuss the goal with them and gain their commitment.

For goals to be useful, they have to link directly to the final vision. To stay ahead of the competition, or simply to remain in business, organizations create compelling visions and then management and employees work together to set and achieve the goals to realize those visions. Look over these examples of compelling visions that drive the development of goals at several successful enterprises. These visions are, perhaps, even more important as the organizations fight to thrive in the face of depressed telecommunications and technology sectors.

▲ Samsung is the $35 billion, Korean-based manufacturer of electronics, chemicals, and heavy machinery, as well as architectural and construction services. At Samsung, management created a clear and compelling vision that drives the goals of the organization. Samsung's vision is to become one of the world's ten largest "technological powerhouses."

▲ Motorola, long known for its obsession with quality, has set a truly incredible vision for where it wants to be in the next decade. Motorola has set a target of no more than two manufacturing defects per billion.

> ## FOR EXAMPLE
>
> ### Visions Can Change
>
> Almost a century ago, the chair of AT&T created this vision for the organization: the dream of good, cheap, and fast worldwide telephone service. Now, with the explosion of information technology creating incredible new opportunities for the telecommunications industry, AT&T has had to create a new vision. AT&T's new vision is to be a "major factor in the worldwide movement and management of information."

3.1.3 Different Visions and Different Goals for Different Purposes

Although most of the examples in this chapter will relate to businesses, non-profits and educational institutions have visions and goals as well. However, their vision may be very different from what you would find in a business. For example, the Michael J. Fox Organization, an organization devoted to the elimination of Parkinson's disease, wants to fund a cure for Parkinson's and go out of business as quickly as possible. Everyone in the organization understands this, believes in the cause, and works hard to make the jobs obsolete. The staff sets short-term goals that are aligned with this vision.

Educational institutions also have different visions and goals. For example, the Yale Medical School's vision is "to educate and inspire scholars and future leaders who will advance the practice of medicine and the biomedical sciences."[3] The faculty and staff of Yale Medical School work on short-term goals that align with this vision.

SELF-CHECK

1. What is the difference between a **vision** and a **goal**?
2. The best goals are those that are difficult to achieve. True or false?
3. A(n) _____ _____ requires someone to work beyond his or her normal level of performance.
4. For goals to be effective, they must be aligned with a company's _____.

3.2 Identifying SMART Goals

You can find all kinds of goals in all types of organizations. Some goals are short-term and specific. An example would be the statement, "starting next month, we will increase production by two units per employee per hour." Other goals may be vague and subject to interpretation; for instance, "within the next five years, we will become a learning organization." Employees easily understand some goals like in the first example; but other goals can be difficult to fathom and subject to much interpretation. Some goals can be accomplished relatively easily, whereas others are virtually impossible to attain.

How do you know what kind of goals to set? The whole point of setting goals, after all, is to achieve them. It does you no good to call meetings, hack through the needs of your organization, and burn precious time, only to end up with goals that aren't acted on or completed. Unfortunately, this scenario describes what far too many managers do with their time.

The best goals are *smart* goals—actually, SMART goals is more like it. **SMART** refers to a handy checklist for the five characteristics of well-designed goals.

▲ **Specific:** Goals must be clear and unambiguous; broad and fuzzy thinking has no place in goal setting. When goals are specific, they tell employees exactly what's expected, when, and how much. Because the goals are specific, you can easily measure your employees' progress toward their completion.

▲ **Measurable:** What good is a goal that you can't measure? If your goals aren't measurable, you never know whether your employees are making progress toward their successful completion. Not only that, but your employees may have a tough time staying motivated to complete their goals when they have no milestones to indicate their progress.

▲ **Attainable:** Goals must be realistic and attainable by average employees. The best goals require employees to stretch a bit to achieve them, but they aren't extreme. That is, the goals are neither out of reach nor below standard performance. Goals that are set too high or too low become meaningless, and employees naturally come to ignore them.

▲ **Relevant:** Goals must be an important tool in the grand scheme of reaching your company's vision and mission. It's said that 80 percent of workers' productivity comes from only 20 percent of their activities. This relationship comes from Italian economist Vilfredo Pareto's **80-20 rule,** which states that 80 percent of the wealth of most countries is held by only 20 percent of the population. This rule has been applied to many other fields since its discovery. Relevant goals address the 20 percent of workers' activities that have such a great impact on performance and bring an organization closer to its vision.

▲ **Time-bound:** Goals must have starting points, ending points, and fixed durations. Commitment to deadlines helps employees focus their efforts on completion of the goal on or before the due date. Goals without deadlines or schedules for completion tend to be overtaken by the day-to-day crises that invariably arise in an organization.

SMART goals make for smart organizations. Many supervisors and managers neglect to work with their employees to set goals together. And in the ones that do, goals are often unclear, ambiguous, unrealistic, immeasurable, demotivating, and unrelated to the organization's vision. By developing SMART goals with your employees, you can avoid these traps while ensuring the progress of your organization and its employees.

Although the SMART system of goal setting provides guidelines to help you frame effective goals, you have additional considerations to keep in mind. These considerations (explained in the following list) help you ensure that the goals, which you and your employees agree to, can be easily understood and acted on by anyone in your organization.

▲ **Ensure that goals are related to your employees' role in the organization.** Pursuing an organization's goals is far easier for employees when those goals are a regular part of their jobs. For example, suppose you set a goal for employees who solder circuit boards to "raise production by 2 percent per quarter." These employees spend almost every working moment pursuing this goal, because the goal is an integral part of their job. If, however, you give the same employees a goal of "improving the diversity of the organization," what exactly does that have to do with your line employees' role? Nothing. The goal may sound lofty and may be important to your organization, but because your line employees don't make the hiring decisions, you're wasting your time and their time with that particular goal.

▲ **Whenever possible, use values to guide behavior.** What is the most important value in your organization? Honesty? Fairness? Respect? Whatever it is, ensure that leaders model this behavior, and reward employees who live it.

▲ **Simple goals are better goals.** The easier your goals are to understand, the more likely the employees are to work to achieve them. Goals should be no longer than one sentence; make them concise, compelling, and easy to read and understand.

3.2.1 Setting Goals: Less Is More

Avoid taking on too many goals in your zeal to get as many things done as quickly as you can. Too many goals can overwhelm you, and they can overwhelm your employees, too. You're far better off if you set a few significant goals and then concentrate your efforts on attaining them. Don't forget that management isn't a game of huge success after huge success. Instead, it's a daily meeting of challenges and opportunities—gradually, but inevitably, improving the organization in the process. Remember that too many goals can overwhelm you, so set your goals accordingly.

The following guidelines can help you select the right goals—and the right number of goals—for your organization:

▲ **Pick two to three goals to focus on.** You can't do everything at once, and you can't expect your employees to either. A few goals are the most you should attempt to conquer at any one time. Picking too many goals dilutes the efforts of you and your staff and can result in a complete breakdown in the process.

▲ **Pick the goals with the greatest relevance.** Certain goals take you a lot farther down the road to attaining your vision than do other goals. Because you have only so many hours in your workday, it clearly makes sense to concentrate your efforts on a few goals that have the biggest payoff—rather than on a boatload of goals with relatively less payoff.

▲ **Focus on the goals that tie most closely to your organization's mission.** Don't be tempted to take on goals that are challenging, interesting, and fun to accomplish but that are far removed from your organization's mission.

▲ **Periodically revisit the goals and update them as necessary.** Business is anything but static, and periodically assessing your goals is important to making sure that they're still relevant to the vision you want to achieve. If so, great—carry on. If not, meet with your employees to revise the goals and the schedules for attaining them.

3.2.2 Following Through on Goals

Don't let all your hard work go for naught. When you go through the trouble of setting goals, keep them to a manageable number that can realistically be followed up on. And, when you finish one goal, move on to the next. To examine follow-through, let's look at the fictional case of ACME, a pharmaceutical company. ACME lost two major patents in the past year and was losing market share as a result. ACME had determined that it needed to develop a long-range, strategic plan. The entire management team was marshaled for this effort—the team scheduled several all-day planning sessions, retained a high-priced consultant, and pronounced to the workers that something major was brewing at the top.

The management team threw itself wholeheartedly into the planning effort. The managers wanted to answer questions like:

▲ Why does the organization exist?
▲ Who are its customers?
▲ What are its values?
▲ What is its mission?
▲ What are its goals?
▲ How can the organization know when it achieves the goals?

Session after session, they had great idea after great idea. Before long, they had more than twelve poster-sized flip-chart pages taped to the walls of the meeting room, each brimming with goals for the organization: "Improve customer service." "Provide quicker project turnaround." "Fix the heating and air conditioning system at corporate headquarters." And many more—in all, more than two hundred!

FOR EXAMPLE

The Power of the Annual Goal at Marmot Mountain

When Steve Crisafulli was brought on a number of years ago as president of Marmot Mountain Ltd., a California-based producer of super-high-quality outdoor clothing, he quickly discovered that Marmot was in big trouble. According to Crisafulli, Marmot "had no credit records, an unusable computer inventory system, and financial statements that were six months late. I had never before seen a company this screwed up from an operational standpoint." Crisafulli planned to develop specific goals to lead the company to his vision of profitability. However, the job wasn't done immediately, but one step at a time. "The way to run a small business is to concentrate on one or two small things," Crisafulli said.

The first problem to receive Crisafulli's attention was the firm's traditional difficulties making deliveries to customers on time. In one particularly bad example of Marmot's problems in this area, the entire winter clothing line—due to arrive in stores by Labor Day—was not delivered until January of the next year. As a result, business dropped precipitously. Soon, Crisafulli made timely delivery of Marmot products the firm's number one priority. Employees agreed to a goal of getting the next winter clothing line out no later than mid-September. To meet the goal, the management team implemented daily meetings, managers began to communicate with each other and with workers, quality control inspectors went out to check on key suppliers, and marketing budgets were increased.

"Most of what you lack in a small business is resources. People often say, 'I don't have enough money,' but the real thing you lack is time. People are doing a once-over-lightly on too many things. Trying to advance on too broad a front, they don't go anywhere," Crisafulli said.

Not only did Marmot achieve its goal, but also the entire winter clothing line was shipped out two weeks ahead of the mid-September deadline. Even today, the company and its president retain the single-mindedness that delivered it from the brink of disaster years ago. At its annual strategic meeting, Marmot's management team decides on one goal for the following year. According to Crisafulli, "It hasn't failed to work yet. That's the beauty of the system: If you focus on only one thing, it's not difficult to achieve. It's much easier than trying to meet 20 different goals."[4]

When the last planning meeting ended, the managers congratulated each other over their collective accomplishment and went back to their regular office routines. Before long, the goals were forgotten: the pages on which they were recorded were neatly folded and stored away in someone's file cabinet. Meanwhile, business went on as usual, and the long-range planning effort went into long-term hibernation. Soon, the organization's employees who knew that the management team had embarked on a momentous process of strategic planning finally tired of asking about it.

ACME not only failed to achieve its goals but also wasted time in the process and lowered employee morale. Employees were hopeful that things would change for the better as a result of the meeting and were enthusiastic about the plans, but the plans never came to fruition.

SELF-CHECK

1. The **80-20 rule** was originally developed when Vilfredo Pareto observed that in any organization 20 percent of the employees do 80 percent of the work. True or false?

2. The *M* in **SMART** stands for_____.

3. What criteria should you use when choosing the most important goals to focus on?

4. Why is following through on goals important?

3.3 Communicating Your Goals to Your Team

Having goals is great, but how do you get the word out to your employees? As you know, goals grow out of an organization's vision. Establishing goals helps you ensure that employees focus on achieving the vision in the desired time frame. You have many possible ways to communicate goals to your employees, but some ways are better than others. In every case, you must communicate goals clearly, the receiver must understand the goals, and the goals must be followed through.

Goals are personal, and the methods you use to communicate them must be much more formal and direct. The following guidelines can help you:

▲ Make sure that the goals are written down.

▲ Always conduct one-on-one, face-to-face meetings with your employees to introduce, discuss, and assign goals. If physical distance prohibits—or for any reason you can't conduct—a face-to-face meeting, conduct your meeting over the phone. The point is to make sure that your employees receive the goals, understand them, and have the opportunity to ask for clarifications.

▲ Call your team together to introduce team-related goals. You can assign goals to teams instead of to individuals. If this is the case, get the team together and explain the role of the team and each individual in the successful completion of the goal. Make sure that all team members understand exactly what they are to do and are excited about it.

▲ Gain the commitment of your employees, whether individually or on teams, to the successful accomplishment of their goals.

Ask your employees to prepare and present plans and milestone schedules explaining how they can accomplish the assigned goals by the deadlines that you agreed to. After your employees embark on the pursuit of their goals, regularly monitor their progress to ensure that they're on track and meet with them to help them overcome any problems.

Communicating your organization's vision is as important as communicating specific goals. You can communicate the vision in every way possible, as often as possible, throughout your organization and to significant others such as clients, customers, suppliers, and so forth. You also need to be aware of possible obstacles: Often an organization's vision is pounded out in a series of management meetings that leave the participants beaten and tired. By the time the managers reach their final goal of developing a company's vision, they are sick of it and ready to go on to the next challenge.

Many organizations drop the ball at this crucial point and are thereby slow to communicate the vision. Also, each succeeding layer of an organization has the natural tendency to draw some of the energy from the vision so that, by the time it filters down to the frontline employees, the vision has become dull and lifeless.

When you communicate vision and goals, do it with energy and with a sense of urgency and importance. You are talking about the future of your organization and your employees. If your employees don't think that you care about the vision, why should they? Simply put, they won't.

Companies usually announce their visions with much pomp and fanfare. The following are different ways that companies commonly announce and communicate their vision:

▲ By conducting huge employee rallies where the vision is unveiled in inspirational presentations.

▲ By printing their vision on anything possible—business cards, letterhead stationery, massive posters hung in the office, newsletters, employee name tags, and more.

▲ By encouraging managers to "talk up" the vision in staff meetings or other verbal interactions.

To avoid a cynical "fad" reaction from employees who are suspicious of management's motives when unveiling a new initiative, consistent, casual reference to it is much more effective than a huge, impersonal event. Again, in this case, less is often better.

FOR EXAMPLE

Hallmark Communicates Its Goals in Many Different Ways

The management of Hallmark Cards, Inc., the world's largest producer of greeting cards, firmly believes in the value of communicating the organization's vision, goals, and vital business information to its employees. According to former Hallmark president and CEO Irvine O. Hockaday Jr., "The only sustainable edge for a corporation is the energy and cleverness of its people. To tap that, a chief executive must craft a vision, empower employees, encourage teamwork, and kindle the competitive fires."

To back up its commitment to getting the word out to employees, Hallmark developed an elaborate portfolio of formal employee publications. In addition to distributing a daily newsletter, *Noon News,* for all employees, Hallmark publishes *Crown,* a bimonthly magazine for employees, and a newsletter for managers titled *Directions.* However, Hallmark's commitment to communicating doesn't end with newsletters and magazines: when Hockaday worked at Hallmark, he regularly invited workers from throughout the organization to join him for a meal to share information.

SELF-CHECK

1. You should always write down your goals. True or false?
2. Goals can be set for individuals or for _____ within companies, or they can be companywide.
3. To track the progress toward achieving goals, there should be a(n) _____ schedule.
4. It is not important for you to communicate goals face-to-face to employees, as long as employees know what the goals are. True or false?

3.4 Juggling Priorities: Keeping Your Eye on the Ball

After you've decided the goals that are important to you and to your organization, you come to the difficult part. How do you maintain the focus of your employees—and your own focus, for that matter—on achievement of the goals that you've set?

The process of goal setting often generates a lot of excitement and energy within employees, whether the goals are set in large group meetings or in one-on-one encounters. This excitement and energy can quickly dissipate as soon as everyone gets back to his or her desk. You, the manager, must take steps to ensure that the organization's focus remains centered on the goals and not on other matters (which are less important but momentarily more pressing). Of course, this task is much easier said than done.

Staying focused on goals can be extremely difficult—particularly when you're a busy person and the goals are added on top of your regular responsibilities. Think about situations that fight for your attention during a typical day at work:

▲ How often do you sit down at your desk in the morning to plot out your priorities for the day only to have them pushed aside five minutes later when you get a call from your boss?

▲ How many times has an employee come to you with a problem?

▲ Do you remember getting caught in a fifteen-minute meeting that dragged on for over an hour?

In unlimited ways, you or your employees can fall off track and lose the focus that you need to get your organization's goals accomplished. One of the biggest problems that employees face is confusing activity with results. Do you know anyone who works incredibly long hours—late into the night and on weekends—but never seems to get anything done? Although this employee always seems to be busy, the problem is that he or she is working on the wrong things.

We previously discussed the general rule that says that 80 percent of workers' productivity comes from 20 percent of their activity. The flip side of this rule is that only 20 percent of workers' productivity comes from 80 percent of their activity. This statistic illustrates the activity trap at work. What do you do in an average day? More important, what do you do with the 80 percent of your time that produces so few results? You can get out of the activity trap and take control of your schedules and priorities. However, you have to be tough, and you have to be single-minded in pursuit of your goals.

Achieving your goals is all up to you. No one, not even your boss (perhaps especially not your boss), can make it any easier for you to concentrate on achieving your goals. You have to take charge, and you have to take charge now! If you aren't controlling your own schedule, you're simply letting everyone else control your schedule for you. Following are some tips to help you and your employees work on the items that help all of you achieve the company's goals:

▲ **Do your number one priority first!** With all the distractions that compete for your attention, with the constant temptation to work on the easy stuff first and save the tough stuff for last, and with people dropping into your office just to chat or to unload their problems on you, concentrating on your number one priority is always a challenge. However, if you don't do your number one priority first, you're almost guaranteed to find yourself in the trap. That is, you're almost guaranteed to find the same priorities on your list of tasks to do day after day, week after week, and month after month. If your number one priority is too big, divide it into smaller chunks and focus on the most important one of those.

▲ **Get organized!** Getting organized and managing your time effectively are incredibly important pursuits for anyone in business. If you're organized, you can spend less time trying to figure out what you should be doing and more time doing what you should be doing.

▲ **Just say no!** If someone tries to make his or her problems your problems, just say no! If you're a manager, you probably like nothing more than taking on new challenges and solving problems. The conflict arises when solving somebody else's problems interferes with solving your own. You have to constantly be on guard and fight the temptation to fill your day with meaningless activities. Always ask yourself, "How does this help me achieve my goals?" Focus on your own goals and refuse to let others make their problems your own.

SELF-CHECK

1. Twenty percent of workers' productivity comes from 80 percent of their activity. True or false?
2. Achieving goals is easier when you are _____ and use your time efficiently.

3.5 Using Your Power for Good: Making Your Goals Happen

After you create a wonderful set of goals with your employees, how do you make sure that they get done? How do you turn your priorities into your employees' priorities? The best goals in the world mean nothing if they aren't achieved. You can choose to leave this critical step in the process to chance, or you can choose to get involved.

You have the power to make your goals happen. Power has gotten a bad rap lately. In reaction to the autocratic leadership styles that often ruled the roost in many American corporations, employees have increasingly demanded, and organizations have increasingly provided, management that is principle centered and that has a more compassionate, human face.

Nothing is inherently wrong with power—everyone has many sources of power within them. Not only do you have power but you also exercise power to control or influence people and events around you on a daily basis. Generally, power is a positive thing. However, power can be a negative thing when abused. Manipulation, exploitation, and coercion have no place in the modern workplace.

You can use the positive power within you to your advantage—and to the advantage of the people around you—by tapping into it to help achieve your organization's goals. People and systems often fall into ruts or into nonproductive patterns of behavior that are hard to break. Power properly applied can jump-start these people and systems and move them in the right direction: the direction that leads to the accomplishment of goals.

Everyone has five primary sources of power, and each of you has specific strengths and weaknesses related to these sources. Recognize your strengths and weaknesses and use them to your advantage. As you review the five sources of power that follow, consider your own personal strengths and weaknesses.

▲ **Personal power:** This is the power that comes from within your character. Your passion for greatness, the strength of your convictions, your ability to communicate and inspire, your personal charisma, and your leadership skills all add up to personal power.

▲ **Relationship power:** Everyone has relationships with others at work. These interactions contribute to the relationship power that you wield in your offices. Sources of relationship power include close friendships with top executives, partners, or owners; people who owe you favors; and coworkers who provide you with information and insights that you would normally not get through your formal business relationships.

▲ **Knowledge power:** To see knowledge power in action, notice what happens the next time your organization's computer network goes down! Then you'll see who really has the power in an organization (in this case, your computer network administrator). Knowledge power comes from the special expertise and knowledge that you have gained during the course of your career. Knowledge power also comes from obtaining academic degrees (think MBA) or special training.

▲ **Task power:** Task power is the power that comes from the job or process that you perform at work. As you have undoubtedly witnessed on many occasions, people can facilitate or impede the efforts of their coworkers and others through the application of task power. For example, when you submit a claim for payment to your insurance company and months pass with no action ("Gee, we don't seem to have your claim in our computer—are you sure you submitted one? Maybe you should send us another one just to be safe!"), you are on the receiving end of task power.

▲ **Position power:** This kind of power derives strictly from your rank or title in the organization and is a function of the authority that you wield to command human and financial resources. Although the position power of the receptionist in your organization is probably quite low, the position power of the president or owner is at the top of the chart. The best leaders seldom rely on position power to get things done today.

If you're weak in certain sources of power, you can increase them if you want. For example, work on your weakness in relationship power by making a concerted effort to know your coworkers better and to cultivate relationships with higher-ranking managers or executives. Instead of passing on the invitations to get together with your coworkers after work, join them—have fun and strengthen your relationship power at the same time.

Be aware of the sources of your power and use it in a positive way to help you and your employees accomplish the goals of your organization. For getting things done, a little power can go a long way.

SELF-CHECK

1. A CEO always has _____ power.
2. What is **personal power**?
3. Power is always used in a negative way. True or false?
4. The CEO's personal assistant has _____ _____.

SUMMARY

An organization can live up to its full potential only if it sets and strives toward goals that are closely aligned with the company's vision. These goals should be SMART goals. SMART goals are specific, measurable, attainable, relevant, and time-bound. As you have learned, these goals must be communicated effectively and prioritized. You and other managers can use different sources of power to ensure the goals have buy-in from all employees.

KEY TERMS

80-20 rule	Eighty percent of the wealth of most countries is held by only 20 percent of the population; the rule has been applied to many other fields since its discovery.

Goal	The specific result of an effort to improve an organization in some way. Goals can be short-term or long-term and should align with the vision of the organization.
Knowledge power	Authority that comes from the special expertise and knowledge gained during one's career. Also comes from obtaining academic degrees or special training.
Personal power	Authority that comes from within someone's character.
Position power	Authority that comes from rank or title in the organization.
Relationship power	Authority that comes from close friendships with top executives, partners, or owners; people who owe you favors; and coworkers who provide privileged information and insights.
SMART goals	Goals that have the following five characteristics: specific, measurable, attainable, relevant, and time-bound.
Stretch goal	Goal that requires you to work beyond your normal level of performance.
Task power	Authority that comes from the job.
Vision	The overall purpose of the organization. A vision is a long-term, broad, strategic direction that will take several years to achieve. The vision is usually set by the CEO, president, or another top-level executive.

ASSESS YOUR UNDERSTANDING

Go to www.wiley.com/college/nelson to evaluate your knowledge of goal setting. *Measure your learning by comparing pre-test and post-test results.*

Summary Questions

1. The *M* in *SMART* stands for "many." True or false?
2. The organization's overall purpose is its _____.
3. _____ _____ can come from academic degrees.
4. An effort that requires someone to work beyond his or her normal level of performance is a:
    (a) vision.
    (b) stretch goal.
    (c) SMART goal.
    (d) simple goal.
5. CEOs who are well liked by the employees have _____ _____ in addition to having position power.
6. After setting goals, the most important goal should be concentrated on first. True or false?
7. Goals _____ everyone's role within the organization.
8. SMART stands for:
    (a) smart, measurable, accurate, relevant, timely.
    (b) specific, measurable, accurate, relevant, timely.
    (c) specific, many, attainable, relevant, time-bound.
    (d) specific, measurable, attainable, relevant, Time-bound.
9. After setting goals, managers must gain _____ from the employees that they will work toward these goals.
10. Simple goals are the best goals. True or false?
11. What characteristics do specific goals have?

Applying This Chapter

1. You work for a computer manufacturer that prides itself on customer service. Write down a sample vision for the organization and three sample goals the company might have that relate to customer service.
2. You are the manager in a call center that includes top performers, mediocre performers, and poor performers. As a result, the average wait time that a customer is on the phone is twenty minutes. You set a goal

to cut that time in half. How do you communicate this goal to all the employees?

3. You work in a marketing department for an athletic wear company. Your goal is to increase market share by 5 percent. How do you take this goal and turn it into a SMART goal?

4. You are the director of human resources for a school system. You have one important goal: to recruit a new principal for an underperforming school. You try to work on this goal every day, but you are constantly interrupted by your boss and by employees. Furthermore, you have so much work on your desk that you are overwhelmed. How can you ensure that you achieve your goal?

5. You are the director of a large accounting firm and you have set two goals for the next year. How do you ensure these goals are achieved and there is follow-through?

YOU TRY IT

Vision and Goals

You decide to go into business for yourself and you buy a restaurant. Write down what your overall vision for the restaurant is and what your goals would be for its first year of operation.

Communicating Goals

You are the manager of a small consulting firm and your company has the goal to increase the number of billable hours by 50 percent. This will mean more client time as well as more travel time away from the office for every consultant. Write a communications plan as to how you will communicate these goals effectively and enthusiastically.

Sources of Power

Compare and contrast the sources of power that autocratic and unpopular executives use with those sources of power that democratic, well-liked executives use.

4

EFFECTIVE COMMUNICATION

Improving Performance through Listening and Providing Feedback

Starting Point

Go to www.wiley.com/college/nelson to assess your knowledge of effective communication.

Determine where you need to concentrate your effort.

What You'll Learn in This Chapter

▲ The difference between informal and formal communication
▲ The importance of communication as a management tool
▲ The common barriers to effective communication
▲ How to provide effective feedback to employees
▲ The difference between active and passive listening

After Studying This Chapter, You'll Be Able To

▲ Assess the different communication methods
▲ Decide when to use verbal communication instead of written communication
▲ Support your employees by being an active listener
▲ Construct methods for overcoming common barriers to effective communication
▲ Select ways to provide effective feedback to employees

INTRODUCTION

Excellent interpersonal or human relations skills are required if you hope to eventually become a successful supervisor, manager, or owner of a profitable business. This is especially true for both lower-level managers and owners who have daily contact with employees and valued customers. Since the communication process contributes significantly to our overall interpersonal skills, our ability to communicate effectively will undoubtedly play a huge role in the success or failure of the operation. Communication is all-important for the growth and survival of today's organizations. How big or how small the organization is doesn't matter—communication must be the cornerstone of every organization.

In business, communication takes place in a variety of formats. Table 4-1 shows the order in which the bulk of business communication occurs. However, the formal training that most Americans receive in school reverses this order. Table 4-2 illustrates the focus of formal communication training.

As you can see, informal communication—not formal communication—is most important in business. Many managers fail because they don't understand this critical point. The occasional speeches you make, the beautifully crafted memos you write, and the many articles on chaos theory that you read don't have any effect on how you really communicate with your employees. You can make a difference when you talk to your employees one-on-one, face-to-face, day in and day out. Listening to them and really hearing what they have to say is vital.

Over the past couple of decades, a fundamental change in the style of business communication has occurred. Long ago, most business communication—whether verbal or in writing—was very formal and constrained. This style came out of the old view of business where workers were little more than cogs in a vast machine.

Today, the way that business people communicate has changed. In fact, the wrong way is now the right way. Business communication today is, above anything else, informal and nonhierarchical. Fast and furious, quick and dirty—sure, formal communication still has its place in contracts, licensing agreements, and nasty letters to wayward suppliers, for example.

Table 4-1: The Format of Business Communications

Communication Format	Frequency of Use
Listening	Most frequent
Speaking/presentation	Next most frequent
Writing	Next most frequent
Reading	Least frequent

Table 4-2: Formal Education Provided in Communications

Communication Format	Training Provided
Reading	4 years English
Writing	4 years English
Speaking/presentation	Optional class
Listening	Little formal training offered

This chapter is about communicating with others and, in particular, the way in which you do it. In this chapter, you will assess different communication methods, learn when to use written and verbal communications, and find out how to overcome common communication barriers and provide effective feedback to your employees.

4.1 Using Different Communication Methods

The **communication process** is simply the sending and receiving of information, which is a powerful thing. Information enables managers and supervisors to make sound business decisions. Without it, important decisions about the organization, its environment, its products and services, and its employees and customers are made in a vacuum; nothing could be more dangerous for a hospitality business. Information is also an important key to employee satisfaction. For employees, a lack of sufficient information will often lead to high stress levels and low morale among workers, two significant causes of turnover.

If information is the engine that drives the business, then the **communication systems** that management puts into place are what fuel the engine. Communication systems may be written or verbal and can be a combination of both formal and informal methods for circulating information throughout the organization.

The extent to which management needs to convey or receive information as well as the type of information that needs conveying will best determine the optimal form of communication. Clearly, matters affecting policy, procedures, and other issues of importance will require more formal methods of delivery. The intended audience, or those who will receive the information, will also determine whether a more formal or informal approach is necessary. **Formal communication** often addresses task-related issues and tends to span the organization's chain of command. Examples include the following:

▲ A supervisor gives directions to an employee about how to greet a guest.
▲ An employee offers advice to a work team in her department.
▲ An employee suggests a way to improve productivity to his supervisor.

FOR EXAMPLE

Management-by-Walking-Around

When J. W. Marriott Jr. tours one of his hotels, he likes to stroll the entire property with the general manager at his side. Marriott is not only interested in the hotel's "numbers," but he also pays attention to the way the general manager interacts with the hotel's staff. Speaking of one such stroll, Marriott said that he and the hotel's general manager were "greeted by smiles, teasing, and hellos from just about every Marriott associate we passed. What's the big deal? Why was I so pleased? At Marriott, the reaction of staff to the GM is the ultimate litmus test of how well a hotel is run."[1]

This hands-on, management-by-walking-around (MBWA) approach has been an important part of Marriott's corporate culture for over seventy-five years. It also illustrates an effective informal communication method.

▲ A supervisor interacts with other supervisors at a weekly staff meeting.

▲ An employee responds in writing to a request made by his supervisor.

Informal communication may or may not follow the chain of command; it may move in any direction, and it is as likely to satisfy social needs as it is to facilitate the functions of business. Informal communication methods include **management-by-walking-around (MBWA)**, a hands-on approach that encourages effective two-way communication among staff as well as between managers and subordinates. The traditional **open-door policy**, where employees are free to walk into any manager's office with their problems, is another way to foster informal communication. Most workers are reluctant to take a problem to their boss, or even to their boss's boss, so the best open-door policy is the one where the manager gets up from her desk and walks out of her office to talk to employees in their space. Other examples of informal communication may include the employee grapevine. Formal communication methods may consist of such things as memos, reports, employee suggestion boxes, and employee newsletters or bulletin boards.

4.1.1 Using the Employee Grapevine

Perhaps the least understood method of informal communication is the **employee grapevine** and the rumors and gossip it provides. When two employees chat in the break room about their trouble with a supervisor, this is grapevine communication. Some managers see this as a positive source of informal communication, and they have an interest in the grapevine because it provides useful, off-the-record feedback from employees—if managers are prepared to listen, understand, and interpret the information.

Managers who keep their employees in the dark about company concerns have the potential to breed anxiety and fuel gossip and rumors, a generally less positive form of grapevine communication. A recent study conducted by ISR, a global employee research and consulting firm headquartered in Chicago, found that the majority of employees view the employee grapevine as more informative than what they hear from their boss when it comes to work issues, and 63 percent of workers said that rumors are usually how they first hear about important business matters.[2] Good leaders are good communicators, and this research shows that some managers have a lot to learn when it comes to communicating with their employees. One thing is certain: the employee grapevine will never go away, so wise managers will learn to tap into the grapevine's value as a way of identifying key issues of importance to employees.

4.1.2 Using Downward and Upward Communication

The most effective hospitality managers and supervisors make use of extensive communication systems to keep people informed. Although the goal is to facilitate an open, two-way flow of information, most messages are of the top-down variety.

▲ **Downward communication** is information that begins at some point in the organizational structure and cascades down the chain of command to inform or influence others. Downward communication is necessary to execute decisions and to give employees information about the organization. Successful hospitality operations should use a variety of downward communication methods because the diversity of multiple communication channels is more likely to overcome barriers and reach the intended receivers.[3] Examples of downward communication include company and department newsletters and bulletin boards, email and recorded messages, reports, booklets, and meetings held to inform employees about company issues.

▲ **Upward communication** originates within the organization's lower levels and filters to its higher levels. This sort of communication is initiated by employees who seek to inform or influence those who are higher up in the organization's hierarchy. In many businesses, there is probably no area of communication that is more in need of improvement than upward communication. When supervisors have a good relationship with their employees, and when two-way communication between these groups flows freely, upward communication is very powerful in that it allows employees to participate in the day-to-day decision making that goes on in the organization.

Some businesses encourage this form of communication by using **employee suggestion boxes.** Workers are encouraged to write down their ideas or concerns and to drop them in a special box, sometimes anonymously, where upper management will later retrieve them and, hopefully, act on them. In some instances, organizations will reward an employee who has come up with a cost-saving idea or with an idea to increase business and revenue.

SELF-CHECK

1. A company newsletter is an example of **upward communication.** True or false?
2. Company gossip is also known as the _____ _____.
3. An **open-door policy** is an example of _____ communication.
4. What is the difference between **formal** and **informal communication?**

4.2 Choosing When to Use Verbal vs. Written Communication

Managers and supervisors must constantly rely on their verbal communication skills. Meeting with an employee, training a new hire, and instructing staff members are all superb examples of instances where excellent communication skills are essential for managers and supervisors to work effectively with their employees as well as their guests.

There are many benefits to delivering information to others orally. Certainly, the ease and speed with which large amounts of information can be conveyed is one benefit. One's facial expressions and body language as well as the tone of voice used will also add depth to the information being delivered. Many would argue that because of the evolution of email and other electronic means of communication, verbal communication provides a more personal interaction and fosters feelings of trust and goodwill.

If the message you need to send is somewhat complex and official, or is intended for a more formal audience, then written communication is generally the method that should be used. Forms of written communication include memos, reports, presentations, and so forth. Generally, the lengthier and more involved the message, the greater the need for presenting the information in written form. This method also provides an official record or other such documentation, which may be important in the future for substantiating facts and information. Providing communication in writing also helps eliminate confusion and ambiguity over the message that is being sent.

4.2.1 The Information Superhighway

Email, voice mail, cell phones, pagers, the Internet, and even corporate intranets have forever changed the way in which individuals communicate with each

FOR EXAMPLE

Monitoring Internet Use

A large percentage of companies are monitoring Internet use by workers. Although some organizations still allow some personal use of the Web, many companies will ask employees to limit the amount of time they spend at online shopping sites, and some companies will block employee access to some Web locations altogether. Companies are taking advantage of new Web-filtering software programs that allow management to retain and review employees' e-mail messages, and most companies have some kind of policy regarding personal e-mail use. Other types of monitoring software allow organizations to monitor and track e-mail content, keystrokes, and the time an employee spends at the keyboard. Plenty of workers have been fired for misusing the Internet. A good rule of thumb for managers and employees is to apply good judgment when accessing the Internet and to keep focused on the task at hand.

other. Hospitality businesses large and small increasingly rely upon these electronic means of sending and receiving information. Today's technology enables key staff members to be in constant contact with management—and vice versa—no matter where in the world each person is located. Of all these electronic methods of communication now available, email is probably the most popular Internet application because it extends and enhances our ability to communicate with others regardless of physical geography. E-mail encourages informal communication. The ease of quickly typing a reply to a message and zapping it off within minutes of receiving the initial message is a powerful and efficient way to communicate. However, such ease and informality may create problems for those using e-mail, so it is necessary to use judgment, restraint, and thoughtfulness when communicating by e-mail.

In business, the formality of e-mail messages tends to vary, between the semiformal approach, previously the domain of the interoffice memo, and the chatty exchanges that you might have with someone over the telephone or while sitting in the break room. The approach you take when e-mailing will depend upon your intended audience. Remember, because e-mail messages are surprisingly permanent, since they are technically online written messages, a good rule of thumb is to think before you press the Send button.

4.2.2 Harnessing the Power of the Written Word

At first glance, you may think that the information revolution has made the written word less important. Nothing is further from the truth. Indeed, instead of making the written word less important, the information revolution has increased the variety of written media at your beck and call and increased the speed at which the written word travels. Writing well in business is more important than ever—you need to write concisely and with impact.

Regardless of whether you're writing a one-paragraph e-mail message or a hundred-page report for your boss, business writing shares common characteristics. Review the list of writing tips that follows and don't forget to practice these tips every opportunity you get. The more you write, the better you get at it. So write, write, and then write some more.

▲ **What's the point? (Get to it!):** Before you set pen to paper (or fingertip to keyboard), think about what you want to achieve. What information are you trying to convey, and what do you want the reader to do as a result? Who is your audience, and how can you best reach it?

▲ **Get organized:** Organize your thoughts before you start to write. Jotting down a few notes or creating a brief outline of your major points may be beneficial. Bounce your ideas off coworkers and business associates or find other ways to refine them and get the all-important reality check.

▲ **Write the same way that you speak:** Written communication and spoken communication have a lot more in common than many people think—the best writing most closely resembles normal, everyday speech. Writing that is too formal or stilted is less accessible and harder to understand than conversational writing. Although this doesn't mean that you should start using slang like "gonna" and "ain't" in your reports and memos, it does mean you should loosen up!

▲ **Make it brief and concise:** Write every word with a purpose. Make your point, support it, and then move on to the next point. Don't repeat, and don't fill your memos, letters, and other correspondence with needless fluff simply to give them more weight or to make them seem more impressive. If you can make your point in three sentences, then don't write three paragraphs or three pages to accomplish the same goal.

▲ **Keep it simple:** Simplicity is a virtue. Avoid the tendency to use a fifty-cent word when a simpler one works. Be alert to the proliferation of cryptic acronyms and jargon that mean nothing outside of a small circle of industry insiders and replace them with more common terminology whenever possible.

▲ **Write and then rewrite:** Few writers can get their thoughts into writing perfectly on the first try. The best approach is to write your first draft without worrying too much about whether you've completed it perfectly. Next, read through your draft and edit it for content, flow, grammar, and readability. Keep polishing your work until it shines.

▲ **Convey a positive attitude:** No one likes to read negative memos, letters, reports, or other business writing. Instead of making the intended points with their intended targets, negative writing often only reflects poorly on its author, and the message gets lost in the noise. Be active, committed, and positive in your writing. Even when you convey bad news, your writing can indicate that a silver lining follows even the worst storm.

SELF-CHECK

1. List two advantages that verbal communication has over written communication.
2. List and describe two ways you can improve your written communications.
3. The approach you take to writing e-mails will depend on your_____.

4.3 Common Obstacles to Effective Communication

The messages that we send are not always the messages that are received. It is easy for our communications to be rendered ineffective if the sender and/or the receiver interpret the message in a way that distorts or obscures the intended meaning. For example, if your new friend Cameron phones you and says, "Hey, I thought I'd come over and knock you up!" this message may be deemed as either extremely offensive or at the very least, quite confusing. Once you realize that Cameron is from New Zealand and in the vernacular of that country, to "knock someone up" means to go knock on their door and pay them a visit, the message is no longer unclear.

Obstacles, or barriers, to effective communication can take many forms. Examples include cultural differences, which can affect attitudes, opinions, and values; differences in background, which include education, past experiences, and intelligence; our prejudices and perceptions; our assumptions and expectations; and our emotions.

4.3.1 Cultural Differences

When individuals have different cultural backgrounds, effective communication can be challenging because differences in backgrounds will affect our attitudes, opinions, and values. Two individuals may even share the same cultural backgrounds, but still differ in the way they think about things and look at certain issues. The old adage that one can talk about anything but religion and politics has a ring of truth to it, as people have strong feelings about these issues. Never

---

FOR EXAMPLE

Language Differences

Even between two English-speaking countries there may be many terms that mean different things. For example, in England the word *ace* means "brilliant." The word *rubber* means "eraser," and the word *barmy* means "mad or crazy."

---

tell off-color jokes, ethnic-based jokes, and so forth. Not only does this behavior put you at risk of losing the respect of your coworkers and subordinates, but it could get you into legal trouble as well.

4.3.2 Differences in Background

People sometimes struggle with the communication process when they do not share similar backgrounds. Someone's background might include the level of education attained, the past experiences encountered, and the person's overall level of intelligence. These inherent differences do not suggest that the individual with more education is better than the individual with less, or that the person who has had a wider variety of unique experiences is better than the person who has had fewer.

Obviously, it is important to be aware of such differences and adjust your approach to the communication process appropriately. Slang can be difficult for newcomers to grasp, and often, modern slang falls on deaf ears if the receiver of the message is significantly older than the sender. The reverse is true when older slang is directed at a younger audience. Consider the plight of the fifteen-year-old who worked the counter at his parent's diner after school: A customer walked in, plopped down on a lunch counter stool, and said, "Gimme some Joe." "My name's Luke," said the kid, somewhat perplexed. "No," the guy said, "Joe, you know, coffee."

4.3.3 Prejudices and Perceptions

Aside from differences in age, education, and culture, prejudices and perceptions can also distort communication. Workers are often drawn from diverse backgrounds, which will, of course, influence the language they use and the meanings that they give to words. We often think of prejudice as biases certain individuals have against people of a specific race, sex, sexual orientation, and so forth. Prejudice may also include biases against certain religions, against people who are overweight, against people whose political opinions differ from our own, and even against people who grew up in different parts of the United States. It is important not to form wide-sweeping opinions about members of a certain group. Words should be chosen carefully so as not to offend; otherwise, the message you are sending will simply stir up anger and cause your message to be rejected.

An individual's perceptions can be a barrier to effective communications. People tend to see and sense things differently. Using words that have no real, concrete meaning will often lead to confusion and chaos. When giving direction and instructions to your staff, it is best to use language that is measurable, concrete, and not open to interpretation.

4.3.4 Assumptions and Expectations

When you assume listeners know what you are talking about, you are simply asking for trouble. If, in fact, the listener is oblivious, the entire message may be lost. It is best to know for certain that the listener is on the same page as you are to avoid anger and confusion when your message is not properly acted on. This is especially true in operations that may have employees who do not speak English as a first language. People who come from certain cultural backgrounds may be reluctant to tell you that they do not understand something. Misguided assumptions may also lead to jumping to inaccurate conclusions, which prevents effective communication. Where expectations are concerned, we often get exactly what we expect to get. In other words, if you expect very little from your employees, then that is exactly what you are likely to get. We communicate our expectations all the time, whether we realize it or not. Communicating high expectations will often result in high achievement on the part of your employees.

4.3.5 Emotions

Emotions are a powerful force, but they have no real place in effective communication at work. In fact, emotions may be one of the most difficult obstacles to overcome, particularly the emotion of anger. Things said in anger tend to bury the message entirely, leaving the listener as well with feelings of anger, fear, or anxiety. A good rule of thumb is to regain your composure before speaking.

4.3.6 Overcoming Barriers to Effective Communication

Some of these barriers and obstacles may never be completely overcome. People are different, and that is unlikely to change anytime soon. Having employees from diverse backgrounds can tend to complicate the communication process further. Being aware of these obstacles is the first step to overcoming them. There are some other actions that effective managers and supervisors can take to overcome the barriers to effective communication. These actions include the following:

▲ **Think about what you are going to say.** If the message you intend to deliver is not entirely clear to you, then it certainly will not be clearly conveyed or received by the listener. If your message is to be delivered in writing, jot down some notes and reread what you have written, ensuring clarity of the message.

▲ **Keep your emotions under control.** No one will be rational 100 percent of the time, but it is a good practice to maintain rationality *most* of the time. Remember that extreme emotions will cloud your message and misconstrue meaning. When in doubt, calm down first.

▲ **Be a good listener.** Most people are not very good listeners. We hear things, but that is not necessarily the same as listening. Active listening is the key to being a good listener, and we will examine active and passive listening techniques in the next section of this chapter.

▲ **Actions speak louder than words.** Be sure that your actions and your body language match your message. Nonverbal cues carry a lot of weight, so the effective manager must be tuned in to body language, both his own and that of the listener.

▲ **Provide and ask for feedback.** It is important to provide employees with feedback, whether it is positive or negative. It is also important to ask for feedback to ensure that messages sent have been properly received.

SELF-CHECK

1. People sometimes struggle with the communication process when they do not share similar _____.

2. _____, such as anger, may be the most difficult obstacle to overcome in providing effective communication.

3. You should avoid talking about _____ and politics in the workplace.

4. _____ can be difficult for nonnative English speakers to grasp.

5. Communicating high expectations will often result in high _____ on the part of your employees.

6. Name and describe one way you can overcome barriers for effective communication.

4.4 Active and Passive Listening

Much of the information presented in this chapter thus far has focused on communication methods that involve sending or delivering information. Although these skills are certainly necessary in order to achieve effective communication, they paint only half of the picture. The other half of the picture is, of course, your ability to listen effectively.

▲ **Passive listening** is simply hearing; in other words, you are not really processing the entire message. You may get bits and pieces, but more than likely you will not process the information that was sent.

▲ **Active listening,** on the other hand, requires effort and concentration because you want to fully understand what the speaker is saying.

There are generally four requirements for active listening:

1. **Listen with intensity.** Because it is easy for the mind to wander, active listening requires concentration and focus. Instead of thinking about what you will make for dinner, or what you will wear to next week's party, you are an active listener if your thought process involves summarizing and integrating what is being said.

2. **Listen with empathy.** Your ability to put yourself in the speaker's shoes means that you must put your own thoughts and assumptions on hold and try to understand what the speaker wants to communicate rather than what you want to understand.

3. **Listen with acceptance.** This means that you are objective about the message being sent and that you do not prejudge the speaker or the content of the information being delivered. Distractions occur when you disagree and begin to compose some objection or retort in your mind. It is more effective to concentrate on the entire message as it is delivered and to withhold objections until the speaker is finished.

4. **Take responsibility for the message.** In other words, now may be the time to ask for clarification, to disagree with a point made, to agree, or simply to respond in some meaningful manner. Active listeners take responsibility to ensure that they have received the speaker's full, intended meaning.

Of course, making an effort to give your full attention is easier said than done. How can you focus on the other person and not allow all the people and tasks that are vying for your attention distract you? You have a tough job, but someone has to do it. And that someone is you! The following tips may help:

▲ **Express your interest:** One of the best listening techniques is to be interested in what your counterpart has to say. For example, give your counterpart your full attention and ask questions that clarify what he or she has to say. You can say, "That's really interesting. What brought you to that particular conclusion?" There is no bigger turnoff to communication than for you to yawn, look around the room aimlessly, or otherwise show that you're not interested in what your coworker is saying. The more interest you show your counterpart, the more interesting he or she becomes.

▲ **Maintain your focus:** People speak at the rate of approximately 150 words per minute. However, people think at approximately 500 words per minute. This gap leaves a lot of room for your mind to wander. Make a point of keeping your mind focused on listening to what the other person has to say. If your mind starts to wander, then rein it back in right away.

▲ **Ask questions:** If something is unclear or doesn't make sense to you, then ask questions to clarify the subject. Not only does this practice keep communication efficient and accurate, but it also demonstrates to the speaker that you're interested in what he or she has to say. *Reflective listening*—summarizing what the speaker has said and repeating it back to him or her—is a particularly effective way of ensuring accuracy in communication and demonstrating your interest. For example, you can say, "So you mean that it's your belief that we can sell our excess capacity to other firms?"

▲ **Seek the key points:** What exactly is your counterpart trying to tell you? Anyone can easily get lost in the forest of details of a conversation and miss seeing the trees as a result. As you listen, make a point of categorizing what your speaker has to say into information that is key to the discussion and information that isn't really relevant. If you need to ask questions to help you decide which is which, then don't be shy—ask away! "What does that have to do with meeting our goals?"

▲ **Avoid interruptions:** Although asking clarifying questions or employing reflective listening techniques is okay, constantly interrupting the speaker or allowing others to do so is not okay. When you're having a conversation with an employee, make him or her the most important thing in your life at that moment. If someone telephones you, don't answer it; that's what voice mail is for, after all. If someone knocks on your door and asks whether he or she can interrupt, say no, but that you can talk after you finish your current conversation. If your building is on fire, then you may interrupt the speaker.

▲ **Listen with more than your ears:** Communication involves a lot more than the obvious, verbal component. According to communications experts, up to 90 percent of the communication in a typical conversation is nonverbal! Facial expressions, posture, position of arms and legs, and much more add up to the nonverbal component of communication. Because this is the case, you must use all your senses when you listen—not just your ears.

▲ **Take notes:** Remembering all the details of an important conversation hours, days, or weeks after it took place can be quite difficult. Be sure to take notes when necessary. Jotting down notes can be a terrific aid to listening and remembering what was said. Plus, when you review your notes later, you can take the time to organize what was said and make better sense of it.

SELF-CHECK

1. _____ _____ means hearing.
2. _____ _____ requires concentration and effort.
3. People speak at the rate of 500 words a minute, whereas people listening can process only 150 words per minute. True or false?

4.5 Providing Effective Feedback

Some inexperienced managers and supervisors believe that managing means strolling out of the office once or twice a day and trying to catch an employee doing something wrong. That way, the manager can manage things by telling the employee what he has done wrong. This action is usually followed by the manager making a hasty retreat back to the office, leaving the employee in the dust with a bewildered look on his face. Effective managers realize that there will be times when they will need to correct employee behavior so that standards of performance are being met, but these managers also spend a great deal of time trying to catch employees doing things right. When this occurs, and it *will* occur often if the manager is truly doing her job, it presents an opportunity to provide some positive feedback and thus reinforce positive behavior. Believe it or not, negative feedback can also change behavior when properly directed.

4.5.1 The Role of Positive Feedback

Telling your employees that they are doing a good job and then pointing out specific examples is providing **positive feedback.** When the executive housekeeper says to the room attendant "Great job! This room is perfect. I can see that you take a lot of pride in your work," the manager has left the room attendant with a feeling of pride for a job well done, and the manager has also reinforced the importance of properly cleaning the hotel's guest rooms. Such feedback takes only a moment to deliver, but its effects can last a very long time.

Positive feedback is easy to deliver, so it's unclear why many managers and supervisors fail miserably in this area. Employees in some hospitality operations get so little feedback from management that they begin to wonder whether the work that they do even matters. These are the employees who quickly get frustrated and leave the company for greener pastures—not in the sense that they leave for more money, but that they prefer to work for an organization where what they do is important to the overall success of the operation, that what they do matters. Delivering positive feedback usually feels good, both to the deliverer and to the receiver. Positive feedback is almost always well received because it reinforces what people want to hear or what they already believe to be true about themselves.

4.5.2 The Role of Negative Feedback

Strolling out of the office and barking at the employee who has done something wrong is not **negative feedback.** It certainly is negative, but the missing element would be the feedback. Managers often avoid negative feedback because they know that it will be met with resistance by their employees. Most people want to hear only the good things, not the bad. Negative feedback should not be avoided, however, but simply reworked in such a way that it becomes an effective management tool. The ultimate goal of negative feedback is to change incorrect behavior or performance, so it is best used when you are dealing with absolutes such as hard numbers, data, and other specifics. Telling an employee that she has a bad attitude is not telling that employee anything at all. What does *bad* mean exactly? Did she come to work somewhat grouchy and a few minutes late, or did she get into a screaming match with a customer?

4.5.3 Guidelines for Providing Feedback That Works

The goal of feedback is to either enforce behavior (positive feedback), or change behavior (negative feedback). For feedback to be effective, you should remember the following points:

▲ **Be specific.** This is most important when the feedback is meant to correct behavior or actions that do not meet performance standards. Even when you are providing positive feedback, specifics are important so that the employee knows exactly which behavior to repeat.

▲ **It's not personal.** Don't attack the person; attack the behavior. Rather than saying "You're doing a bad job," choose wording that focuses on the behavior, *not* on the employee's personality. Focusing on the person rather than the behavior will rarely be met with anything but a negative reaction and is hardly productive.

▲ **Be in the moment.** Feedback that is either negative or positive must be delivered in a timely manner. It does no good to delay negative feedback, because much information can be lost over time. It's best to correct inappropriate behavior at the moment it occurs. This principle also applies to positive feedback.

▲ **Keep the goal in mind.** Negative feedback should be offered only when doing so can change behavior. What is your goal in delivering negative feedback? Do you just need to dump on someone, or can you pinpoint specific behavior that needs improving and offer reasons for why it should be improved?

One final thing to keep in mind when offering negative feedback is that the feedback should be directed at something over which the employee has control. Negative feedback also presents management with a good opportunity to offer suggestions on how the employee can change behavior for the better.

SELF-CHECK

1. Yelling at an employee who has done something wrong is **negative feedback?** True or false?
2. When providing feedback, you should be _____ and detail what you want to see changed.
3. _____ feedback should be offered only when doing so it can change behavior.
4. _____ feedback is easy to deliver.

SUMMARY

Effective managers and supervisors need excellent interpersonal or human relations skills to communicate with employees and to provide the kind of work environment where talented employees can self-motivate.

The communication process—sending and receiving information—contributes significantly to one's human relations skills. When employees lack sufficient information, the result can be stress and low morale, which leads to high employee turnover rates. Communications systems drive the communication process; these systems may be written, verbal, formal, and informal. The extent to which you need to convey or receive information as well as the type of information that needs to be conveyed will determine whether formal or informal methods should be used. Formal communication may be written or verbal, and it usually follows the chain of command. Informal communication may also be written or verbal, but it may not follow the chain of command; it may move in any direction.

In this chapter, you assessed how to overcome common barriers to effective communication by keeping your emotions under control, being a good listener, matching your actions with your words, and providing feedback to employees and asking for feedback from them as well. When providing either positive or negative feedback, you should be specific and focus on the behavior and not on the employee personally. You should also be sure that the feedback is timely, and should keep the end goal in mind.

KEY TERMS

Active listening	A concentrated effort to focus and to fully understand the message that is being sent.
Communication process	The method by which information is delivered from a sender to a receiver.
Communication systems	Provide formal and informal methods for moving information throughout an organization.
Downward communication	Information that flows down the chain of command to set policy, to provide information, and to influence others.
Employee grapevine	Informal communication that arises spontaneously from the social interaction of people in the organization.
Employee suggestion box	A common tool used to seek employee input where employees write suggestions or cost-saving ideas and drop them in a box. Management will later retrieve the suggestions submitted by employees and review them.
Formal communication methods	May be written or verbal; examples include memos, reports, employee suggestion boxes, newsletters, and meetings.
Informal communication methods	May be written or verbal; examples include open-door policies, the employee grapevine, and MBWA.
Management-by-walking-around (MBWA)	Managers exhibit this method of management when they leave their offices and engage employees one-on-one at their workstations.
Negative feedback	Employee feedback that serves to correct behavior that is unacceptable and that does not conform to performance standards. It is essential that negative feedback focus on the employee's behavior rather than on the employee personally.

Open-door policy   A company policy whereby the manager's door is always open to employees who may wish to voice a complaint or state an issue.

Passive listening   Hearing but not processing the information being sent.

Positive feedback   Employee feedback that seeks to boost morale and to reinforce positive behavior or actions.

Upward communication   Information that flows from the lower levels of the organization to the higher levels. This often represents information initiated by employees who seek to inform or influence those who are higher in the corporate hierarchy.

ASSESS YOUR UNDERSTANDING

Go to www.wiley.com/college/nelson to evaluate your knowledge of effective communication.
Measure your learning by comparing pre-test and post-test results.

Summary Questions

1. Management-by-walking-around (MBWA) is a formal, written communication system that has been in place at the Marriott Hotel Corporation for over seventy-five years. True or false?

2. Formal communication systems are always preferred to informal communication systems because otherwise, employees will not pay attention to the information being sent. True or false?

3. In organizations with open-door policies, employees are sometimes reluctant to take a problem to their boss or to their boss's boss. True or false?

4. Keeping employees in the dark about company concerns will often fuel gossip and rumors, but that is okay because most managers find this information useful. True or false?

5. Downward communication is normally initiated by employees who are lower in the organization's hierarchy. True or false?

6. Which of the following is *not* a key benefit of verbal communication?
   (a) It works well when the message is complex.
   (b) It works well because it can deliver large amounts of information with speed and ease.
   (c) It works well because of the added benefit of tone of voice.
   (d) It works well because of the added benefit of body language.

7. Differences in background are a common obstacle to effective communication because of all the following *except:*
   (a) individuals may not share the same education levels.
   (b) individuals may not share the same emotions.
   (c) individuals may not share the same past experiences.
   (d) individuals may not share the same level of intelligence.

8. Active listening techniques involve all the following *except:*
   (a) listening with empathy.
   (b) listening with acceptance.
   (c) listening with intensity.
   (d) listening with emotion.

9. Positive feedback seeks to accomplish which of the following?

(a) Ignore employee morale

(b) Reinforce negative stereotypes

(c) Reinforce positive behavior or actions

(d) All of the above

10. Which of the following is *not* a guideline for providing effective feedback?

(a) Always wait a few days before delivering negative feedback to keep your emotions in check.

(b) Focus on specific behavior whether your feedback is positive or negative.

(c) Feedback should either seek to change or reinforce actions and behavior.

(d) Negative feedback regarding something over which the employee has no control should not be given.

Applying This Chapter

1. Provide some examples of how information has flowed through the employee grapevine where you work now or where you have worked in the past. Was the information gathered from the employee grapevine accurate or inaccurate? How do you know this? If you have not had work experience, use the *student grapevine* as your source for this assignment. Be prepared to share your findings with the class.

2. In your own words, explain the difference between active and passive listening. At what times might passive listening be preferred to active listening, and vice versa? Provide examples of a conversation you have had with a friend or a coworker when it was clear to you that the person to whom you were speaking was passively listening. How did this make you feel? Why?

3. Construct three separate email messages that would properly address each of the following scenarios: (1) a message to your boss explaining why last month's costs were eleven percentage points over budget, (2) a message to all eight of your front-office employees requiring them to attend a mandatory meeting at which you plan on discussing methods to increase profit, and (3) a reply email message to a travel agent who has emailed you requesting a travel agent discount for a night on which the hotel will likely be sold out. Compare your messages with those of at least one other student. How are they similar? How are they different? Be specific.

4. You own a day spa and have received several complaints from the customers that the relaxation room and massage rooms are not clean. Give examples of the feedback that you would give to the housekeeping staff.

5. You manage an IT department and you have five employees: two are Native American, one is Indian, one is Mexican, and one is Iraqi. What steps can you take in your communication to ensure it is understood by everyone regardless of their different cultural backgrounds?

YOU TRY IT

Netiquette

Do your own Web research on Internet etiquette, or netiquette. Give examples of the types of communication shortcuts that can be used when sending or replying to e-mail. How do these shortcuts impede the communication process, or do they? Be specific and be prepared to share your work with the class.

Improving Employee Morale

You own a marketing firm and you can sense that many of the employees are unhappy. Write a paper listing and describing some ways you can institute a system for informal, upward communication so you can understand why the employees are unhappy.

5

EMPLOYEE DISCIPLINE
Managing Conflict

Starting Point

Go to www.wiley.com/college/nelson to assess your knowledge of discipline.
Determine where you need to concentrate your effort.

What You'll Learn in This Chapter

▲ The difference between discipline and punishment
▲ How to focus on performance and not personalities
▲ How to discipline employees with performance problems
▲ How to discipline employees who engage in misconduct
▲ The five steps in creating a discipline script
▲ How to make and implement a performance plan

After Studying This Chapter, You'll Be Able To

▲ Discipline employees for performance problems
▲ Discipline employees who engage in misconduct
▲ Write a discipline script using five steps
▲ Create and implement a performance improvement plan
▲ Support employees by following up on their performance improvement plans

INTRODUCTION

It is human nature to want to avoid conflict. However, as a manager, you will have conflict. Good managers will handle the conflict in a manner that improves the organization. Every organization has employees (and managers) who exhibit varying degrees of these behaviors, but don't worry too much about it. However, when your employees make repeated, serious mistakes, when they fail to meet their performance goals and standards, or when it seems that they'd rather be working somewhere else (and they prove that by ignoring company policies), you have to take action to stop the offending behaviors—immediately and decisively. Why?

First, when employees aren't performing up to standard, or when they allow a poor attitude to overcome their ability to pull with the rest of the team, these employees cost an organization more than do the employees who are working at or above standard and pulling their share of the load. Poor performance and poor attitudes directly and negatively affect your work unit's efficiency and effectiveness.

Second, if other employees see that you're letting their coworkers get away with poor performance, they have little reason to maintain their own standards. Not only do you create more management headaches, but also the morale and performance of your entire work unit decreases as a result.

In this chapter, you will discover the importance of dealing with employee performance issues before they become major problems. You will find out why you need to focus on performance and not personality. You also will discover and implement a consistent system of discipline that can work for you, regardless of your line of business.

5.1 Understanding Employee Discipline

Employee discipline has lately gotten something of a black eye. Because of the abuses that more than a few overzealous supervisors and managers have committed, for many workers, the word *discipline* conjures up visions of crazed management tirades, embarrassing public scoldings, and worse.

What does discipline mean to you? What does discipline mean in your organization? Do your employees look forward to being disciplined? Do you?

The reality is that far too many employees confuse the following terms:

▲ **Discipline** is defined as actions taken with the purpose of correcting problems and improving performance.

▲ **Punishment** consists of actions taken with the purpose of causing pain or embarrassment to someone in retribution for some perceived error.

The whole point of this little digression is that employee discipline can be a positive experience. At least it should be when you do it the right way! Through discipline, you bring problems to your employees' attention so that they can take actions to correct them before they become major problems. Remember, however, to build a strong foundation of positives and trust that can be drawn upon when dealing with the negatives. The primary goal of discipline isn't to punish your employees; you want to help guide them back to a satisfactory job performance. Of course, sometimes this step isn't possible, and you have no choice but to terminate employees who can't perform satisfactorily.

Two main reasons to discipline your employees exist:

▲ **Performance problems:** All employees must meet goals as a part of their jobs. For a receptionist, a goal may be to always answer the telephone on the second ring or sooner. For a sales manager, a goal may be to increase annual sales by 15 percent. When employees fail to meet their performance goals, administering some form of discipline is required.

▲ **Misconduct:** Sometimes employees behave in ways that are unacceptable to you as a manager and to the organization. For example, if an employee abuses the company sick leave policy, you have a valid reason for disciplining that employee. Similarly, discipline employees who sexually harass or threaten other employees.

Discipline ranges from simple verbal counseling ("William, you turned in the report a day late. I expect future reports to be submitted on time.") to termination ("Sorry, Mary, I warned you that I wouldn't tolerate any further insubordination. You're fired."). A wide variety of options lie between these two extremes, the use of which depends on the nature of the problem, its severity, and the work history of the employee involved. For example, if the problem is an isolated incident, and the employee normally performs well, the discipline will be less severe than if the problem is repeated and persistent.

Always carry out discipline as soon after the incident as possible—you can deal with problems before they escalate. And, as with rewarding employees, your message is much stronger and relevant when it has the immediacy of a recent event. If too much time lapses between an incident and the discipline that you conduct afterward, your employee may forget the specifics of the incident. Not only that, but you also send the message that the problem isn't that serious because you don't bother doing anything about it for so long.

Managers practice effective discipline by noticing performance shortcomings or misconduct before these problems become serious. Effective managers help guide their employees along the right path. Managers who don't discipline their employees have only themselves to blame when poor performance continues unabated or acts of misconduct escalate and get out of hand. Employees need the active support and guidance of their supervisors and managers to know what's expected of them. Without the guidance, employees sometimes find it difficult to keep from straying from the right path.

FOR EXAMPLE

Labor Unions Are Different

If you're dealing with union-represented employees, you're likely required to work within the system proscribed by the contract between the union and your firm. You may, for example, be required to allow a union representative to sit in on any discipline sessions that you conduct with union-represented employees. Whatever the case, review your organization's policies and labor relations practices and procedures before you embark on the task of disciplining your employees.

And don't forget: You get what you reward. Take a close look at the behavior you're rewarding in your employees. You may be surprised to find that you're inadvertently reinforcing negative behaviors and poor performance.

Don't put off discipline. Don't procrastinate. Don't look the other way and hope that your employees' bad behavior disappears. If you do look the other direction (or think you just don't have the time), you're doing a disservice to the employees who need your guidance, to the employees who are working at or above standard, and to your organization. Discipline your employees before you run out of time. Do it now.

SELF-CHECK

1. Punishment and discipline are two interchangeable words that mean the same thing. True or false?
2. Name two negative outcomes resulting from a manager's failure to discipline his or her employees.
3. What is the difference between performance problems and misconduct?

5.2 Focusing on Performance, Not Personalities

You're a manager (or a manager-to-be). You're not a psychiatrist or psychologist—even if you feel that you sometimes do nothing but counsel your employees. Your job isn't to analyze your workers' personalities or to attempt to understand why your employees act the way they do: it's impossible to read minds about things like "attitude." Your job is to assess your employees' performance against the standards that you and your employees agree to and to be alert to employee violations of company policy. If your employees are performing above standard, reward them for their efforts. If, on the other hand, they're performing below standard, you need to find out why (possibly a process, motivation, or training problem is out of your employees' control) and, if necessary, discipline them.

That's not to say you shouldn't be compassionate. Sometimes performance suffers because of family problems, financial difficulties, or other non-job-related pressures. Although you can give your employees the opportunity to get through their difficulties—you may suggest some time off or a temporary reassignment of duties—they eventually have to return to meeting their performance standards.

If an employee is overwhelmed by personal problems or other difficulties, encourage him or her to seek confidential help from professional sources through your organization's employee assistance program (EAP), a therapist, or other professional counselor.

To be fair, and to be sure that discipline focuses on performance and not on personalities, ensure that all employees fully understand company policies and that you communicate performance standards clearly. When your organization hires new employees, do they get an orientation to key company policies? When your human resources representative drops off new employees at your door, do you (or someone in your department) take the time to discuss your department's philosophy and practices? Do you periodically sit down with your employees to review and update their performance standards? If you say no to any of these questions, you need to get to work!

When you apply discipline, use it consistently and fairly. Although you must always discipline your employees soon after a demonstrated shortfall in performance or act of misconduct, rushing to judgment before you have a chance to get all the facts is a mistake. Although proving that an employee submitted a report a week late is simple, uncovering the facts in a case of sexual harassment may not be so simple. When you discipline employees, know the facts and act impartially and without favoritism for certain employees. If one employee does something wrong, you can't ignore the same behavior in your other employees. To do so certainly risks the loss of employee respect for your management, and it definitely invites lawsuits.

Remember, although your job is to point out your employees' shortcomings and to help guide your employees in their efforts to perform to standard, your employees are ultimately responsible for their performance and their behavior. You can't, and shouldn't, do their work for them, and don't cover for their mistakes and misdeeds. Sure, you can excuse an occasional mistake, but you must deal with an ongoing pattern of substandard performance or misconduct.

FOR EXAMPLE

Underperformance Places Everyone at Risk

A branch of a local regional telephone company was lagging in its sales numbers. The performance puzzled the national sales managers. On close inspection, the managers found that the head of the branch had many employees who had personal problems. The director of the branch was allowing these employees to use their personal problems for excuses for underperformance. When the company was bought by a larger corporation, the larger corporation warned that it would be the first branch that would be shut down in the merger. The director of the branch had to make a decision: either discipline the underperformers or do nothing and put everyone's job at risk.

SELF-CHECK

1. Managers should be consistent in their discipline. True or false?
2. The first step in discipline is finding out why employees are performing below standards. True or false?
3. _____ are ultimately responsible for employees' performance and behavior.

5.3 Identifying the Two Tracks of Discipline

As the beginning of this chapter explains, two key reasons for disciplining employees exist: performance problems and misconduct. The two-track system of discipline includes one set of discipline options for performance problems and another for misconduct. These tracks reflect the fact that misconduct, usually an employee's willful act, is considered a much more serious transgression than a shortfall in performance. Performance problems often aren't the employee's direct fault and can usually be corrected with proper training or motivation.

These two tracks reflect the concept of progressive discipline. **Progressive discipline** means that you always select the least severe step that results in the behavior that you want. For example, if your employee responds to a verbal warning and improves as a result, then you can move on to your next management challenge. However, if the employee doesn't respond to a verbal warning, you then progress to the next step—a written warning—and give that step a try. The hope is that your employee gets the hint and corrects his or her behavior before you get to heavy-handed steps, such as reductions in pay, demotions, or terminations.

As you prepare to discipline your employees, first decide whether you're trying to correct performance-related behaviors or misconduct. After you figure that out, decide the best way to get your message across. If the transgression is minor—a lack of attention to detail, for example—you may need only to conduct a verbal counseling. However, if you catch an employee sleeping on the job, you may decide to suspend your employee without pay for some period of time. The choice is yours.

In any case, make sure that the discipline takes place as soon as possible after the transgression occurs. You want to correct your employee's performance before the problem becomes significant. You definitely don't want to make discipline only an annual event by saving all your employee's problems for his or her periodic performance appraisal.

5.3.1 Dealing with Performance Problems: The First Track

If you've done your job right, each of your employees has a job description and a set of performance standards. The job description is simply an inventory of all the different duties that accompany a particular position. **Performance standards,** on the other hand, are the measurements that you and your employees agree to use in assessing your employees' performance. Performance standards form the basis of periodic performance appraisals and reviews. They also make great filler for your personnel files.

Although every organization seems to have its own unique way of conducting performance assessments, employees usually fall into one of three broad categories:

▲ Outstanding performance
▲ Acceptable performance
▲ Unacceptable performance

When it comes to employee discipline, you're primarily concerned with correcting unacceptable performance. You always want to help your good employees become even better employees, but your first concern has to be to identify employees who aren't working up to standard and to correct their performance shortcomings.

The following steps are listed in order of least to most severe. Don't forget: Use the least severe step that results in the behavior you want. If that step doesn't do the trick, move down the list to the next step:

▲ **Verbal counseling:** This form of discipline is certainly the most common, and most managers take this step first when they want to correct an employee's performance. A manager verbally counsels a variety of employees many times a day. Verbal counseling can range from a simple, spontaneous correction performed in the hallway ("Marge, you need to let me know when our clients call with a service problem.") to a more formal, sit-down meeting in your office ("Sam, I am concerned that you don't understand the importance of checking the correct address prior to shipping orders. Let's discuss what steps you're going to take to correct this problem and your plan to implement them."). You usually don't document verbal counseling in your employees' files.

▲ **Written counseling:** When employees don't respond favorably to verbal counseling, or when the magnitude of performance problems warrants its use, consider written counseling. Written counseling formalizes the counseling process by documenting your employees' performance shortcomings in a written memo. Written counseling is presented to employees in one-on-one sessions in the supervisor's office. After the employees have an opportunity to read the document, verbal discussions regarding the employees' plans to improve their performance ensue. This documentation becomes a part of your employees' personnel files.

▲ **Negative performance evaluation:** If verbal and written counseling fail to improve your employees' performance, the situation warrants a negative performance evaluation. Of course, because performance evaluations are generally given only annually, if at all, they're not usually very useful for dealing with acute situations. However, if you give verbal and written counseling to no avail, negative performance evaluations are the way to go.

▲ **Demotion:** Repeated negative performance evaluations or particularly serious performance shortcomings may warrant demoting your employees to a lower rung on the organizational ladder. Often, but not always, the pay of demoted employees is also reduced at the same time. Face it: some employees are hired or promoted into positions that they just can't handle. This situation isn't their fault, but you can't let your employees continue to fail if you have no hope of bringing performance up to an acceptable level with further training or guidance. Although demoralizing, demotions at least allow your employees to move into positions that they can handle. Before you resort to demotion, always first try to find a position at an equivalent level that the employee can handle. This step may help to improve your employee's motivation and self-confidence and result in a situation that is a "win" for both the employee and the organization.

▲ **Termination:** When all else fails, termination is the ultimate form of discipline for employees who are performing unsatisfactorily. As any manager who has fired an employee knows, terminating employees isn't fun. Consider it as an option only after you exhaust all other avenues. Perhaps needless to say, in these days of wrongful termination lawsuits and multimillion-dollar judgments, you must document employees' performance shortcomings very well and support them by the facts.

> ## FOR EXAMPLE
>
> ### Are the Right People on the Bus?
>
> Jim Collins, author of *Good to Great,* writes that one of the characteristics of "great" companies (in terms of sales) is that they have the right people working for them, the right people are in the right position, and they are unafraid to let the wrong people go. If you have an employee who you think just isn't a right fit, or was the product of a hiring decision, then you need to ask yourself two questions. First, would you hire this person for this job today? Second, if the person were to resign would you be disappointed or relieved?[1]

5.3.2 Dealing with Misconduct: The Second Track

Misconduct is a whole different animal from performance problems, so it has its own discipline track. Although both misconduct and performance problems can have negative effects on a company's bottom line, misconduct is usually considered a much more serious offense than performance shortcomings because it indicates a problem with your employees' attitudes or ethical beliefs. And modifying performance behaviors is a great first step in eventually modifying workers' attitudes or belief systems.

Even the terminology of the different steps in the second track indicates that something serious is going on. For example, although the first step on the first track is called verbal counseling, the first step on the second track is called verbal warning. You need to deal with misconduct more severely than you deal with performance problems.

The discipline that results from misconduct also has much more immediate consequences to your employees than the discipline that results from performance problems. Although performance may take some time to bring up to standard—with preparing a plan, scheduling additional training, and so forth—misconduct has to stop right now! When you discipline your employees for misconduct, you put them on notice that you won't tolerate their behavior. Repeated misconduct can lead quickly to suspension and termination.

As in the first track, the following discipline steps are listed from least severe to most severe. Your choice depends on the severity of the misconduct and the employee's work record:

▲ **Verbal warning:** When employees' misconduct is minor or a first offense, the verbal warning provides the least severe option for putting your employees on notice that their behavior won't be tolerated. ("John, I understand that you have continued to pressure Susan into going to lunch with you—even though she has told you on numerous occasions that she is not interested. This isn't acceptable. I expect you to stop this harassing behavior immediately.") In many cases of misconduct, a verbal warning that demonstrates to your employees that you're aware of the misconduct is all the situation requires.

▲ **Written warning:** Unfortunately, not all your employees get the message when you give them a verbal warning. Also, the magnitude of the offense may require that you skip the verbal warning and proceed directly to the written warning. Written warnings signal to your employees that you're serious and that you're documenting their behavior for their personnel files. An employee's immediate supervisor gives the written warning.

▲ **Reprimand:** Repeated or serious misconduct results in a reprimand. A reprimand is generally constructed in the same format as a written warning. However, a manager higher up in the organization gives the reprimand instead of the employee's immediate supervisor. The reprimand is the employee's last chance to correct the behavior before suspension, demotion, or termination.

▲ **Suspension:** A suspension, or mandatory leave without pay, is used in cases of very serious misconduct or repeated misconduct that hasn't been corrected as a result of other, less severe attempts at employee discipline. You may have to remove employees from the workplace for a period of time to ensure the safety of your other employees or to repair your work unit's morale. Employees may also be given nondisciplinary suspensions while they're being investigated on charges of misconduct. During a nondisciplinary suspension, employees are usually paid while the manager, human resources representative, or other company official reviews the case.

▲ **Termination:** In particularly serious cases of misconduct, termination may be your first choice in disciplining a worker. This rule is particularly true for extreme violations of safety rules, theft, gross insubordination, and other serious misconduct. Termination may also be the result of repeated misconduct that less severe discipline steps don't correct.

SELF-CHECK

1. _____ _____ means that you always select the least severe step that results in the behavior that you want.

2. In particularly serious cases of _____, termination may be your first choice in disciplining a worker.

3. _____ is the ultimate form of discipline for employees who are performing unsatisfactorily.

4. A _____ is a mandatory leave without pay.

5.4 Disciplining Employees: A Suite in Five Parts

A right way and many wrong ways to discipline employees exist. Forget the many wrong ways for now and focus on the right way.

Regardless of which kind of discipline you select for the particular situation, the approach that you take with your employees remains the same—whether you conduct verbal counseling or give a suspension or demotion (because of their finality, terminations are an exception here). Five steps must always form the basis of your discipline script. By following these steps, you can be sure that your employees understand what the problem is, why the problem exists, and what they need to do to correct the problem.

5.4.1 Describing the Unacceptable Behavior

Exactly what is your employee doing that is unacceptable? When describing unwanted behavior to an employee, make sure that you're excruciatingly specific. You don't have time for mushy, vague statements such as "You have a bad attitude," or "You make a lot of mistakes," or "I don't like your work habits."

Always relate unacceptable behaviors to specific performance standards that haven't been met or to specific policies that have been broken. Specify exactly what the employee did wrong and when the behavior occurred. Focus on the behavior and not on the individual.

Following are some examples for you to consider:

▲ "Your performance last week was below the acceptable standard of 250 units per week."
▲ "You failed the drug test that you took on Monday."
▲ "The last three analyses that you submitted to me contained numerous computational errors."
▲ "You have been late to work three out of four days this week."

5.4.2 Expressing the Impact to the Work Unit

When an employee engages in unacceptable behavior—whether his or her work doesn't meet standards or whether he or she engages in misconduct—the behavior typically affects a work unit negatively. When an employee is consistently late to work, for example, you may have to assign someone else to cover your employee's position until the offender arrives. Doing so takes your other employee away from the work that he or she should be doing, reducing the efficiency and effectiveness of the work unit. And if an employee engages in sexual harassment, the morale and effectiveness of the workers who are subjected to the harassment unnecessarily suffer.

Continuing with the examples that we used in the preceding section, following are the next steps in your discipline script:

▲ "Because of your below-standard performance, the work unit didn't meet its overall targets for the week."
▲ "This violation specifically breaks our drug-free workplace policy."
▲ "Because of these errors, I now have to take extra time to review your work much more thoroughly before I can forward it up the chain."
▲ "Because of your tardiness, I had to pull Marge from her position to cover yours."

5.4.3 Specifying the Required Changes

Telling your employee that he or she did something wrong does little good if you don't also tell that employee what he or she needs to do to correct the behavior. As a part of your discipline script, tell your employee the exact actions that you want him or her to adopt. Tell the employee that his or her behavior must be in accordance with an established performance standard or company policy.

Following are some examples of the third part of your discipline script:

▲ "You must bring your performance up to the standard of 250 units per week or better immediately."
▲ "You will be required to set an appointment with the company's employee assistance program for drug counseling."
▲ "I expect your work to be error free before you submit it to me for approval."
▲ "I expect you to be in your seat, ready to work, at 8:00 every morning."

5.4.4 Outlining the Consequences

Of course, if the unacceptable behavior continues, you need to have a discussion about the consequences. Make sure that you get the message across clearly and unequivocally and that your employee understands it.

Here are some possibilities for the fourth part of your script:

▲ "If you can't meet the standard, you'll be reassigned to the training unit to improve your skills."
▲ "If you refuse to undergo drug counseling, you'll be suspended from work without pay for five days."
▲ "If the accuracy of your work doesn't improve immediately, I'll have to issue a written counseling to be placed in your employee file."
▲ "If you're late again, I will request that the general manager issue a formal reprimand in your case."

5.4.5 Providing Emotional Support

Give your employee an emotional boost by expressing your support for his or her efforts. Make this support sincere and heartfelt—you do want your employee to improve, right?

Finally, the icing on the pineapple upside-down cake that is employee discipline:

▲ "But let's try to avoid that—I know you can do better!"

▲ "I really want this to work out—let's find you the help you need."

▲ "Is there anything I can do to help you avoid that outcome?"

▲ "There's no reason we can't avoid that situation—I'm counting on you to turn this around!"

5.4.6 Molding It All Together

After you develop the five parts of your discipline script, put them together into a unified statement that you deliver to your wayward employees. Although you'll undoubtedly discuss the surrounding issues in some detail, make the script be the heart of your discipline session.

The five parts of the script work together to produce the final product as follows:

▲ "Your performance last week was below our standard of 250 units per week. Because of your below-standard performance, the work unit didn't meet its overall targets for the week. You must bring your performance up to the standard of 250 units per week or better immediately. If you can't meet the standard, you'll be reassigned to the training unit to improve your skills. But let's try to avoid that—I know you can do better!"

▲ "You failed the drug test that you took on Monday. This violation specifically breaks our drug-free workplace policy. You'll be required to set an appointment with the company's employee assistance program for drug counseling. If you refuse to undergo drug counseling, you'll be suspended from work without pay for five days. I really want this to work out—let's find you the help you need."

▲ "The last three analyses that you have submitted to me contained numerous computational errors. Because of these errors, I now have to take extra time to review your work much more thoroughly before I can forward it up the chain. I expect your work to be error free before you submit it to me for approval. If the accuracy of your work doesn't improve immediately, I'll have to issue written counseling to be placed in your employee file. Is there anything I can do to help you avoid that outcome?"

> ### FOR EXAMPLE
>
> ### Mitigating and Litigating Circumstances
>
> If the employee you need to discipline has filed discrimination or sexual harassment charges or has claimed to be the victim of discrimination or sexual harassment, then you need to talk to human resources and possibly the company's legal team before pursuing discipline. The employee can claim that the disciple was retaliation for his or her complaints. The U.S. Supreme Court has ruled in favor of the employee in past lawsuits.[2]

▲ "You have been late to work three out of four days this week. Because of your tardiness, I had to pull Marge from her position to cover yours. I expect you to be in your seat, ready to work, at 8:00 every morning. If you're late again, I will request that the general manager issue a formal reprimand in your case. There's no reason we can't avoid that situation— I'm counting on you to turn this around!"

SELF-CHECK

1. The statement "you have a bad attitude" is acceptable in outlining employee behavior. True or false?

2. When disciplining employees, you should always specify what needs to _____ about their performance or conduct.

3. You should always end a discipline conversation by providing emotional _____.

4. In disciplining an employee, you should ensure that the employee understands how his or her actions impact the work unit. True or false?

5.5 Making and Implementing a Plan for Improvement

Managers have many types of plans: plans for completing projects on time, plans for meeting the organization's financial goals in five years, and plans to develop more plans. In the case of employee discipline, one more plan exists. The **performance improvement plan (PIP)** is a crucial part of the discipline process because it sets definite steps for the employee to undertake to improve performance within a fixed period of time.

If your employee's performance transgressions are minor, and you're giving only verbal counseling, working up a performance plan is probably overkill. Also, because most instances of misconduct must by nature be corrected right now or else, PIPs generally aren't appropriate for correcting employee misconduct. However, if your employee's poor performance is habitual and you've selected counseling or more severe discipline, a performance plan needs to be put into place.

A PIP consists of the following three parts:

▲ **Goal statement:** The **goal statement** provides clear direction to your employees about what it takes to make satisfactory improvement. The goal statement, which is tied directly to your employee's performance standards, may be something along the lines of "Completes all his assignments on or before agreed deadlines," or "Is at her station ready to work at exactly 8:00 a.m. every day."

▲ **Schedule for attainment:** What good is a plan without a schedule? Not having a schedule is like eating an ice cream cone without the ice cream or like watching TV with the sound turned off. Every good plan needs a definite completion date with fixed milestones along the way if the plan for goal attainment is complex.

▲ **Required resources/training:** The PIP must also contain a summary of any additional resources or training that will be brought to bear to help your employee bring his or her performance up to snuff.

Here's a sample PIP for a worker who makes repeated errors in typed correspondence:

Performance Improvement Plan
Jack Smith

Goal statement:
Complete all drafts of typed correspondence with two or fewer mistakes per document.

Schedule for attainment:
Jack must meet the above goal within three months after the date of this plan.

Required resources/training:
Jack will be enrolled in the company refresher course in typing and reviewing correspondence. This training must be successfully completed no later than two months after the date of this plan.

After you put PIP in place, your job is to ensure that it is followed. Follow up with your employees to make sure that they're acting on their plans and making progress toward the goals that you both agreed to. Yes, following up on improvement plans takes time, but that time is well spent. Besides, if you can't find the time to check your employees' progress on their improvement plans, don't be surprised if they can't find the time to work on them.

Are your employees following through with the goal statements that you agreed to? Do they even have the goal statements that you agreed to? Are they keeping to their schedules, and are they receiving the training and other resources that you agreed to provide? If not, you need to emphasize the importance of the improvement plans with your employees and work with them to figure out why they haven't been implemented as agreed.

To assist your employees in implementing their improvement plans, schedule regular progress reporting meetings with them on a daily, weekly, or monthly basis. More extensive improvement plans necessitate more frequent follow-up. Progress meetings serve two functions.

▲ They provide you with the information that you need to know to assess your employees' progress toward meeting their plans.

▲ They demonstrate to your employees—clearly and unequivocally—that their progress is important to you. If you demonstrate that the plans are important to you, your employees can make the plans a priority in their busy schedules.

Set up PIPs with your employees and stick with them. One of the most difficult challenges of management is dealing with a poor performer who improves under scrutiny, and then lapses again. Stick with your plan. If an employee can't maintain necessary performance standards, then you may want to consider whether he or she is really suited for continued employment.

SELF-CHECK

1. Name and describe the three parts of a **performance improvement plan (PIP)**.

2. A PIP is always necessary when disciplining employees. True or false?

3. It is the _____ responsibility to ensure the PIP is followed.

SUMMARY

Although disciplining an employee can be an unpleasant experience, it can also be an opportunity for growth for yourself and the employee. The employee will learn how to improve his or her performance, and you will gain practice in dealing with conflict in a positive, manageable way. After reading this chapter, you can now follow the steps in the disciplining employees for performance problems and misconduct. Using the five steps outlined, you can write a discipline script. You can create and implement a performance improvement plan. After implementing the plan, you can support employees (and the company) by following up and ensuring the correct actions are implemented.

KEY TERMS

Discipline	Actions taken with the purpose of correcting problems and improving performance.
Goal statement	Clear directions for employees about what actions are needed for them to improve.
Performance improvement plan (PIP)	Plan designed to improve an employee's job performance. It consists of a goal statement, a schedule of attainment, and a listing of the required resources or training.
Performance standards	Measurements that management and employees agree to use in assessing performance.
Progressive discipline	Selecting the least severe step that results in improved behavior or purpose.
Punishment	Actions taken with the purpose of causing pain or embarrassment to someone in retribution for some perceived error.

ASSESS YOUR UNDERSTANDING

Go to www.wiley.com/college/nelson to evaluate your knowledge of discipline.
Measure your learning by comparing pre-test and post-test results.

Summary Questions

1. If an employee does not meet his job-related goals, then he has _____ _____.

2. Stealing a coworker's wallet is an example of _____.

3. If you do not like an employee's personality, then you can punish him in hopes that he will change. True or false?

4. If you do not like an employee's personality, then you can discipline her. True or false?

5. Verbal counseling is always documented in an employee's file. True or false?

6. _____ means that the employee is moved to a lower-level job, and usually, the pay is reduced.

7. If an employee physically abuses another employee, then that employee should:
   (a) receive a warning.
   (b) receive a demotion.
   (c) receive a suspension.
   (d) be terminated immediately.

8. Part of a discipline script is outlining the _____.

9. The statement, "I expect you to answer the phone before it gets to the third ring regardless of what you are doing," is an example of which part of the discipline script?
   (a) Providing emotional support
   (b) Outlining the consequences
   (c) Addressing the impact to the work unit
   (d) Specifying the required change

10. Why is a goal statement important?

Applying This Chapter

1. You work for an Internet service provider in the sales department. Part of the success in sales is dependent on the employees' belief that they can reach the lofty goals set every month. You have one employee who comes

in every day and complains loudly that the goals are unreasonable and will never be reached. Do you discipline the employee? Why or why not?

2. You are the manager in a call center that includes two employees who are consistently late in arriving to work in the morning. You give them both verbal counseling. Neither responds to the verbal counseling. What do you do next?

3. You work in a consulting firm. Two consultants, one male and one female, have to travel to a client's location. The female consultant comes back from the trip and claims that the male consultant "hit on her" during the trip. What are your options for discipline?

4. You work at a manufacturing company and you learn that one of the machine operators has a drug addiction. The company has a drug-free policy. What are your options for discipline?

5. You have given two employees performance improvement plans due to their failure to meet company standards. How do you implement and follow up to ensure the employees are improving their performance?

YOU TRY IT

Discipline and Compassion

Your secretary, Mary, who has been a strong employee for a number of years, suddenly begins showing up for work an hour late several times a month. When asking around, you learn that her mother is very ill and she is taking care of her. You call Mary into your office. Write down what your next steps with Mary would be and why.

Discipline Script

You are the manager of a small accounting firm. One of the accountants, Lori Brown, completed taxes for five companys. Three of the tax returns were perfect. Two of the returns, however, had sloppy, glaring mathematical errors. Write a discipline script for your session with Lori.

Performance Improvement Plan

You work in a factory that makes milk jugs. The plastic bottle machine operator, Mike Stuart, is supposed to be turning out 250 plastic bottles an hour without any defects, but he is turning out 200 bottles per hour and 10 percent of these have defects. Write a performance improvement plan for Mike.

6

BUILDING A TEAM
Hiring the Best

Starting Point

Go to www.wiley.com/college/nelson to assess your knowledge of building a team.
Determine where you need to concentrate your effort.

What You'll Learn in This Chapter

- ▲ How to approach the hiring process
- ▲ How to determine the personal and job-specific qualities needed in an employee
- ▲ How to define a job
- ▲ How to recruit talented employees
- ▲ What to look for in résumés, cover letters, and applications
- ▲ Steps in the interview process
- ▲ How to make a job offer

After Studying This Chapter, You'll Be Able To

- ▲ Write a job description
- ▲ Use different resources and organizations to recruit talented employees
- ▲ Evaluate applicants and determine which ones are qualified for the next step in the job application process
- ▲ Conduct a successful interview
- ▲ Prepare a job offer and present it to a prospective employee

INTRODUCTION

Good employees are hard to find. If you've had the recent privilege of advertising for a job opening, you know good employees aren't easy to come by. Here's the scenario: You place the advertisement and then wait for the résumés of the best and brightest candidates to find their way into your mailbox. In just a couple days, you're pleased beyond your wildest dreams as you see the stack of résumés awaiting your review. How many are there—100? 200? Wow! What a response!

Your glee quickly turns to disappointment, however, as you begin your review. "Why did this guy apply? He doesn't have half the required number of years of experience!" "What? She's never even done this kind of work before." "Is this guy joking? He must have responded to the wrong advertisement!"

Finding and hiring the best candidates for a job has never been easy. Unfortunately, with all the streamlining, downsizing, and rightsizing going on in business nowadays, a lot of people are looking for work—and, chances are, very few of them have the exact qualifications that you're looking for. Your challenge is to figure out how to pluck the best candidates out of the sea strewn with the wreckage of corporate castoffs. The lifetime earnings of the average American worker are calculated at approximately $1 million. Hiring really is a million-dollar decision!

6.1 Approaching the Hiring Process

Hiring the right people is one of the most important tasks that managers face. You can't have a great organization without great people. Unfortunately, managers traditionally give short shrift to this task—devoting as little time as possible to preparation and to the actual interview process. As in much of the rest of your life, the results that you get from the hiring process are usually in direct proportion to the amount of time that you devote to it. If you devote yourself to finding the best candidates for a position, you're much more likely to find them. If you rely on chance to bring them to you, you may be disappointed by what and whom you find.

When you begin the hiring process, you have to understand your goals. The company will have goals for the new employee and you will have specific goals for your employee. Ultimately, however, in general the goal is for an employee to either provide an internal service to other employees or customers or to generate revenue for the company. Companies generally divide employees into two groups:

▲ A **cost center** is a department within a company that provides services to customers or employees that cost the company in terms of salaries, benefits, and equipment, without adding revenue directly to the bottom line.

▲ A **profit center** is a department within a company that generates revenue above and beyond the costs of operation. An example of a profit center is the sales department.

However, and companies may not admit this, in either capacity the new employee will be expected to contribute to the bottom line. If the employee is in customer service, for example, that employee's job is to retain customers by solving their problems in an efficient, friendly manner. Studies show that it takes ten times more money in advertising to recruit a new customer than it does to retain an existing customer. Let's look at another example. If the employee is in IT, his or her job is to fix the network and personnel computer problems quickly so no productivity, and therefore money, is lost.

Your goal in the hiring process is to represent the company and its best interests. You want someone who will contribute to the growth of the company; as the company prospers, you will prosper as well either in bonuses, raises, or just being able to keep your job. Your goal is not to make a new friend. Your goal is not to find a warm body. Your goal is not to find someone just because you have the budget for it. Your goal is to find the right person to help the company secure its future.

6.1.1 Defining the Characteristics of Your New Employees

Employers look for many qualities in candidates. There are general qualities and specific qualities. For example, if you are looking for an IT administrator, the general quality you are looking for may be experience in the IT field whereas the specific quality may be having Cisco certification. The following list gives you an idea of the general qualities that employers consider most important when hiring new employees. Other specific characteristics may be particularly important to you.

▲ **Hardworking:** Hard work can often overcome a lack of experience or training. You want to hire people who are willing to do whatever it takes to get the job done. Conversely, no amount of skill can make up for a lack of initiative or work ethic. Although you won't know for sure until you make your hire, careful questioning of candidates can give you some idea of their work ethic (or, at least, what they want you to believe about their work ethic).

▲ **Good attitude:** Although what constitutes a "good" attitude is different for different people, a positive, friendly, willing-to-help perspective makes life at the office much more enjoyable and makes everyone's job easier. When you interview candidates, consider what they'll be like to work with for the next five or ten years. Skills are important, but attitude is even more important. This is the "mantra" for the success of Southwest

Airlines: "Hire for attitude, train for success." And consider what the new CEO of General Electric says: With every hire the company makes, they look for *givers*, not *takers*.

▲ **Experienced:** When new graduates enter the workforce, many naively believe they will be hired immediately based on the weight of their institution's diploma. However, they lack a critical element—experience—that's so important in the hiring process. An interview gives you the opportunity to ask very pointed questions that require your candidates to demonstrate to you that they can do the job.

▲ **Go-getter:** The ability to take initiative to get work done. In a recent Internet survey, initiative was ranked as the top reason that employees were able to get ahead where they work.

▲ **Team player:** Teamwork is critical to the success of today's organizations that must do far more with far fewer resources than their predecessors. The ability to work with others effectively is a must for employees today.

▲ **Smart:** Smart people can often find better and quicker solutions to the problems that confront them. In the world of business, work smarts are more important than book smarts.

▲ **Responsible:** You want to hire people who are willing to take on the responsibilities of their positions. Questions about the kinds of projects that your candidates have been responsible for, and the exact roles they played in the success of these projects, can help you determine this important quality. Also, evidence that a candidate has researched the company is a key indicator of his or her sense of responsibility.

▲ **Stable:** You don't want to hire someone today and then find out that he or she is already looking for the next position tomorrow. You can get some indication of a person's potential stability (or lack thereof) by asking how long he or she worked with the previous employer and the reason for leaving.

6.1.2 The Consequences of a Poor Hiring Decision

Likewise, bad hires can make working for an organization an incredibly miserable experience. The negative impacts of hiring the wrong candidate can reverberate throughout an organization for years. If you, as a manager, ignore the problem, you put yourself in danger of losing your good employees. We can't overemphasize the importance of hiring the right people. Do you want to spend a few extra hours up front to find the best candidates, or do you later want to devote countless hours trying to straighten out a problem employee? Following is an example of some of the consequences of a poor hiring decision.

▲ **Loss of investment.** You spent countless hours looking for Ms. Perfect, countless more hours training her, and she does not work out. You have to terminate her and start again.

▲ **Lower employee morale.** Your current employees will be aggravated that the new employee is not pulling his weight. Even when you terminate the new employee, your current employees may be upset and feel that you were not fair to him.

In most companies, after an employee's probationary period, it is difficult to terminate him or her except under extreme circumstances. Therefore, you have to hang on to a poor employee for months while you document deficiencies. During this time, the following could happen:

▲ **Loss of good employees.** No one likes working with a difficult person, and good employees can find jobs elsewhere and will not tolerate an uncomfortable working environment. The rate a company losses employees is **employee turnover.**

▲ **Low productivity.** The new employee does not pull her weight and drags down your entire department in terms of numbers. This makes you look bad and can affect your department's ability to meet its goals and qualify for bonuses and so forth.

FOR EXAMPLE

Employee Turnover Costs

If you make a poor hiring decision and the employee leaves the company, you have employee turnover. Some industries, such as the fast-food industry, have very high employee turnover. Employee turnover costs can be damaging to a company's bottom line. The PricewaterhouseCoopers Saratoga Institute has a formula to calculate the turnover cost. This formula is:

$$\text{Total employee turnover cost} = \text{Costs of hiring new employees} + \text{Costs of training new employees}$$

In this formula, you have two types of costs: the costs of hiring new employees and the costs of training new employees. The costs of hiring new employees include advertising, bonus signing, relocation pay, time for interviewing, travel expenses, and pre-employee assessments. The costs of training new employees include training materials, technology, employee benefit setup, and time for trainers. All these costs can exceed 100 percent of an employee's salary.[1]

▲ **Low morale.** Your current employees will wonder why they are working so hard when the new employee isn't and they are all getting paid the same. Your good employees will ask, Is this fair? Does what I do really matter?

6.1.3 Steps in the Hiring Process

As with any process, there are steps that must be taken. These may vary from company to company in terms of the order they are performed, but the basic steps are the same.

Step 1: **Define the need.** You have to first determine, in general terms, what position you need filled. Are you filling a position because someone left or creating a new position or expanding the department?

Step 2: **Get approval.** You may know there is a need. Your overworked employees may know there is a need. However, you have to convince management that there is a need and you must get approval to hire someone. You must also get approval for the specific salary range of a new employee.

Step 3: **Write the job description.** You must clearly define the job before you can begin recruiting new talent. The job description is discussed more thoroughly in Section 6.2.

Step 4: **Place an ad and ask for referrals.** You may place the ad or your human resources department may place the ad. Ask people within the industry and employees if they know of any good candidates.

Step 5: **Read the résumés and cover letters and call the candidates who look the most promising.** First impressions are important. If you are not impressed by the candidates' letters or qualifications, then there is no need to waste your time and theirs in an interview. This is the first step in screening applicants.

Step 6: **Either interview the candidates over the phone first or ask the candidates to come in.** Some employers prefer short phone interviews as the second screening step and others prefer a face-to-face meeting.

Step 7: **Ask the candidates to fill out the application and take any necessary tests.** Most companies have employment applications already created for potential employees. Some jobs may require exams. For exam, a potential copyeditor would need to take a copyediting test. A potential IT help desk clerk may need to take a test that covers his knowledge of basic software and hardware issues. Some companies also require psychological tests and/or profiles.

Step 8: **Conduct a first interview with a promising candidate.** If you did not complete a phone interview with the candidate, then this will be your first chance to talk to the candidate and get a feel for her personality. Keep in mind that you should also be selling the company to the candidate, so it is a place where they want to work.

Step 9: **Conduct a second interview with the candidate.** This will be your chance to get any clarification on any unresolved questions from the first interview. It is also your chance to dig deeper into areas that you have concerns about. In this interview you should be trying to sell the company as well.

Step 10: **If necessary, conduct a third interview with the candidate.** If you don't love the candidate after this interview, then do not offer the job. The third interview may be a chance for your supervisor or your employees to meet the candidate. Everyone who interviews the candidate at this point should spend a lot of time selling the applicant on the company and extolling its great benefits package, location, training program, and other selling points.

Step 11: **Check the candidate's references.** This may be done by you or the human resources department. Section 6.6.1 discusses this process in more detail.

Step 12: **Make the job offer.** Be prepared for the candidate to try to negotiate the compensation and benefits package. Also, it is customary to give the candidate twenty-four to forty-eight hours to consider the offer. If the candidate rejects the offer, then you can decide if you want to make an offer to your second-choice candidate.

SELF-CHECK

1. List the ideal qualities of an employee.
2. Discuss the consequences of hiring the wrong employee.
3. List and define the steps in the hiring process.

6.2 Defining the Job Before You Start

Is the position new, or are you filling an existing one? In either case, before you start the recruiting process, you need to know exactly what standards you're going to use to measure your candidates. The clearer you are about what you need, the easier and less arbitrary your selection process becomes.

If the job is new, now is your opportunity to design your ideal candidate. Draft a job description that fully describes all the tasks and responsibilities of the position and the minimum necessary qualifications and experience. If the job requires expertise in addition and subtraction, for example, then say so. Don't be shy! You're not going to fill the position with the right hire if you don't make it a key part of the job description. The more work you put into the job description now, the less work you have to do after you make your hire.

If you're filling an existing position, review the current job description closely and make changes where necessary. Again, make the job description reflect exactly the tasks and requirements of the position. When you hire someone new to fill an existing position, you start with a clean slate. For example, you may have had a difficult time getting a former employee to accept certain new tasks—say, taking minutes at staff meetings or filing travel vouchers. By adding these new duties to the job description before you open recruitment, you make the expectations clear, and you won't have to struggle with your new hire to do the job.

Finally, before you start recruiting, use the latest and greatest job description to outline the most important qualities that you're seeking in your new hire. Consult and compare notes with other managers on your team to get input on your descriptions, and ask employees for their feedback as well. Use this outline to guide you in the interview process. Keep in mind, however, that job descriptions may give you the skills you want, but they do not automatically give you the kind of employee you want—that's much more difficult to accomplish (and the reason that you spend so much time recruiting in the first place).

Making an interview outline carries an additional benefit: You can easily document why you didn't hire the candidates who didn't qualify for your positions. Pay close attention here. If a disgruntled job candidate ever sues you for not hiring him, and such lawsuits are more common than you may suspect, you'll be eternally thankful that you did your homework in this area of the hiring process.

SELF-CHECK

1. Why is a job description important?
2. What is the purpose of an interview outline?

6.3 Recruiting Talent

People are the heart of every business: the better the people running your business, the better the business you have. Some people are just meant to be in their jobs. You may know such an individual—someone who thrives as a receptionist or someone who lives to sell. Think about how great your organization would be if you staffed every position with people who lived for their jobs.

Of course, as important as the interview process is to selecting the best candidates for your jobs, you won't have anyone to interview if you don't have a good system for finding qualified candidates. So where can you find the best candidates for your jobs?

The simple answer is everywhere. Some places are better than others—you probably won't find someone to run your lab's fusion reactor project by advertising on the backs of matchbooks—but you never know where you can find your next star programmer or award-winning advertising copywriter. Who knows, he or she may be working for your competitors right now! You will find that your best experience comes when you do a broad search for the new hire, involving other employees in the process. The short-term, "we gotta have somebody right away" approach often results in selecting an applicant who is the lesser of a number of evils—and whose weaknesses soon become problems to the organization.

The following list presents some of the best ways to find candidates for your positions. Your job is to develop a recruitment campaign that can find the kinds of people that you want to hire. Don't rely solely on your human resources department to develop this campaign for you; you're in the field, so you probably have a better understanding of where to find the people you need. Finally, make sure that your input is heeded.

▲ **Within the organization:** Typically, the first place to look for candidates is within the organization. If you do your job in training and developing employees, then you probably have plenty of candidates to consider for your job openings. Only after you exhaust your internal candidates should you look outside your organization. Not only is hiring people this way less expensive and easier, but you also get happier employees, improved morale, and have new hires who are already familiar with your organization.

▲ **Personal referrals:** Whether from coworkers, professional colleagues, friends, relatives, or neighbors, you can find great candidates by referrals. Who better to present a candidate than someone whose opinion you already value and trust? You get far more insight about the candidates' strengths and weaknesses from the people who refer them than you ever get from résumés alone. Not only that, but research shows that people hired through current employees tend to work out better, stay with the company longer, and are happier. When you're getting ready to fill a position, make sure that you let people know about it.

▲ **Temporary agencies:** Hiring *temps,* or temporary employees, has become routine for many companies. When you simply have to fill a critical position for a short period, temporary agencies are the way to go—no muss, no fuss. And the best part is that when you hire temps, you get the opportunity to try out employees before you buy them. If you don't like the temps you get, no problem. Simply call the agency, and it sends replacements before you know it. But if you like your temps, most agencies allow you to hire them at a nominal fee or after a minimum time commitment. Either way, you win.

▲ **Professional associations:** Most professions have their accompanying associations that look out for their interests. Whether you're a doctor (and belong to the American Medical Association), or a truck driver (and belong to the Teamster's Union), you can likely find an affiliated association for whatever you do for a living. Associations even have their own associations. Association newsletters, journals, and magazines are great places to advertise your openings when you're looking for specific expertise, because your audience is prescreened for you.

▲ **Employment agencies:** If you're filling a specialized position, are recruiting in a small market, or simply prefer to have someone else take care of recruiting and screening your applicants, employment agencies are a good, albeit pricey (with a cost of up to one-third of the employee's first-year salary, or more), alternative. Although employment agencies can usually locate qualified candidates in lower-level or administrative positions, you may need help from an executive search firm or **headhunter** (someone who specializes in recruiting key employees away from one firm to place in a client's firm) for your higher-level positions.

▲ **The Internet:** Every day, more and more companies discover the benefits of using the Internet as a hiring tool. Although academics and scientists have long used Internet newsgroups to advertise and seek positions within their fields, corporations are now following suit. The proliferation of corporate web pages and online employment agencies and job banks has brought about an entirely new dimension in recruiting. Web pages let you present almost unlimited amounts and kinds of information about your firm and about your job openings—in text, audio, graphic, and video formats. Your pages work for you twenty-four hours a day, seven days a week.

▲ **Want ads:** Want ads can be relatively expensive, but they're an easy way to get your message out to a large cross section of potential candidates. You can choose to advertise in your local paper or in nationally distributed publications such as *The Wall Street Journal*. On the downside, you may find yourself sorting through hundreds or even thousands of unqualified candidates to find a few great ones. But that's what your human resources department is for, right?

A *great* test of your supervision skills is what actions you take if you do not find the right candidate. Do you proceed if you don't find the right candidate and hire someone you do not have confidence in? It's a real testament to your values and prework to stick with your plan and either extend the candidate recruiting period to allow for additional candidates, or delay the recruitment for another time.

> ## FOR EXAMPLE
>
> ### Using the Internet to Recruit Talent
>
> Companies have different Internet strategies when it comes to recruiting talent. Large corporations, such as drug maker Eli Lilly and Company (www.lilly.com), not only advertise positions primarily on their Web site, but they will also only accept résumés through their Web site. Other smaller companies may advertise only in employment Web sites such as www.career-builder.com or www.monster.com.

SELF-CHECK

1. Hiring temporary workers has become routine for many companies. True or false?
2. How can you use the Internet to recruit talent?
3. What are the advantages of using a temporary agency?
4. One drawback in using a **headhunter** is the fee that you must pay. True or false?

6.4 Reviewing Applications

Typically, prospective employees will send in a résumé and a cover letter in response to a job opening. If the résumé and cover letter pass the test, then you will ask the employee to come in and fill out a job application. All these pieces of information provide clues as to whom you should hire.

6.4.1 Reviewing Résumés

Creating an accurate job description and using it in your advertisement to acquire the right talent has yet another benefit: it helps you quickly screen résumés. If the candidate's objective or experience does not fit with the job description, then there is no need to waste your time and the candidate's in setting up an interview. Below are a few examples using very abbreviated job descriptions.

Example 1, Nursing

Job Description: A registered nurse to provide, coordinate, and direct the provision of home nursing care.

Applicant: You read the résumé of Suzy Jones, which begins as follows:

Suzy Jones

Objective: To provide quality care to patients in an intensive care unit.

Disconnect: You are looking for an RN who wants to work in homes, not someone who wants to work in an intensive care unit of a hospital. The two settings are so different that this is not a good match. This is also an example of where you should be wondering, "What is Suzy thinking?" If Suzy really wanted the job then she should have taken the time to read the job description and changed her objective appropriately.

Example 2, Editing

Job Description: A copyeditor who reads textbooks for spelling, style, grammar, and flow. Must be able to manage several projects simultaneously.

Applicant: You read Dan Carson's résumé:

Dan Carson

Objective: To serve as a copyeditor for a publishing company.

Professional Experience: Professional profreader for Arcadia Publishing. 2005–2006

Disconnect: You notice that in listing his professional experience he misspells *proofreader*. This may be acceptable for an engineering position, but not a copyeditor position. Again, you ask yourself, "What was Dan thinking?" Even if Dan used spell check, he would have caught this typo.

Example 3, Customer Service

Job Description: Provide excellent customer care to customers regarding daily transactions, addressing inquiries, and problem resolution, in accordance with bank policies. Refer customers to the appropriate business partner for products and services uncovered during business interactions and/or conversations.

Applicant: You read Lori Chandler's résumé. She chose not to have an objective, so you read through her professional experience:

Lori Chandler

Professional Experience: Manager at USA bank. 2002–2007
- Managed ten employees.
- Increased bank revenue by 20 percent over a three-year period (2004–2007).
- Designed and initiated profitable points program that rewards customer use of debit cards.

Disconnect: Lori sounds great. The problem is you are hiring for an entry-level position. It is highly unlikely that Lori would be happy both in terms of duties and compensation. There are three reasons why Lori would have applied for this job. The first one is that she misread the ad. The second is that she is out of work and is desperate. The third is that she thinks she can come in, interview, and wow you with her experience so that you will hire her as a manager. Any of these three scenarios would not work. However, if you also have a management position open or if there is a department you could forward her résumé to, then she could potentially be a viable candidate. She is not, however, a viable candidate for the job you have advertised.

Other Red Flags in Résumés

The résumé can provide several pieces of information about the candidate. For example, does the candidate have a history of staying with one company for a long time or does he or she change jobs every two years? If the candidate changes jobs often and you still want to hold an interview, ask the reason for moving so often. Also, if you interview someone with gaps in employment, ask for the reasons. You may also see overlapping dates indicating that the person was working two jobs at once. Is this true or is it a mistake? For example, if the candidate performed freelance work while working for the last employer then you would be right to question how committed the person would be to the job you are offering. Also look for tasks and achievements that are aligned closely with the potential job. You will want to use some of these as the basis for your questions during the interview. For example, if you have a sales job open and you see that someone achieved a 10 percent increase in sales, then you will want to ask, "How did you achieve a 10 percent increase in sales?"

6.4.2 Reviewing Cover Letters

There are different schools of thought as to how the cover letter should be approached. Professional job coaches will tell you that it should be short and to the point. Other professional coaches will tell you that it should be in paragraph form and make cases as to how the candidate's previous experience fits the tasks of the open position. However, there are three things that are universally agreed upon. The first rule is that there should always be a cover letter accompanying the résumé. The second rule is that the cover letter should not say anything in direct contradiction to the job itself. For example, if you have an opening in the sales department, then you should dismiss an applicant who sends a cover letter expressing his interest in finance. The third rule is that the cover letter should have a professional tone and presentation and be error free. Applicants who send a professional cover letter on flowered stationery, and it has happened, cannot be taken seriously. Nor can the applicants who misspell the company's name be seriously considered.

6.4.3 Reviewing Applications

Most companies will want prospective employees to fill out some standard forms. If an applicant refuses to fill out the form, then you know that he or she would not be an easy employee to deal with. Other applicants will reveal a lot about themselves on these forms. For example, some will write down reasons for being fired from a past job. Others will specify high salary expectations. Consider all this information as more evidence that supports your gut feeling that either this applicant is a good fit and will do a good job, or that you should keep looking.

SELF-CHECK

1. What are the three rules universally agreed upon about cover letters?
2. What should you look for in a résumé?
3. What are some examples of red flags in a cover letter, résumé, and application?

6.5 Interviewing the Best

After you narrow the field to the top three or five applicants, you need to start interviewing. What kind of interviewer are you? Do you spend several hours preparing for interviews—reviewing résumés, looking over job descriptions, writing and rewriting questions until each is as finely honed as a razor blade? Or are you the kind of interviewer who, busy as you already are, starts preparing for the interview when you get the call from the receptionist that the candidate has arrived?

The secret to becoming a great interviewer is to spend some serious time preparing for your interviews. Remember how much time you spent preparing to be interviewed for your current job? You didn't just walk in the door, sit down, and get offered the job, did you? You probably spent hours researching the company, it products and services, financials, market, and other business information. You probably brushed up on your interviewing skills and may have even done some role-playing with a friend or in front of a mirror. Don't you think that you should spend at least as much time getting ready for the interview as the people whom you're going to interview?

Every interview consists of five key steps. They are:

Step 1: Welcome the applicant. Greet your candidates warmly and chat with them informally to help loosen them up. Questions about the weather, the difficulty of finding your offices, or how they found out about your position are old standbys.

Step 2: Summarize the position. Briefly describe the job, the kind of person you're looking for, and the interview process that you use.

Step 3: Ask your questions (and then listen!). Questions should be relevant to the position and should cover the applicant's work experience, education, and other related topics. Limit the amount of talking you do as an interviewer. Many interviewers end up trying to sell the job to an applicant instead of probing whether he or she is a good fit.

Step 4: Probe experience and find out the candidate's strengths and weaknesses. The best predictor of future behavior is past behavior, which is why exploring an applicant's experience can be so helpful to see what he or she did and how! And, although asking your candidates to name their strengths and weaknesses may seem cliché, the answers can be very revealing.

Step 5: Conclude the interview. Allow your candidates the opportunity to offer any further information that they feel is necessary for you to make a decision, and to ask questions about your firm or about the job. Thank them for their interest and let them know when they can expect your firm to contact them.

6.5.1 Asking the Right Questions

More than anything else, the heart of the interview process is the questions that you ask and the answers that you receive in response. You get the best answers when you ask the best questions. Lousy questions often result in lousy answers—answers that don't really tell you whether the candidate is going to be right for the job.

A great interviewer asks great questions. According to Richard Nelson Bolles, author of the perennially popular job-hunting guide *What Color Is Your Parachute?*,[2] you can categorize all interview questions under one of the following four headings:

▲ **Why are you here?** Why is the person sitting across from you going to the trouble of interviewing with you today? You have just one way to find out—ask. You may assume that the answer is because he or she wants a job with your firm, but you may be surprised at what you find. Consider the story of the interviewee who forgot that he was interviewing for a job with Hewlett-Packard. During the entire interview, the applicant referred to Hewlett-Packard by the name of one of its competitors.

▲ **What can you do for us?** This is always an important consideration! Of course, your candidates are all going to dazzle you with their incredible personalities, experience, work ethic, and love of teamwork—that almost goes without saying. However, despite what many job seekers seem to believe, the question is not "What can your firm do for me?"—at least not from your perspective. The question that you want an answer to is "What can you do for us?" One recruiter shares a story about the job applicant who slammed his hand on her desk and demanded a signing bonus. And this was before the interview had even started! Is it a surprise that this particular candidate landed neither the job nor the bonus?

▲ **What kind of person are you?** Few of your candidates will be absolute angels or demons, but don't forget that you'll spend a lot of time with the person whom you hire. You want to hire someone whom you enjoy being with during the many work hours, weeks, and years that stretch before you—and the holiday parties, company picnics, and countless other events that you're expected to attend. (Okay, at least someone you can tolerate being with for a few hours every once in a while.) You also want to confirm a few other issues: Are your candidates honest and ethical? Do they share your views in regard to work hours, responsibility, and so forth? Are they responsible and dependable employees? Of course, all your candidates will answer in the affirmative to mom-and-apple-pie questions like these. So, how do you find the *real* answers? You can try to "project" the applicant in a typical, real-life scenario and then see how he or she would think it through. This way, there is no "right" answer and the candidate is forced to expose his or her thinking process. For example, these scenarios can reveal the questions the applicant would ask, strategies they would consider, people they would involve, and so forth. Ask open-ended questions and let your candidates do most of the talking!

▲ **Can we afford you?** It does you no good to find the perfect candidate and then, at the end of the interview, discover that you're far apart in terms of salary. Keep in mind that the actual wage you pay to workers is only part of an overall compensation package. Although you may not be able to pull together more money for wages for particularly good candidates, you may be able to offer them better benefits, a nicer office, a more impressive title, or a key to the executive sauna.

6.5.2 Interviewing Do's

So, what can you do to prepare for your interviews? The following handy-dandy checklist gives you ideas on where to start:

▲ **Review the résumé of each interviewee the morning before interviews start.** Not only is it extremely poor form to wait to read an interviewee's résumé until during the interview, but it will also cause you to miss out on the opportunity to tailor your questions to those little surprises that you invariably discover in the résumé.

▲ **Become intimately familiar with the job description.** Are you familiar with all the duties and requirements of the job? Telling interviewees that the position requires duties that it really doesn't is poor form. Surprising new hires with duties that you didn't tell them about—especially when they are major duties—is definitely poor form.

▲ **Draft your questions before the interview.** Make a checklist of the key experience, skills, and qualities that you seek in your candidates and use it to guide your questions. Of course, one of your questions may trigger other questions that you didn't anticipate. Go ahead with such questions as long as they provide you with additional insights regarding the candidates and help illuminate the information that you've outlined on your checklist.

▲ **Select a comfortable environment for both of you.** Your interviewee will likely be uncomfortable regardless of what you do. You don't need to be uncomfortable, too. Make sure that the interview environment is well ventilated, private, and protected from interruptions. You definitely don't want your phone ringing off the hook or employees barging in during your interviews. You get the best performance from your interviewees when they aren't thrown off track by distractions.

▲ **Avoid playing power trips during the course of the interview.** Forget the old games of asking trick questions, turning up the heat, or cutting the legs off their chairs (yes, some managers still do this game playing!) to gain an artificial advantage over your candidates.

▲ **Take lots of notes.** Don't rely on your memory when it comes to interviewing candidates for your job. If you interview more than a couple of people, you can easily forget who said exactly what and what your impressions were of their performances. Not only are your written notes a great way to remember who's who, but also they're an important tool to have when you're evaluating your candidates. Plus, they look impressive when you route them to your boss.

As you have no doubt gathered by now, interview questions are one of your best tools for determining whether a candidate is right for your company. Although some amount of small talk is appropriate to help relax your candidates, the heart of your interviews should focus on answering the questions just listed. Above all, don't give up! Keep asking questions until you're satisfied that you have all the information you need to make your decision.

And don't forget to take lots of notes as you interview your candidates. Try to avoid the temptation to draw pictures of little smiley faces or that new car you've been lusting after. Write the key points of your candidates' responses and their reactions to your questions. For example, if you ask why your candidate left her previous job, and she starts getting really nervous, make a note about this reaction. Finally, note your own impressions of the candidates.

6.5.3 Interviewing Don'ts

The topic of interviewing don'ts is probably worth a chapter of its own. If you've been a manager for any time at all, you know that you can run into tricky situations during an interview and that certain questions can land you in major hot water if you make the mistake of asking them.

Some interviewing don'ts are merely good business practice. For example, accepting an applicant's invitation for a date is probably not a good idea. After a particularly drawn-out interview at a well-known high-tech manufacturer, a male candidate asked out a female interviewer. The interviewer considered her options and declined the date; she also declined to make Prince Charming a job offer.

Then you have the blunders of the major legal type—the kind that can land you and your firm in court. Interviewing is one area of particular concern in the hiring process as it pertains to the possibility of discrimination. For example, although you can ask applicants whether they are able to fulfill job functions, in the United States you can't ask them whether they are disabled. Because of the critical nature of the interview process, you must know the questions that you absolutely should never ask a job candidate. Here is a brief summary of the kinds of topics that may, depending on the exact circumstances, get you and your firm into trouble:

▲ Applicant's race or skin color
▲ Applicant's national origin
▲ Applicant's sex

> ### FOR EXAMPLE
>
> **When Candidates Share Too Much**
>
> There are people who, when interviewing, try to become friendly with the interviewer and share information about themselves such as their health problems, age, marital status, and their religious beliefs. When this happens, you should not comment on the remarks but quickly switch the topics and steer the conversation to the professional requirements for the job. Even though the candidate may have volunteered the information, he or she can still try to sue for discrimination if not selected for the job.

▲ Applicant's sexual orientation
▲ Applicant's marital status
▲ Applicant's religion (or lack thereof)
▲ Applicant's arrest and conviction record
▲ Applicant's height and weight
▲ Applicant's debts
▲ Applicant's age
▲ Applicant's disability

Legal or illegal, the point is that none of the preceding topics are necessary to determine the applicants' ability to perform their jobs. Therefore, ask questions that directly relate to the candidates' ability to perform the tasks required. To do otherwise can put you at definite legal risk. In other words, what *does* count are job-related criteria—that is, information that's directly pertinent to the candidates' ability to do the job (you clearly need to decide this *prior* to interviewing!).

SELF-CHECK

1. List three interview *do's* and *don'ts*.
2. What types of questions can you *not* ask an applicant?
3. How can you prepare for an interview?
4. What types of questions *should* you ask in an interview?
5. List the steps in the interview process.

6.6 Evaluating Your Candidates Further

Now comes the really fun part of the hiring process—evaluating your candidates. If you have done your homework, then you already have an amazing selection of candidates to choose from, you've narrowed your search to the ones showing the best potential to excel in your position, and you've interviewed them to see whether they can live up to the promises that they made in their résumés. Before you make your final decision, you need a little bit more information.

6.6.1 Checking References

Wow! What a résumé! What an interview! What a candidate! Would you be surprised to find out that this shining employee-to-be didn't really go to Yale? Or that he really wasn't the account manager on that nationwide marketing campaign? Or that her last supervisor was not particularly impressed with her analytical skills?

A résumé and interview are great tools, but a reference check is probably the only chance you have to find out whether your candidates are who they say they are before you make a hiring decision. Depending on your organization, you may be expected to do reference checks. Or maybe your human resources department takes care of that task. Whichever the case, don't hire new employees without first doing an exhaustive check of their backgrounds.

The twin goals of checking references are to verify the information that your candidates have provided and to gain some candid insight into who your candidates really are and how they really behave in the workplace. When you contact a candidate's references, limit your questions to those that are related to the work to be done. As in the interview process, asking questions that can be considered discriminatory to your candidates is not appropriate.

Here are some of the best places to do your reference checking:

▲ **Check academic references.** A surprising number of people exaggerate or tell outright lies when reporting their educational experience. Start your reference check here. If your candidates didn't tell the truth about their education, you can bet that the rest of their experience is suspect, too, and you can toss the candidate into the discard pile before you proceed.

▲ **Call current and former supervisors.** Getting information from employers is becoming more difficult. Many business people are rightfully concerned that they may be sued for libel or defamation of character if they say anything negative about current or former subordinates. Still, it doesn't hurt to try. You get a much better picture of your candidates if you speak directly to their current and former supervisors instead of to their firms' human resources department—especially if the supervisors you

> ### FOR EXAMPLE
>
> **Don't Be Fooled by Diploma Mills**
>
> The number of companies that grant undergraduate and graduate diplomas in exchange for money have proliferated in recent years. You will want to ensure that the college listed on an applicant's resume is accredited.
>
> In Indianapolis, Indiana, the man named to run the Marion County Juvenile Detention Center was chosen because he claimed that he completed course work for a master's degree. County court officials were forced to withdraw their offer of employment after *The Indianapolis Star* reported that the university listed, the University of Ravenhurst, was a diploma mill that was shut down by the Federal Trade Commission in 2003. The University of Ravenhurst had an online presence, did not have a campus, and sold degrees through call centers in Israel and Romania.[3]

speak to have left their firms. The most you are likely to get from the human resources folks is a confirmation that the candidate worked at the firm during a specific period of time.

▲ **Check your network of associates.** If you belong to a professional association, union, or similar group of like-minded careerists, you have the opportunity to tap into the rest of the membership to get the word on your candidates. For example, if you're a certified public accountant (CPA) and want to find out about a few candidates for your open accounting position, you can check with the members of your professional accounting association to see whether anyone knows anything about them.

▲ **Do some surfing.** On the Web, plug the candidate's name into a search engine such as Google (www.google.com), perhaps along with the name of the company where he or she last worked or the city in which he or she lives. You never know what can turn up!

6.6.2 Reviewing Your Notes

You did take interview notes, didn't you? Now's the time to drag them out and look them over. Review the information package for each candidate—one by one—and compare your findings against your predetermined criteria. Take a look at the candidates' résumés, your notes, and the results of your reference checks. How do they stack up against the standards that you set for the position? Do you see any clear winners at this point? Any clear losers? Organize your candidate packages into the following stacks:

▲ **Winners:** These candidates are clearly the best choices for the position. You have no hesitation in hiring any one of them.

▲ **Potential winners:** These candidates are questionable for one reason or another. Maybe their experience isn't as strong as that of other candidates, or perhaps you weren't impressed with their presentation skills. Neither clear winners nor clear losers, you hire these candidates only after further investigation or if you can't hire anyone from your pool of winners.

▲ **Losers:** These candidates are clearly unacceptable for the position. You simply don't consider hiring any of them.

6.6.3 Conducting a Second (or Third) Round of Interviews

When you're a busy manager, you have pressure to get things done as quickly as possible, and you're tempted to take shortcuts to achieving your goals. It seems that everything has to be done yesterday—or maybe the day before. When do you have the opportunity to spend as much time as you want to complete a task or project? Time is precious when you have ten other projects crying for your attention. Time is even more valuable when you're hiring for a vacant position that's critical to your organization and needs to be filled right now.

Hiring is one area of business where you can't take shortcuts. Remember: Hire slowly, fire quickly. Finding the best candidates for your vacancies requires a real investment of time and resources to be successful. Your company's future depends on it.

Depending on your organization's policies or culture, or because you're undecided as to the best candidate, you may want to bring in candidates for several rounds of interviews. In this kind of system, lower-level supervisors, managers, or interview panels conduct initial screening interviews. Candidates who pass this round are invited back for another interview with a higher-level manager. Finally, the best two or three candidates interview with the organization's top manager.

But, keep in mind, the timeline for an offer is very different depending on the job you're interviewing for. Lower-level job hunters cannot afford to be unemployed (if they are) for long, and they often get and accept job offers quickly. A higher-level position—say, a general manager—gives you more time.

The ultimate decision on how many rounds and levels of interviews to conduct depends on the nature of the job itself, the size of your company, and your policies and procedures. If the job is simple or at a relatively low level in the company, a single phone interview may be sufficient to determine the best candidate for a job. However, to determine the best candidate, you may need several rounds of testing and personal interviews if the job is complex or at a relatively high level in the organization.

SELF-CHECK

1. List three methods of checking references.
2. Why should you check references?
3. Under what circumstances should you conduct a second or third round of interviews?

6.7 Hiring the Best (and Leaving the Rest)

The first step in making a hiring decision is to rank your candidates within the groups of winners and potential winners that you established during the evaluation phase of the hiring process. You don't need to bother ranking the losers because you wouldn't hire them anyway—no matter what. The best candidate in your group of winners is first, the next best is second, and so on. If you have done your job thoroughly and well, the best candidates for the job should be readily apparent at this point.

The next step is to get on the phone and offer your first choice the job. Don't waste any time—you never know whether your candidate has interviewed with other employers. It would be a shame to invest all this time in the hiring process only to find out that she just accepted a job with one of your competitors. If you can't come to terms with your first choice in a reasonable amount of time, then go on to your second choice. Keep going through your pool of winners until you either make a hire or exhaust the list of candidates.

The following sections give you a few tips to keep in mind as you rank your candidates and make your final decision.

6.7.1 Being Objective

In some cases, you may prefer certain candidates because of their personalities or personal charisma—regardless of their abilities or work experience. Sometimes the desire to like these candidates can obscure their shortcomings, whereas a better qualified, albeit less socially adept, candidate may fade in your estimation.

Be objective. Consider the job to be done and consider the skills and qualifications that being successful requires. Do your candidates have these skills and qualifications? What would it take for your candidates to be considered fully qualified for the position?

Don't allow yourself to be unduly influenced by your candidates' looks, champagne-like personalities, high-priced hairstyles, or dangerously named colognes. None of these characteristics can tell you how well your candidates will perform the job. The facts are present for you to see in the résumés, interview notes, and reference checks. If you stick to the facts, you can still go wrong, but the chances are diminished.

One more thing: Diversity in hiring is positive for any organization—both for the business and for society in general. Check your bias at the door!

6.7.2 Trusting Your Gut

Sometimes you're faced with a decision between two equally qualified candidates, or with a decision about a candidate who is marginal but shows promise. In such cases you have weighed all the objective data and you have given your analytical side free rein, but you still have no clear winner. What do you do in this kind of situation?

Listen to yourself. Unlock your heart, your feelings, and your intuition. What do you feel in your gut? Although two candidates may seem equal in skills and abilities, do you have a feeling that one is better suited to the job than the other? If so, go with it. As much as you may want your hiring decision to be as objective as possible, whenever you introduce the human element into the decision-making process, a certain amount of subjectivity is naturally present.

In reality, rarely are two candidates equally qualified, although some people seem to have more to bring to the job than anticipated (for example, industry focus, fresh ideas, previous contacts, and so forth). Again, this is where your pre-work can be so valuable in keeping you focused. Can they both do the job? If so, the bonus traits can tip the scale.

Other options:

▲ Give them each a nonpaid assignment and see how they do.
▲ Try them each on a paid project.

6.7.3 Adjusting after the Offer

What do you do if you can't hire anyone from your group of winners? This unfortunate occurrence is a tough call, but no one said that management is an easy task. Take a look at your stack of potential winners. What would it take to make your top potential winners into winners? If the answer is as simple as a training course or two, then give these candidates serious consideration—with the understanding that you can schedule them for the necessary training soon after hire. Perhaps they just need a little more experience before you can put them in the ranks of the winners. You can make a judgment call as to whether you feel that their current experience is sufficient to carry them through until they gain the experience you are looking for. If not, you may want to keep looking for the right candidate. After all, this person may be working with you for a long time; waiting for the best candidate only makes sense.

If you're forced to go to your group of almost winners, and no candidate seems up to the task, then don't hire someone simply to fill the position. If you do, you probably are making a big mistake. Hiring employees is far easier than unhiring them. The damage that an inappropriate hire can wreak—on coworkers, your customers, and your organization (not to mention the person you hired!)—can take years and a considerable amount of money to undo. Not only that, but it also can be a big pain in your neck! Other options are to redefine the job, reevaluate other current employees, or hire on a temporary basis to see whether a risky hire works out.

SELF-CHECK

1. What is the first step in choosing which candidate to make an offer to?
2. What can you do if you don't find someone that you want to hire?

SUMMARY

Finding good employees can take many hours of effort and a substantial financial investment. However, the investment of time and money can pay off when the right decision is made. The payoff is a productive, happy employee who can do the job well and add to the success of the company. During this chapter, you have assessed how to write a job description. Once the job description is written, you can use different resources and organizations to recruit talented employees. Once you receive employment applications, you review them according to the criteria reviewed in this chapter. The next step, the interview, consists of specific steps that you have evaluated. Finally, you have assessed how to present a job offer.

KEY TERMS

Cost center	Department within a company that provides services to customers or employees that cost the company in terms of salaries, benefits, and equipment, without adding revenue directly to the bottom line.
Employee turnover	The rate at which a company loses employees.
Headhunter	Someone who specializes in recruiting key employees away from one firm to place in a client's firm.
Profit center	Department within a company that generates revenue above and beyond the costs of operation. An example of a profit center is the sales department.

ASSESS YOUR UNDERSTANDING

Go to www.wiley.com/college/nelson to evaluate your knowledge of building a team.

Measure your learning by comparing pre-test and post-test results.

Summary Questions

1. A sales department is an example of a cost center. True or false?
2. A customer service department has no impact on a company's profits and/or losses. True or false?
3. When a company loses employees, it is referred to as _____ _____.
4. The first step in the hiring process is:
   (a) writing the job description.
   (b) getting approval.
   (c) defining the need.
   (d) recruiting talent.
5. A job description should include which of the following?
   (a) Responsibilities, qualifications, and experience required for the new position
   (b) Responsibilities, qualifications, experience, and salary of the new position
   (c) Responsibilities, salary, and reporting structure of the new position
   (d) Salary and reporting structure of the new position
6. The first place you can look for candidates is:
   (a) personal referrals.
   (b) within the company.
   (c) temporary agencies.
   (d) professional associations.
7. In searching for an executive, many companies use _____ _____ or headhunters.
8. Want ads are an easy way to get a company's message out to a large cross section of potential candidates. True or false?
9. Creating an accurate job description allows you to quickly screen _____.
10. After welcoming the applicant, the next step in the interview process is:
    (a) asking questions.
    (b) summarizing the position.

(c) determining the candidate's strengths and weaknesses.

(d) none of the above.

11. You can ask about a candidate's marital status in an interview. True or false?

12. It is important to be _____ when determining which candidate to hire.

13. A _____ _____ is a company that offers college degrees for money.

14. If you cannot find the perfect candidate for the open position, then you should hire the best candidate out of the candidate pool that you have. True or false?

Applying This Chapter

1. You are the manager in a call center that is always overwhelmed. As a result, your staff members cannot answer customer phone calls as quickly as you would like them too. What arguments can you make to your boss in order to receive permission to hire another employee?

2. You are the manager for an intensive care unit at the local hospital and you need two more nurses for the night shift. You place the ad and are inundated with résumés. How can you sort through these quickly and what specific qualities do you look for?

3. You are the manager for a software company that is rapidly growing. Your boss has given you the budget to add five more people to your team. What steps do you take to define the positions before you begin recruiting candidates?

4. You are the director of human resources for a school system. In the past, your department has advertised for employees only in the Sunday newspaper. Although this used to work well, you are noticing that you are not reaching the kinds of candidates you would like to by relying on print advertising. How would you find candidates and why would you use these methods?

5. You are the director of a large accounting firm and you need to hire seven people to help prepare taxes for clients during tax season. You know these positions will require overtime and the ability to keep information confidential. What types of questions do you ask applicants for this specific position during an interview?

6. You are the manager of an advertising firm and you have interviewed several candidates for an open receptionist position. For various reasons, you were not comfortable with any of the candidates. What do you do?

YOU TRY IT

Training Others to Interview

You are the manager of a small marketing group and you are hiring an entry-level marketing associate. You are also on the search committee to find a new vice president of marketing. Write a sample recruitment plan for both, listing the sources you would use to find candidates.

Writing Job Descriptions

You are the manager of a small doctor's office and you need to hire a receptionist. Write a list of personal and professional qualities the ideal candidate would have.

Creating an Interview Outline

You are the manager of a customer support call center for computers. Your customer service representatives take many calls, troubleshoot technical problems, and have to remain patient with people at all times. Create an interview outline for this position to be used when interviewing candidates.

7

TRAINING A TEAM
Organizing Teams and Coaching Employees

Starting Point

Go to www.wiley.com/college/nelson to assess your knowledge of training teams.
Determine where you need to concentrate your effort.

What You'll Learn in This Chapter

▲ The difference between vertical and horizontal organizations
▲ How empowerment transforms an organization
▲ The advantages of organizing employees into teams
▲ How to organize and support teams
▲ How to run effective meetings
▲ The characteristics of a good coach
▲ Coaching methods and tools

After Studying This Chapter, You'll Be Able To

▲ Assess how to flatten an organization
▲ Empower employees
▲ Propose a team structure for your organization
▲ Evaluate the advantages of teams
▲ Design and hold effective meetings
▲ Develop basic coaching skills
▲ Use coaching methods and tools to improve your organization

INTRODUCTION

A revolution is going on in business today. The revolution is deciding what work to do, how to accomplish it, what goals an organization strives for, and who's responsible for achieving them. The revolution also is touching everyone in an organization—from the very top to the very bottom. What is this revolution? The revolution is called teams. A **team** is two or more people who work together to achieve a common goal.

Why use teams? Teams offer an easy way to tap the knowledge and resources of all employees—not just supervisors and managers—to solve the organization's problems. A well-structured team draws together employees from different functions and levels of the organization to help find the best way to approach an issue. Companies have discovered that to remain competitive, they can no longer rely solely on management to guide the development of work processes and the accomplishment of organizational goals. The companies need to involve those employees who are closer to the problems and to the customers as well.

This chapter discusses the changes in today's global business environment that set the stage for the movement toward teams; the major kinds of teams and how they work; the impact of the new, computer-based technology on teams; and insights for conducting the best team meetings ever.

The best managers of teams are **coaches**—that is, individuals who guide, discuss, and encourage others on their journey. With the help of coaches, employees can achieve outstanding results and organizations can perform to their full potential.

Coaching plays a critical part in the learning process for employees who are developing their skills, knowledge, and self-confidence. Your employees don't learn effectively when you simply tell them what to do. In fact, they usually don't learn at all. Neither do your employees learn effectively when you throw a new task at them with no instruction or support. Sure, good employees eventually can figure things out, but they waste a lot of time and energy in the process. Between these two extremes—being told what to do and being given no support—is a happy medium where employees can thrive and the organization can prosper. This happy medium happens with coaching.

7.1 Phasing Out the Old Hierarchy

The last couple of decades have seen a fundamental shift in the distribution of power and authority in organizations. Until recently, most organizations were **vertical organizations:** they had many layers of managers and supervisors between top management and frontline workers. The classic model of a vertical organization is the traditional military organization. In the old army, privates report to corporals, who report to sergeants, who report to captains, and so on, up to the top general. When a general gives an order, it passes down the line from person to person until it reaches the person who is expected to execute it.

Until recently, large companies such as Ford, Exxon, and AT&T weren't that different from this rigid, hierarchical model. Employing hundreds of workers, these companies depended—and in many cases still depend—on legions of supervisors and managers to control the work, the workers who did it, and when and how they did it. The primary goal of top management was to command and control workers' schedules, assignments, and decision-making processes very closely to ensure that the company met its objectives.

The hierarchical model has one fundamental flaw: Many supervisors and managers made little direct contribution to the production of a company's products or services. Instead of producing things, in many cases managers merely managed other managers or supervisors and served as liaisons between levels. They did little more than push paper from one part of their desks to another. In the model's worst scenario, the levels of supervisors and managers actually impeded their organizations' capability to get tasks done—dramatically adding to the cost of doing business and slowing down the response time of decision making. Although this problem was overlooked as the global economy continued to expand in the last half of the twentieth century, the economic slowdown in the late 1980s and once again after the dot-com bust that hit full force in 2001 made for quite a wake-up call to those companies with unproductive middle management.

Although the downsizing of corporate workforces after economic downturns had obvious negative effects on the employees who lost their jobs—and in many cases, their hopes for comfortable retirement—this dark cloud had a silver lining. In these new, flatter organizations, a new life (and quicker pace) came in the following important areas:

▲ **Decision making:** Decisions, which may have taken weeks or even months to make in the old, bloated bureaucracy, are made in hours or minutes.

▲ **Communicating:** Instead of being intercepted and possibly distorted by middle managers at numerous points along its path, communication now travels a more direct and speedier route from frontline workers to top management and vice versa, or to whomever the person needs to get information from. There's nothing like cutting six layers of management out of an organization to improve communication!

Also, this transformation from vertical to **horizontal organizations** (organizations with minimal levels of management) has had a fundamental impact on financial and organizational elements:

▲ **Quantifiable benefits to the bottom line:** By cutting out entire layers of management employees, many companies saved money in the way of substantially reduced costs of personnel, facilities, and benefits.

▲ **Movement of authority and power:** The move happened from the very top of the organization down to the frontline employees who interact with

> ## FOR EXAMPLE
>
> ### Why Use Teams
>
> Perhaps management expert Peter Drucker best answered the question "Why use teams?" when he considered the importance of ranking knowledge over ego in the modern organization. According to Drucker, "No knowledge ranks higher than another; each is judged by its contribution to the common task rather than by any inherent superiority or inferiority. Therefore, the modern organization cannot be an organization of boss and subordinate. It must be organized as a team" (*Harvard Business Review*).

customers on a day-to-day basis. With fewer middle managers to interfere, frontline employees are naturally granted more autonomy and authority.

More than ever before, businesses worldwide are rewarding employees for cooperating with each other instead of competing against one another. This innovation in today's business environment is truly amazing! Organizations are no longer measuring employees only by their individual contributions, but also by how effective they are as contributing members of their work teams.

Coupled with this shift of authority is a fundamental change in the way that many businesses structure their organizations. They're moving away from a structure of traditional, functional divisions that once separated departments from each other. In their place are teams whose members work together to perform tasks and achieve common goals. Of course, most businesses still organize their operations by departments, divisions, and so forth, but smart managers now encourage, rather than discourage, their employees to cross formal organizational lines.

Following are benefits that your organization can reap from promoting cooperation:

▲ **Reducing unproductive competition:** Promoting a cooperative, team-oriented work environment reduces the chance that your employees will become overcompetitive.

▲ **Sharing knowledge:** Knowledge is power. If you're in the know, you have a clear advantage over others. In a cooperative work environment, team members work together and thereby share their areas of knowledge and expertise.

▲ **Fostering communication:** The use of teams helps break down the walls between an organization's departments, divisions, and other formal structures to foster communication between organizational units.

▲ **Achieving common goals:** The development of teams with members from various departments encourages workers from all levels and all parts of a company to work together to achieve common goals.

SELF-CHECK

1. What is the difference between **vertical** and **horizontal organizations**?

2. The classic model of a horizontal organization is the traditional military organization. True or false?

3. Horizontal businesses have fewer layers of management than vertical organizations. True or false?

7.2 Empowering Your Teams

With the flattening of organizational structures that accompanied downsizing, employees gained more authority and autonomy from top management. The result: Employees have a better responsiveness to the customers' needs and the resolution of problems at the lowest possible level in the organization. The transfer of power, responsibility, and authority from higher-level to lower-level employees is called **empowerment.**

By empowering workers, managers place the responsibility for decision making with the employees who are in the best position to make the decision. In the past, many managers felt that they were in the best position to make decisions that affected a company's products or customers. Although managers may have been right in some cases, their driving need to control workers and processes often blinded managers—so much so that control became more important than encouraging employee initiative.

Effective managers today know the value of empowering their workers. Not only are customers better served, but also by delegating more responsibility and authority to frontline workers, managers are free to pursue other important tasks that only they can do, such as coaching, "big-picture" communicating, long-range planning, walking the walk, and talking the talk. The result is a more efficient, more effective organization.

Empowerment is also a great morale booster in an organization. Managers who empower their workers show that they trust them to make decisions that are important to the company's success.

Today's businesses have discovered a lot from the improvement movement. Taking a cue from successful Japanese businesses—noted for their high-quality automobiles and innovative consumer electronic products—U.S. businesses embarked on a quality quest in the1980s. U.S. managers quickly discovered that the cornerstone of many Japanese programs was the empowerment of workers to make decisions regarding their work processes.

For example, **quality circles**—groups of employees who meet regularly to suggest ways to improve the organization—have become a much-copied Japanese

FOR EXAMPLE

Empowerment at Work

Fireman's Fund Insurance Company's personal insurance division in Novato, California, divided its employees into work units organized around its customers. The company cut several levels of management, and whenever possible, the company assigned individuals whole jobs instead of fragmented work tasks. With these changes, employees felt they had a real stake in making customers happy, efficiency increased by 35 to 40 percent, systems investments declined by $5 million a year, and endorsement turnaround decreased from twenty-one days to forty-eight hours.

technique of participative decision making. A quality circle's suggestions carry great weight with management.

The management of Motorola considers employee teams to be a crucial part of its strategy for quality improvement. Self-directed teams at its Arlington Heights, Illinois, cellular equipment manufacturing plant not only decide on their own training programs and schedule their own work, but they're also involved in the hiring and firing of coworkers.

SELF-CHECK

1. Name two ways **empowerment** improves an organization.
2. **Quality circles** are an idea borrowed from the _____.

7.3 Identifying Advantages of Teams

Teams not only have the potential to make better decisions, but they can also make faster decisions. Because team members are closest to the problems and to one another, a minimal amount of lag time exists due to communication channels or the need to get approvals from others in the organization.

Large organizations often have a hard time competing in the marketplace against smaller, more nimble competitors. And, smaller units within a large organization—such as teams—are better able to compete. The rate and scope of change in the global business environment has led to increased competitive pressures on organizations in almost every business sector.

As customers can get products and services faster, they demand to have them. As they can buy products more cheaply as a result of technology improvements or global competition, they expect lower prices as well. This expectation of quality in relation to price has dramatically increased over the years—especially with consumers' experience in obtaining more advanced electronics and computer technology for progressively lower prices. In short, customer values are changing so that they now want products and services "anytime, anyplace." Not only that, but they also want to pay less than they did last year.

Teams can also lead to increased innovation. According to then-Harvard economist Robert Reich in the *Harvard Business Review,* "As individual skills are integrated into a group, the collective capacity to innovate becomes something greater than the sum of its parts."

Teams are also more adaptive to the external environment as it quickly or constantly changes. Thus, a team's size and flexibility give it a distinct advantage over the more traditional organizational structure of competing organizations. At Xerox and Hewlett-Packard, for example, design, engineering, and manufacturing functions are now closely intertwined in the development of new products—dramatically shortening the time from concept to production.

Teams used to be considered useful only for projects of short duration. However, many companies no longer follow this thought. According to Drucker, "Whereas team design has traditionally been considered applicable only to short-lived, transitory, exceptional task-force assignments, it is equally applicable to some permanent needs, especially to the top-management and innovating tasks" (*Harvard Business Review*). Indeed, the team concept has proved itself to be a workable long-term solution to the needs of many organizations.

SELF-CHECK

1. Teams may lead to decreased innovation. True or false?
2. The better services and products a customer receives, the more the customer expects and demands. True or false?
3. Name two advantages companies have when they organize their employees into teams.

FOR EXAMPLE

The Advantage of a Team

By putting together a small team of workers and encouraging them to take the initiative to solve problems, helicopter parts manufacturer Lord Aerospace Products, a division of the Lord Corporation in Dayton, Ohio, energized the rest of the company's employees. Productivity went up 30 percent and absenteeism dropped 75 percent.

7.4 Setting Up and Supporting Your Teams

The first point you need to consider when setting up a team is what kind of team to set up. Three major kinds of teams exist: formal, informal, and self-managed. Each type of team offers advantages and disadvantages depending on the specific situation, timing, and the organization's needs.

7.4.1 Formal Teams

A **formal team** is chartered by an organization's management and tasked to achieve specific goals. These goals can range from developing a new product line, determining the system for processing customer invoices, or planning a company picnic. Types of formal teams include:

▲ **Task forces:** Formal teams assembled on a temporary basis to address specific problems or issues. For example, a task force may be assembled to determine why the number of rejects for a machined part has risen from 1 in 10,000 to 1 in 1000. A task force usually has a deadline for solving the issue and reporting the findings to management.

▲ **Committees:** Long-term or permanent teams created to perform an ongoing, specific organizational task. For example, some companies have committees that select employees to receive awards for performance or that make recommendations to management for safety improvements. Although committee membership may change from year to year, the committees continue their work regardless of who belongs to them.

▲ **Command teams:** Made up of a manager or supervisor and all the employees who report directly to him or her. Such teams are by nature hierarchical and represent the traditional way that tasks are communicated from managers to workers. Examples of command teams include company sales teams, management teams, and executive teams.

Formal teams are important to most organizations because much of the communication within an establishment traditionally occurs within the team. News, goals, and information pass from employee to employee via formal teams. And they provide the structure for assigning tasks and soliciting feedback from team members on accomplishments, performance data, and so on.

7.4.2 Informal Teams

Informal teams are casual associations of employees that spontaneously develop within an organization's formal structure. Such teams include groups of employees who eat lunch together every day, form bowling teams, or simply like to hang out together—both during and after work. The membership of informal teams is in a constant state of flux as members come and go and friendships and other associations between employees change over time.

Although informal teams have no specific tasks or goals assigned by management, they are very important to organizations for the following reasons:

▲ Informal teams provide a way for employees to get information outside formal, management-sanctioned communications channels.

▲ Informal teams provide a (relatively) safe outlet for employees to let off steam about issues that concern them and to find solutions to problems by discussing them with employees from other parts of the organization—unimpeded by the walls of the formal organization.

For example, a group of women employees at NYNEX Corporation, a large telecommunications firm, created mentoring circles. The purpose of these informal teams—developed outside the formal NYNEX organization—was to fill the void created by a lack of female top-level managers to serve as mentors for other women in the organization. Organized in groups of eight to twelve employees, the circles provide the kind of career networking, support, and encouragement that mentors normally provide to their charges.

Ad hoc groups are informal teams of employees assembled to solve a problem with only those who are most likely to contribute invited. For example, you may form an ad hoc team when you select employees from your human resources and accounting departments to solve a problem with the system for tracking and recording pay changes in the company's payroll system. You don't invite participants from shipping to join this informal team because they probably can't provide meaningful input to the problem.

7.4.3 Self-managed Teams

Self-managed teams combine the attributes of both formal and informal teams. Generally chartered by management, self-managed teams often quickly take on lives of their own as members take over responsibility for the day-to-day workings of the team. Self-managed teams usually contain from three to thirty employees whose job is to meet together to find solutions to common worker problems. Self-managed teams are also known as high-performance teams, cross-functional teams, or superteams.

To compress time and gain benefits, an organization's self-managing teams must be

▲ Made up of people from different parts of the organization.

▲ Small because large groups create communication problems.

▲ Self-managing and empowered to act because referring decisions back up the line wastes time and often leads to poorer decisions.

▲ Multifunctional because that's the best—if not the only—way to keep the actual product and its essential delivery system clearly visible and foremost in everyone's mind.

American automobile manufacturers' management and their union-dominated workforces have a long history of conflict—often violent and disruptive. However, at Saturn Corporation, the innovative subsidiary of General Motors, teams have helped change this seemingly unchangeable tradition. Teams have led to cooperation between management and workers. Differences of opinion still arise from time to time, according to Michael Bennett, former president of Union Local 1853. Although conflict certainly exists—Saturn is no different in that respect from any other organization—union–management relations are not adversarial as they often are in other unionized workplaces. Each side makes a point of seeking a better solution that benefits everyone.

Being a team member is not optional at Saturn: All employees belong to at least one. On the production floor, employees work in self-managed teams that make decisions regarding training, hiring, budgeting, and scheduling. Each team consists of five to fifteen workers, and instead of being monitored by outsiders, the teams monitor themselves. As a result, team members gain a better appreciation for what the organization has to do and what it costs to do it.

More and more, where management is willing to let go of the reins of absolute authority and turn them over to workers, self-managing teams are rising to the challenge and are making major contributions to the success of their firms. Indeed, the future success of many businesses lies in the successful implementation of self-managed teams.

7.4.4 Encouraging Empowerment

Empowerment is a great thing when it flourishes in an organization. However, real empowerment is still rare. Although many managers talk a good story about how they empower their employees, few actually do it. When they are real and not pale imitations, empowered teams typically

▲ Make the most of the decisions that influence team success.

▲ Choose their leaders.

▲ Add or remove team members.

▲ Set their goals and commitments.

FOR EXAMPLE

Self-managed Teams

Self-managed teams of workers at Johnsonville Foods in Wisconsin increased productivity 50 percent between 1986 and 1990—a much higher rate than chief executive officer Ralph Stayer had imagined possible. As a result of this dramatic productivity gain, Stayer decided to expand the company's sausage production facility.

▲ Define and perform much of their training.

▲ Receive rewards as a team.

Unfortunately, employee empowerment, for the most part, may be only an illusion. A survey of team members showed that plenty of room for change and improvement in the workings of teams still exists. Survey respondents clearly felt that the areas of intragroup trust, group effectiveness, agenda setting/meeting content, and role and idea conformity can use some improvement.

Conducted by management expert Dr. Bob Culver, a recent study of managers, team leaders, and team members at nine different companies discovered that real-world teams are more participative than empowered. Basically, top management is still making the real decisions. Using Culver's study results as a basis, you can apply the following specific recommendations to counter the ineffectiveness of many teams:

▲ **Make your teams empowered, not merely participative:** Instead of just inviting employees to participate in teams, grant team members the authority and power to make independent decisions.
  • Allow your teams to make long-range and strategic decisions, not just procedural ones.
  • Permit the team to choose the team leaders.
  • Allow the team to determine its goals and commitments.
  • Make sure that all team members have influence by involving them in the decision-making process.

▲ **Remove the source of conflicts:** Despite their attempts to empower employees, managers are often unwilling to live with the results. Be willing to start up a team, and then be prepared to accept the outcome.
  • Recognize and work out personality conflicts.
  • Fight turf protection and middle-management resistance.
  • Work to unify manager and team member views.
  • Minimize the stress of downsizing and process improvement tasks.

▲ **Change other significant factors that influence team effectiveness:** Each of these factors indicates that an organization has not yet brought true empowerment to its employees. You have the power to change this situation.
  • Allow the team to discipline poorly performing members.
  • Make peer pressure less important in attaining high team performance.
  • Train as many team members as you train managers or team leaders.

Although clear examples do exist of companies where management has truly empowered its teams, team empowerment doesn't just happen. Supervisors and managers must make concerted and ongoing efforts to ensure that authority and autonomy pass from management to teams.

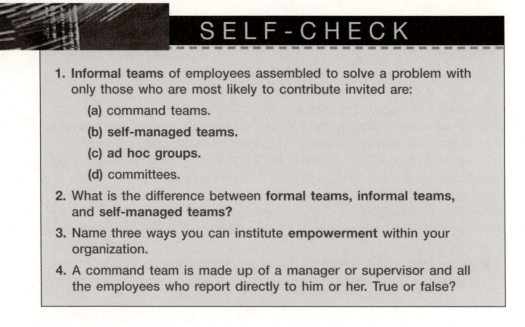

SELF-CHECK

1. **Informal teams** of employees assembled to solve a problem with only those who are most likely to contribute invited are:

    (a) command teams.

    (b) self-managed teams.

    (c) ad hoc groups.

    (d) committees.

2. What is the difference between **formal teams, informal teams, and self-managed teams**?

3. Name three ways you can institute **empowerment** within your organization.

4. A command team is made up of a manager or supervisor and all the employees who report directly to him or her. True or false?

7.5 Meetings: Putting Teams to Work

Meetings are the primary forum in which team members conduct business and communicate with one another. And with the proliferation of teams in business today, it pays to master the basic skills of meeting management.

As organizations continue to flatten their hierarchies and empower frontline workers with more responsibility and authority, teams are the visible and often inevitable result. This transition is good news to the burgeoning industry of consulting and seminars in business team building. Consider the way the best companies run meetings to respond to this new, team-oriented business environment.

▲ Jack Welch, former chair of General Electric, determined that if the company were going to be successful, it had to move away from the old model of autocratic meetings and direction from top management. Welch's solution was to initiate a town-hall concept of meetings throughout the entire organization. These meetings, called "work-out meetings," bring workers and managers together in open forums where workers are allowed to ask any question they want and managers are required to respond.

▲ The company's core business strategies are shaped in regular meetings of senior executives—each of whom represents one of GE's individual business units. In these high-energy meetings, attendees are encouraged to explore every possible avenue and alternative and to be open to new ideas. GE's recent ventures in Mexico, India, and China are a direct result of these meetings.

▲ At GE's Bayamón, Puerto Rico, lightning arrester plant, employees have been organized into teams that are responsible for specific plant functions—shipping, assembly, and so forth. However, instead of tapping only employees from shipping to be on the shipping team for example, teams consist of employees from all parts of the plant. This process enables representatives from all affected departments to discuss how suggested changes or improvements may affect their part of the operation. Hourly workers run the meetings on their own, and advisers—GE's term for salaried employees—participate in meetings only at the team's request.

Results of the Bayamón experiment have produced clear and convincing evidence that GE's approach is quite successful. A year after startup, the plant's employees measured 20 percent higher in productivity than their closest counterpart in the mainland United States. And if that weren't enough, management projected a further 20 percent increase in the following year.

Meetings that produce results like these companies don't just happen by accident. Far too many meetings in organizations today are run poorly. Instead of contributing to an organization's efficiency and effectiveness, most meetings actually make employees less efficient and less effective. How many times have you heard someone complain about getting stuck in one more useless meeting? With today's business imperative to get more done with less, making every meeting count is more important than ever.

7.5.1 Wasting Time with Meetings

Unfortunately, most meetings are a waste of time. Meeting experts have determined that approximately 53 percent of all the time spent in meetings—and this means the time that *you* spend in meetings—is unproductive, worthless, and of little consequence. When you realize that most business people spend at least 25 percent of their working hours in meetings, with upper management spending more than double that time in meetings, you can begin to gain an appreciation for the importance of learning and applying effective meeting skills.

So, what's wrong with meetings anyway? The book *Better Business Meetings*[1] discusses a few of the reasons:

▲ **Too many meetings take place:** When did you last say to yourself, "Gee, I haven't been in any meetings lately. I sure miss them"? Probably never. Indeed, the eternal lament of the manager is something more along the lines of "How am I supposed to get any work done with all these meetings?" The problem is not just that too many meetings take place; the problem is that many meetings are unnecessary, unproductive, and a waste of your time.

▲ **Attendees are unprepared:** Some meetings happen prematurely, before a real reason to meet arises. Other times, individuals, who have prepared neither themselves nor the participants for the topics to be discussed, lead the meeting. What often results is a long period where the participants stumble around blindly trying to figure out why the meeting was called in the first place.

▲ **Certain individuals dominate the proceedings:** You may find one or two in every crowd. You know, the people who think that they know it all and who make sure that their opinion is heard loudly and often during the course of a meeting. These folks may be good for occasional comic relief, if nothing else, but they often intimidate the other participants and stifle their contributions.

▲ **They last too long:** Yes, yes, yes. Make sure a meeting doesn't last longer than it needs to. No less, no more. Despite this fact, most managers let meetings expand to fill the time allotted to them. So rather than let the participants leave after the business at hand is completed, the meeting drags on and on and on.

▲ **The meeting has no focus:** Meeting leadership is not a passive occupation. Many pressures work against keeping meetings on track and on topic, and managers often fail to step up to the challenge. The result is the proliferation of personal agendas, digressions, diversions, off-topic tangents, and worse.

7.5.2 Making Meetings a Success

Although many meetings are a big waste of time, they don't have to be. Take the following steps to make the most of the meetings:

▲ **Be prepared:** You need only a little time to prepare for a meeting, and the payoff is increased meeting effectiveness. Instead of wasting time trying to figure out why you're meeting, your preparation gets results as soon as the meeting starts.

▲ **Have an agenda:** An agenda is your road map, your meeting plan. With it, you and the other participants recognize the meeting goals and know what you're going to discuss. And if you distribute the agenda to participants before the meeting, you multiply its effectiveness many times over because the participants can prepare for the meeting in advance.

▲ **Start on time and end on time (or sooner):** You go to a meeting on time, and the meeting leader, while muttering about an important phone call or visitor, arrives fifteen minutes late. Even worse is when the meeting leader ignores the scheduled ending time and lets the meeting go on and on. Respect your participants by starting and ending your meetings on time. You don't want them spending the entire meeting looking at their watches and worrying about how late you're going to keep them!

▲ **Have fewer but better meetings:** Call a meeting only when a meeting is absolutely necessary. And when you call a meeting, make the meeting a good one. Do you really have to meet to discuss change in your travel reimbursement policy? Wouldn't an e-mail message to all company travelers do just as well? Whenever you're tempted to call a meeting, make sure that you have a good reason for doing so.

▲ **Think inclusion, not exclusion:** Be selective with whom you invite to your meetings—select only as many participants as needed to get the job done. But don't exclude people who may have the best insight into your issues simply because of their ranks in the organization or their lifestyles, appearance, or beliefs. You never know who in your organization is going to provide the best ideas, and you only hurt your chances of getting those great ideas by excluding people for nonperformance-related reasons.

▲ **Maintain the focus:** Ruthlessly keep your meetings on topic at all times. Although doing everything but talking about the topic at hand can be a lot of fun, you called the meeting for a specific reason in the first place. Stick to the topic, and if you finish the meeting early, participants who want to stick around to talk about other topics don't have to hold the other participants hostage to do so.

▲ **Capture action items:** Make sure that you have a system for capturing, summarizing, and assigning action items to individual team members. Flip charts are great for this purpose. Have you ever come out of a meeting wondering why the meeting took place? Was it a meeting with no purpose, no direction, no assignments or follow-up actions? Make sure that your meetings have purpose and that you assign action items to the appropriate people.

▲ **Get feedback:** Feedback can be a great way to measure the effectiveness of your meetings. Not only can you find out what you did right, but you also can find out what you did wrong and get ideas on how to make your future meetings more effective. Ask the participants to give you their honest and open feedback—verbally or in writing—and then use it. You can never see yourself as others do unless they show you.

SELF-CHECK

1. Meetings:
   (a) can be a waste of time.
   (b) can be effective and increase productivity.
   (c) require preparation.
   (d) all of the above.
2. Why is it important to ensure that meetings are effective?
3. How can you measure the effectiveness of your meetings?
4. More meetings are better than fewer meetings. True or false?

7.6 Becoming a Coach

Even if you have a pretty good sense of what it means to be a manager, do you really know what it means to be a coach? A coach is a colleague, counselor, and cheerleader, all rolled into one. Based on that definition, are you a coach? How about your boss? Or your boss's boss? Why or why not?

Coaching a team of individuals isn't easy, and certain characteristics make some coaches better than others. Fortunately, as with most other business skills, you can discover, practice, and improve the traits of good coaches. You can always find room for improvement, and good coaches are the first to admit it. The list that follows highlights important characteristics of coaching:

▲ **Coaches set goals.** Whether an organization's vision is to become the leading provider of wireless telephones in the world, to increase revenues by 20 percent a year, or simply to get the break room walls painted this year, coaches work with their employees to set goals and deadlines for completion. They then go away and allow their employees to determine how to accomplish the goals.

▲ **Coaches support and encourage.** Employees—even the best and most experienced—can easily become discouraged from time to time. When employees are learning new tasks, when a long-term account is lost, or when business is down, coaches are there—ready to step in and help the team members through the worst of it.

▲ **Coaches emphasize team success over individual success.** The team's overall performance is the most important concern, not the stellar abilities of a particular team member. Coaches know that no one person can carry an entire team to success; winning takes the combined efforts of all team members. The development of teamwork skills is a vital step in an employee's progress in an organization.

▲ **Coaches can quickly assess the talents and shortfalls of team members.** The most successful coaches can quickly determine their team members' strengths and weaknesses and, as a result, tailor their approach to each. For example, if one team member has strong analytical skills but poor presentation skills, a coach can concentrate on providing support for the employee's development of better presentation skills.

▲ **Coaches inspire their team members.** Through their support and guidance, coaches are skilled at inspiring their team members to the highest levels of human performance. Teams of inspired individuals are willing to do whatever it takes to achieve their organization's goals.

▲ **Coaches create environments that allow individuals to be successful.** Great coaches ensure that their workplaces are structured to let team members take risks and stretch their limits without fear of retribution if

> ## FOR EXAMPLE
>
> ### Quotes from Coaches
>
> Here are some quotes from famous coaches that are found in Gerald Tomlinson's book *Speaker's Treasury of Sports Anecdotes, Stories, and Humor*[2]:
>
> ▲ Lou Holtz, former head coach of the University of South Carolina football team, said about coaching: "I don't think discipline is forcing someone to do something. It's showing them how this is going to help them in the long run."
>
> ▲ According to former Dartmouth lacrosse coach Whitey Burnham, "Good judgment comes from experience, and experience comes from bad judgment."
>
> ▲ Former Houston Oilers head coach Bum Phillips's theory of football coaching may apply equally well in business: "Two kinds of football players ain't worth a damn: the one that never does what he's told, and the other that never does anything *except* what he's told."

they fail. Coaches are always available to advise their employees or just to listen to their problems if need be.

▲ **Coaches provide feedback.** Communication and feedback between coach and employee is a critical element of the coaching process. Employees must know where they stand in the organization—what they're doing right, and what they're doing wrong. Equally important, employees must let their coaches know when they need help or assistance. And both parties need this dialog in a timely manner, on an ongoing basis—not just once a year in a performance review.

SELF-CHECK

1. List three traits of effective **coaches.**
2. Why is feedback important?

7.7 Coaching Methods, Guidelines, and Tools

Besides the obvious coaching roles of supporting and encouraging employees in their quest to achieve an organization's goals, coaches also teach their employees how to achieve an organization's goals. Drawing from their experience, coaches lead their workers step by step through work processes or procedures.

After the workers discover how to perform a task, the coach delegates full authority and responsibility for its performance to them.

7.7.1 Coaching Using Show-and-Tell

For the transfer of specific skills, you can find no better way of teaching, and no better way of learning, than the **show-and-tell** method. Developed by a post–World War II American industrial society desperate to quickly train new workers in manufacturing processes, show-and-tell is beautiful in its simplicity and effectiveness.

Show-and-tell coaching has three steps:

1. *You do, you say.* **Sit down with your employees and explain the procedure in general terms while you perform the task.** Most businesses today use computers as a critical tool for getting work done. When a manager needs to coach a new employee in the use of an obscure word processing or spreadsheet technique, the first thing she needs to do is to explain the technique to the employee while she demonstrates it. "I click my left mouse button on the Insert command on the toolbar and pull down the menu. Then I point the arrow to Symbol and click again. I choose the symbol I want from the menu, point my arrow to it, and click to select it. I then point my arrow to Insert and click to place the symbol in the document; then I point my arrow to Close and click again to finish the job."

2. *They do, you say.* **Now, have the employee do the same procedure as you explain each step in the procedure.** "Click your left mouse button on the Insert command on the toolbar and pull down the menu. Okay, good. Now point your arrow to Symbol and click again. Good job! Choose the symbol you want from the menu and point your arrow to it. Now click to select it. All right—point your arrow to Insert and click to place the symbol in the document. Okay, you're almost done now. Point your arrow to Close and click again to finish the job. There you are!"

3. *They do, they say.* **Finally, as you observe, have your employees perform the task again as they explain to you what they are doing.** "Okay, Yinka, now it's your turn. I want you to insert a symbol in your document and tell me what you're doing." "All right, Susan. First, I click my left mouse button on the Insert command on the toolbar and pull down the menu. Then I point the arrow to Symbol and click again. I decide the symbol I want from the menu, point my arrow to it, and click to select it. Next, I point the arrow to Insert and click to place the symbol in the document. Finally, I point my arrow to Close and click again to finish the job. I did it!"

It also never hurts to have employees create a "cheat sheet" of the new steps to refer to until they become habit.

Despite popular impressions to the contrary, 90 percent of management isn't the big event—the blinding flash of brilliance that creates markets where none previously existed, the magnificent negotiation that results in unheard of levels of union–management cooperation, or the masterful stroke that catapults the firm into the big leagues. No, 90 percent of a manager's job consists of the daily chipping away at problems and the shaping of talents.

The best coaches are constantly on the lookout for *turning points*—the daily opportunities to succeed that are available to all employees.

The big successes—the victories against competitors, the dramatic surges in revenues or profits, the astounding new products—are typically the result of building a foundation of countless small successes along the way. Making a voice-mail system more responsive to your customers' needs, sending an employee to a seminar on time management, writing a great sales agreement, conducting a meaningful performance appraisal with an employee, meeting a prospective client for lunch—all are turning points in the average business day. Although each event may not be particularly spectacular on its own, when aggregated over time, they can add up to big things.

This is the job of a coach. Instead of using dynamite to transform the organization in one fell swoop, coaches are like the ancient stonemasons who built the great pyramids of Egypt. The movement and placement of each individual stone may not have seemed like a big deal when considered as a separate activity. However, each was an important step in the achievement of the ultimate result: the construction of awe-inspiring structures that have withstood thousands of years of war, weather, and tourists.

7.7.2 Incorporating Coaching in Your Day-to-Day Interactions

Coaches focus daily on spending time with employees to help them succeed—to assess their progress and to find out what they can do to help the employees capitalize on the turning points that present themselves every day. Coaches complement and supplement the abilities and experience of their employees by bringing their own abilities and experience to the table. They reward positive performance and they help their employees learn important lessons from making mistakes— lessons that, in turn, help the employees improve their future performance.

For example, suppose that you have a young and inexperienced, but bright and energetic, sales trainee on your staff. Your employee has done a great job contacting customers and making sales calls, but she has yet to close her first deal. When you talk to her about this, she confesses that she is very nervous about her own personal turning point: She's worried that she may become confused in front of the customer and blow the deal at the last minute. She needs your coaching.

The following guidelines can help you, the coach, handle any employee's concerns:

▲ **Meet with your employee.** Make an appointment with your employee as soon as possible for a relaxed discussion of the concerns. Find a place that is quiet and free of distractions and put your phone on hold or forward it to voice mail.

▲ **Listen!** One of the most motivating things one person can do for another is to listen. Avoid instant solutions or lectures. Before you say a word, ask your employee to bring you up to date with the situation, her concerns, and any possible approaches or solutions she's considered. Let her do the talking while you do the listening.

▲ **Reinforce the positive.** Begin by pointing out the things that your employee did right in the particular situation. Let your employee know when she is on the right track. Give her positive feedback on her performance.

▲ **Highlight areas for improvement.** Point out the things that your employee needs to do to improve and tell her what you can do to help. Agree on the assistance that you can provide, whether your employee needs further training, an increased budget, more time, or whatever is necessary. Be enthusiastic about your confidence in the employee's ability to do a great job.

▲ **Follow through.** After you determine what you can do to support your employee, do it! Notice when she improves! Periodically check up on the progress that your employee is making and offer your support as necessary.

Above all, be patient. Coaching is something that you can't accomplish on your terms alone. At the outset, understand that everyone is different. Some employees catch on sooner than others, and some employees need more time to develop. Differences in ability don't make certain employees any better or worse than their coworkers—they just make them different. Just as you need time to build relationships and trust in business, your employees need time to develop skills and experience.

7.7.3 Identifying a Coach's Tools

Coaching is not a one-dimensional activity. Because every person is different, the best coaches tailor their approach to their team members' specific, individualized needs. If one team member is independent and needs only occasional guidance, recognize where the employee stands and provide that level of support. This support may consist of an occasional, informal progress check while making the rounds of the office. If, on the other hand, another team member is insecure and needs more guidance, the coach recognizes this employee's position and assists as needed. In this case, support may consist of frequent, formal meetings with the employee to assess progress and to provide advice and direction as needed.

Although every coach has his or her own style, the best coaches employ certain techniques to elicit the greatest performance from their team members:

▲ **Make time for team members.** Managing is primarily a people job. Part of being a good manager and coach is being available to your employees when they need your help. If you're not available, your employees may seek out other avenues to meet their needs—or simply stop trying to work with you. Always keep your door open to your employees and remember that they are your number one priority. Manage by walking around. Regularly get out of your office and visit your employees at their workstations.

▲ **Provide context and vision.** Instead of simply telling employees what to do, effective coaches explain the why. Coaches provide their employees with context and a big-picture perspective. Instead of spouting long lists of do's and don'ts, they explain how a system or procedure works and then define their employees' parts in the scheme of things. "Chris, you have a very important part in the financial health and vitality of our company. By ensuring that our customers pay their invoices within thirty days after we ship their products, we're able to keep our cash flow on the plus side, and we can pay our obligations such as rent, electricity, and your paycheck on time."

▲ **Transfer knowledge and perspective.** A great benefit of having a good coach is the opportunity to discover from someone who has more experience than you do. In response to the unique needs of each team member, coaches transfer their personal knowledge and perspective. "We faced the exact situation about five years ago, Dwight. I'm going to tell you what we did then, and I want you to tell me whether you think that it still makes sense today."

▲ **Be a sounding board.** Coaches talk through new ideas and approaches to solving problems with their employees. Coaches and employees can consider the implications of different approaches to solving a problem and role-play customer or client reactions before trying them out for real. By using active listening skills, coaches can often help their employees work through issues and come up with the best solutions themselves. "Okay, David, you've told me that you don't think your customer will buy off on a 20 percent price increase. What options do you have to present the price increase, and are some more palatable than others?"

▲ **Obtain needed resources.** Sometimes, coaches can help their employees make the jump from marginal to outstanding performance simply by providing the resources that their employees need. These resources can take many forms: money, time, staff, equipment, or other tangible assets. "So, Gene, you're confident that we can improve our cash flow if we throw a couple more clerks into collections? Okay, how about giving it a try."

▲ **Offer a helping hand.** For an employee who is learning a new job and is still responsible for performing his or her current job, the total workload

FOR EXAMPLE

Even Coaches Need to Be Coached

Sometimes even coaches need to be coached. Scott McNealy, chair, president, and CEO of Sun Microsystems, has used a combination of drive, passion, and tough financial controls to shepherd his company from $39 million in sales in 1984, when he took over, to more than $18 billion in sales in fiscal year 2001. Calling the stand-alone personal computer a "hairball on the desktop," McNealy has pushed the concept of network computing for years—long before the Internet became the "in" place to be. Sun is the leading maker of UNIX-based servers used to power corporate computer networks and Web sites, and Sun's Internet-ready networks have been adopted for internal use by an increasing number of companies, including Gap, Federal Express, and AT&T Universal Card Services.

However, despite his success, McNealy hired a "CEO coach" to help him become even more effective. The coach, Chuck Raben of Delta Consulting Group, Inc., asked McNealy's managers to report areas where they thought their boss could improve. Raben compiled the surveys and summarized the responses. According to Sun's management team, the result was that McNealy needed to become a better listener. So, McNealy now carries with him a reminder to respond to the points that his managers raise in meetings.
(Source: *BusinessWeek*)

can be overwhelming. Coaches can help workers through this transitional phase by reassigning current duties to other employees, authorizing overtime, or taking other measures to relieve the pressure. "John, while you're learning how to troubleshoot that new network server, I'm going to assign your maintenance workload to Rachel. We can get back together at the end of the week to see how you're doing."

SELF-CHECK

1. What is the **show-and-tell** method?
2. What are the three steps in the show-and-tell method?
3. Name two ways managers can incorporate coaching techniques in their daily job.

SUMMARY

For a team to be successful, it must have a good coach and be trained well. Holding effective meetings, coaching your employees in a positive way, and training your employees to make independent, sound decisions will strengthen the entire organization and improve customer relations. In this chapter, you assessed what characteristics are needed to be a good coach. You also analyzed ways to empower employees. Finally, you evaluated coaching methods and tools to improve your organization.

KEY TERMS

Ad hoc groups	Informal teams of employees assembled to solve a problem with only those who are most likely to contribute invited.
Coaches	Individuals who guide, discuss, and encourage others on their journey.
Empowerment	Transfer of power, responsibility, and authority from higher-level to lower-level employees.
Formal teams	Teams chartered by an organization's management and tasked to achieve specific goals.
Horizontal organization	Organization with minimal levels of management.
Informal teams	Casual associations of employees that spontaneously develop within an organization's formal structure.
Quality circles	Groups of employees who meet regularly to suggest ways to improve the organization.
Self-managed teams	Teams that combine the attributes of both formal and informal teams. They usually contain from three to thirty employees whose job is to meet together to find solutions to common worker problems. They are also known as high-performance teams, cross-functional teams, or superteams.
Show-and-tell	Coaching method developed by a post–World War II American industrial society desperate to quickly train new workers.
Teams	Two or more people who work together to achieve a common goal.
Vertical organization	Organization with many layers of managers and supervisors between top management and frontline workers.

ASSESS YOUR UNDERSTANDING

Go to www.wiley.com/college/nelson to evaluate your knowledge of training teams. *Measure your learning by comparing pre-test and post-test results.*

Summary Questions

1. Coaches should meet regularly with their employees. True or false?

2. _____ between coach and employee is a critical element of the coaching process and allows for open communication.

3. Experts believe that over half of the meetings held in companies are unproductive. True or false?

4. Long-term teams created to perform an ongoing, specific organizational task are:
   (a) ad-hoc groups.
   (b) committees.
   (c) command teams.
   (d) task forces.

5. Teams can lead to increased _____, finding ways to improve the process and products.

6. The transfer of power and responsibility to employees is called _____.

7. A coach is:
   (a) any supervisor.
   (b) an individual who discusses, guides, and encourages employees.
   (c) never someone other than a supervisor.
   (d) a person who trains employees only on the technical aspect of a job.

8. Groups of employees who meet regularly to suggest ways to improve the organization are:
   (a) ad hoc groups.
   (b) quality circles.
   (c) self-managed teams.
   (d) committees.

9. Vertical organizations:
   (a) have few layers of management.
   (b) empower employees.
   (c) have many layers of management.
   (d) are more productive than horizontal organizations.

10. Promoting cooperation can foster unhealthy competitiveness. True or false?

Applying This Chapter

1. You manage a marketing firm and report directly to the CEO. Every week you have a two-hour unproductive meeting with the CEO and staff members, with the CEO running the meeting. The CEO asks you for tips on how to make the meetings more productive. What do you tell her?

2. You are the manager in a call center. You determine that you need a team to study and determine why the average wait time for a customer is so long. This team should also present ideas on how to improve the average wait time. What kind of team do you form and why?

3. You work in a consulting firm. You have just taken over a department that was formerly run by a manager who wouldn't allow the employees to make any of their own decisions. Now your time is taken up with employees asking you before they make any move. How do you empower them?

4. You work at a manufacturing company and you learn that the managers are not spending time with their employees or guiding their careers. You decide to choose a few of them and help them become coaches. What types of things do you try to teach them in terms of how to be a coach?

5. You are a manager at a large public relations firm. You have forty employees to manage and there are groups of employees who do similar functions and have similar qualities. You determine that it would be more efficient if these employees were in teams. What arguments do you present to your boss in support of teams?

YOU TRY IT

Vertical Organizations

You have taken over as CEO of a large corporation that is arranged vertically. In fact, every fifth employee has the title of administrative vice president. What arguments do you present to the board members as to why you should make the organization more horizontal?

Forming a Team

You work for a computer manufacturing company that has fallen on hard times. Not only are you failing to produce products that are priced competitively, but you also lack any new products that are likely to generate enthusiasm in the market. What kind of team or teams do you put together to study the situation and why? What types of goals do you give to the teams? How do you coach the teams?

8

INSPIRING EMPLOYEES TO BETTER PERFORMANCE
Developing and Rewarding Employees

Starting Point

Go to www.wiley.com/college/nelson to assess your knowledge of inspiring employees.
Determine where you need to concentrate your effort.

What You'll Learn in This Chapter

▲ The importance of developing employees
▲ The need for career development plans
▲ How to help employees develop
▲ The need for mentors in the workplace
▲ What motivates employees
▲ What behaviors to reward
▲ Nonmonetary rewards

After Studying This Chapter, You'll Be Able To

▲ Support employees in their professional development
▲ Create a career development plan
▲ Choose mentors for your employees and yourself
▲ Choose which behaviors to reward in the workplace
▲ Predict what will motivate employees
▲ Select rewards for employees that will make a lasting impression

INTRODUCTION

In every organization, you have a lot to figure out: internal and external office politics, formal and informal hierarchies, the right and wrong ways to get important tasks done, which people you should ignore and which people you should pay close attention to. And this list doesn't even take into account the skills that you need to know to do your job: mastering a particular spreadsheet program or getting used to speaking in front of large groups of people, for example. Of course, every time you progress to a new level in the organization or take on a new task, your learning process starts anew. In this chapter, you will examine how to help employees acquire the skills they need to be successful both in their current job and also in their profession. You will also learn about the development process and the importance of mentors, and you will assess career development plans and how to create one.

Trying to develop employees is only half the story; they have to be motivated and want to do a good job. The question of how to motivate employees has loomed large over managers ever since management was first invented. Most of management comes down to mastering skills and techniques for motivating people—to make them better, more productive employees.

You have two ways to motivate employees: rewards and punishments. If employees do what you want them to do, reward them with incentives that they desire—awards, recognition, important titles, money, and so on. These are often called *positive consequences*. Alternatively, if employees don't do what you want, punish them with what they don't desire—warnings, reprimands, demotions, firings, and so on. These are often known as *negative consequences*. By nature, employees are drawn toward positive consequences and shy away from negative consequences.

By leading with positive reinforcers, not only can you inspire your employees to do what you want but you can also develop happier, more productive employees in the process—and that combination is tough to beat! Recognizing your employees for doing a good job is one of the best ways to keep them motivated and engaged in their work. Furthermore, you don't have to break your budget to do it. You have countless ways to thank and appreciate employees for doing a good job, and many of them require little, if any, money. In this chapter, you will examine what behaviors to reward employees for and how to reward them.

8.1 Developing Employees

Employee development doesn't just happen. Managers and employees must make a conscious, concerted effort. Beyond that, it takes time and commitment. When you do employee development right, you don't just talk about it once a year at your employees' annual performance reviews. The best employee development is ongoing and requires that you support and encourage your employees' initiative. Recognize, however, that all development is self-development; you can really only develop yourself. You can't force your employees to develop. They have to want to develop themselves. You can, however, help set an environment that makes it more likely that they will want to learn, grow, and succeed.

Many good reasons exist for helping your employees develop and improve themselves (not the least of which is that they'll perform more effectively in their current jobs). However, despite all the good reasons, development boils down to one important point: As a manager, you're in the best position to provide your employees with the support that they need to develop in your organization. Not only can you provide them with the time and money required for training, but also you can provide them with unique on-the-job learning opportunities and assignments, mentoring, team participation, and more. Besides, you'll need to have someone to take your job when you get promoted, right? Employee development involves a lot more than just going to a training class or two. In fact, approximately 90 percent of development occurs on the job.

The terms *training* and *development* can have two distinctly different meanings:

▲ **Training** usually refers to teaching workers the short-term skills that they need to know right now to do their jobs.

▲ **Development** usually refers to teaching employees the kinds of long-term skills that they'll need in the future as they progress in their careers. For this reason, employee development is often known as *career development*.

Now, in case you don't have any inkling whatsoever why developing your employees is a good idea, the following list provides just a few reasons. Many more exist, depending on your personal situation.

▲ **You may be taking your employees' knowledge for granted.** Have you ever wondered why your employees continue to mess up assignments that you know they can perform? Believe it or not, your employees may not know how to do those assignments. Have you ever actually seen your employees perform the assignments in question?

Say you give a pile of numbers to your assistant and tell him you want them organized and totaled within an hour. However, instead of presenting you with a nice, neat computer spreadsheet, your employee gives you a confusing mess. No, your employee isn't necessarily incompetent; your employee may not know how to put together a spreadsheet on his computer. Find out! The solution may be as simple as walking through your approach to completing the assignment with your employee and then having him give it a try.

▲ **Employees who work smarter are better employees.** Simply put, smarter employees are better employees. If you can help your employees develop and begin to work smarter and more effectively—and doubtless you can—why wouldn't you? No one in your organization knows everything he or she needs to know. Find out what your employees don't know about their jobs and then make plans with them about how and when they can find out what they need to know. When your employees have achieved their development goals, they'll work smarter, your organization will reap the benefits in greater employee efficiency and effectiveness, and you'll sleep better at night.

▲ **Someone has to be prepared to step into your shoes.** Do you ever plan to take a vacation? Or get a promotion? How are you going to go anywhere or do anything outside the office if you don't help prepare your employees to take on the higher-level duties that are part of your job? We all know managers who are so worried about what's going on at the office when they're on vacation that they call the office for a status update several times a day. Whether they're in Niagara Falls, Walt Disney World, or at a beach in Hawaii, they spend more time worrying about the office than they do enjoying themselves.

The reason that many managers don't have to call their offices when they're on vacation is because they make it a point to help develop their employees to take over when they're gone. You can do the same thing, too; the future of your organization depends on it.

▲ **Your employee wins, and so does your organization.** When you allocate funds to employee development, your employees win by learning higher-level skills and new ways of viewing the world—and your organization wins because of increased employee motivation and improved work skills. When you spend money for employee development, you actually double the effect of your investment because of this dual effect. And most important, you prepare your employees to fill the roles into which your organization will need them to move in the future.

▲ **Your employees are worth your time and money.** New employees cost a lot of money to recruit and train. Not only do you have to consider the investment in dollars, but also you and the rest of your staff have to make an investment in time. When you have a trained employee, you should do everything to keep him or her. Constantly training replacements can be disruptive and very expensive.

When employees see that you have their best interests at heart, they're likely to want to work for you and learn from you. As a result, your organization will attract talented people. Invest in your employees now, or waste your time and money finding replacements later.

> ## FOR EXAMPLE
>
> ### Working in the Coal Mine: Not What It Used to Be
>
> Many jobs that were formerly the province of relatively less-educated blue-collar workers are becoming increasingly technical. For example, in coal mining, career development used to mean learning how to use a new type of pickax or pneumatic drill. Now, however, miners are using laptop computers to monitor water quality and equipment breakdowns. At the Twentymile Mine, located near Oak Creek, Colorado, employees of Cyprus Amax Mineral Company have many skills to master in addition to wielding a shovel or driving a tractor. According to an executive of the firm, Cyprus Amax Mineral is looking for employees with "high math skills, more technical background, more comfort with electronics." Indeed, workers at the Twentymile Mine have an average of two years of college under their belts.
> (Source: *BusinessWeek*)

SELF-CHECK

1. What is the difference between **training** and **development**?
2. List and discuss two reasons why managers should develop their employees.

8.2 Creating Career Development Plans

The career development plan is the heart and soul of your efforts to develop your employees. Unfortunately, many managers don't take the time to create development plans with their employees, instead trusting that, when the need arises, they can find training to accommodate the need. This kind of reactive thinking ensures that you will always be catching up to the challenges that your organization will face in the years to come.

Why wait for the future to arrive before you prepare to deal with it? Are you really so busy that you can't spend a little of your precious time planting the seeds that your organization will harvest years from now? No! Although you do have to take care of the seemingly endless crises that arise in the here and now, you also have to prepare yourself and your employees to meet the challenges of the future. To do otherwise is an incredibly shortsighted and ineffective way to run your organization.

All career development plans must contain at minimum the following key elements:

▲ **Specific learning goals:** When you meet with an employee to discuss his or her development plans, you identify specific learning goals. And don't forget: Each and every employee in your organization can benefit from having learning goals. Don't leave anyone out!

For example, say that your employee's career path is going to start at the position of junior buyer and work up to manager of purchasing. The key learning goals for this employee may be to learn material requirements planning (MRP), computer spreadsheet analysis techniques, and supervision.

▲ **Resources required to achieve the designated learning goals:** After you identify your employee's learning objectives, you have to decide how he or she will reach them. Development resources include a wide variety of opportunities that support the development of your employees. Assignment to teams, job shadowing, **stretch assignments** (assignments that aren't too easy or too hard, and involve learning), formal training, and more may be required. Formal training may be conducted by outsiders, by internal trainers, or perhaps in a self-guided series of learning modules. If the training requires funding or other resources, identify those resources and make efforts to obtain them.

▲ **Employee responsibilities and resources:** Career development is a joint responsibility of an employee and his or her manager. A business can and does pay for things, but so can employees (as any employee who has paid out of his own pocket to get a college degree can attest). A good career development plan should include what the employee is doing on his or her own time.

▲ **Required date of completion for each learning goal:** Plans are no good without a way to schedule the milestones of goal accomplishment and progress. Each learning goal has to have a corresponding date of completion. Don't select dates that are so close that they're difficult or unduly burdensome to achieve, or so far into the future that they lose their immediacy and effect. The best schedules for learning goals allow employees the flexibility to get their daily tasks done while keeping ahead of the changes in the business environment that necessitate the employees' development in the first place.

▲ **Standards for measuring the accomplishment of learning goals:** For every goal, you must have a way to measure its completion. Normally, the manager assesses whether the employees actually use the new skills they've been taught. Whatever the individual case, make sure that the standards you use to measure the completion of a learning goal are clear and attainable and that both you and your employees are in full agreement with them.

FOR EXAMPLE

In-House Career Centers

Raychem, a maker of industrial products located in Menlo Park, California, offers its employees the services of an in-house career center. At this center, employees can take courses in résumé writing and interviewing techniques and search for transfer or promotional opportunities within their company.

The career development plan of a junior buyer may look like this:

Career Development Plan
Sarah Smith

Skill goal:

▲ Become proficient in material requirements planning (MRP).

Learning goal:

▲ Learn the basics of employee supervision.

Plan:

▲ Shadow supervisor in daily work for half days, starting immediately.

▲ Attend quarterly supervisor's update seminar on the first Wednesday of January, April, July, and October. (No cost: in-house.)

▲ Complete class "Basics of MRP" no later than the first quarter of fiscal year XX. ($550 plus travel costs.)

▲ Successfully complete class "Intermediate MRP" no later than the second quarter of fiscal year XX. ($750 plus travel costs.)

▲ Continue self-funded accounting certificate program at local community college.

As you can see, this career development plan contains each of the four necessary elements that we describe. A career development plan doesn't have to be complicated to be effective. In fact, when it comes to employee development plans, simpler is definitely better. Of course, the exact format that you decide on isn't so important. The most important point is that you do career development plans.

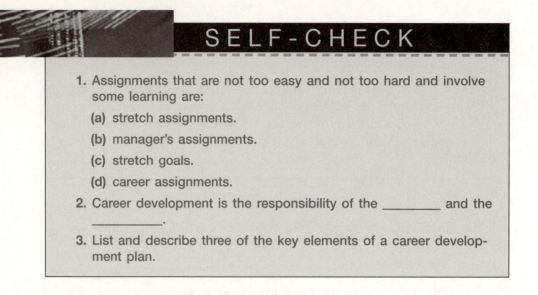

1. Assignments that are not too easy and not too hard and involve some learning are:

   (a) stretch assignments.

   (b) manager's assignments.

   (c) stretch goals.

   (d) career assignments.

2. Career development is the responsibility of the _____ and the _____.

3. List and describe three of the key elements of a career development plan.

8.3 Helping Employees Develop

Employee development takes the deliberate and ongoing efforts of employees with the support of their managers. If either employees or managers drop the ball, then employees won't develop, and the organization will suffer the consequences of not having the employees needed to meet the challenges that the future brings. This outcome definitely isn't good. As a manager, you want your organization to be ready for the future, not always trying to catch up to it.

The employees' role is to identify the areas where development can help to make the employees better and more productive workers and then to relay this information to their managers. After further development opportunities are identified, managers and employees work together to schedule and implement them.

As a manager, your role is to be alert to the development needs of your employees and to keep an eye out for potential development opportunities. Managers in smaller organizations may have the assignment of determining where the organization will be in the next few years. Armed with that information, you're responsible for finding ways to ensure that employees are available to meet the needs of the future organization. Your job is then to provide the resources and support required to develop employees so that they're able to fill the organization's needs.

To develop your employees to meet the coming challenges within your organization, follow these steps:

1. **Meet with your employees about their careers.** After you assess your employees, meet with them to discuss where you see them in the organization and also to find out where in the organization they want to go. This

effort has to be a joint one! Having elaborate plans for an employee to rise up the company ladder in sales management isn't going to do you any good if your employee hates the idea of leaving sales to become a manager of other salespeople.

2. **Discuss your employees' strengths and weaknesses.** Assuming that, in the preceding step, you discover that you're on the same wavelength as your employee, the next step is to have a frank discussion regarding his or her strengths and weaknesses. Your main goal here is to identify areas the employee can leverage—that is, strengths that your employees can develop to allow their continued upward progress in the organization and to meet the future challenges that your business faces. Focus the majority of your development efforts and dollars on these opportunities.

   Most important, you need to spend time developing your strengths than improving your weaknesses. You can be great at something that comes easy to you and this will have more value for you and your organization than forcing yourself to be merely adequate at things others excel in.

3. **Assess where your employees are now.** The next step in the employee development process is to determine the current state of your employees' skills and talents. Does Joe show potential for supervising other warehouse employees? Which employees have experience in doing customer demos? Is the pool of software quality assurance technicians adequate enough to accommodate a significant upturn in business? If not, can you develop internal candidates, or will you have to hire new employees from outside the organization? Assessing your employees provides you with an overall road map to guide your development efforts.

4. **Create career development plans.** Career development plans are agreements between you and your employees that spell out exactly what formal support (tuition, time off, travel expenses, and so on) they'll receive to develop their skills, and when they'll receive it. Career development plans contain milestones.

5. **Follow through on your agreements, and make sure that your employees follow through on theirs.** Don't break the development plan agreement! Make sure that you provide the support that you agreed to provide. Make sure that your employees uphold their end of the bargain, too! Check on their progress regularly. If they miss schedules because of other priorities, reassign their work as necessary to ensure that they have time to focus on their career development plans.

So, when is the best time to sit down with your employees to discuss career planning and development? The sooner the better! Unfortunately, many organizations closely tie career discussions to annual employee performance appraisals. On the plus side, doing so ensures that a discussion about career development happens at least once a year; on the minus side, development discussions become more of an afterthought than the central focus of the meeting. Not only because of that limitation, but also with the current rapid changes in competitive markets and technology, once a year just isn't enough to keep up. Planning for career development only once a year is like watering a plant only once a year!

Conducting a career development discussion twice a year with each of your employees isn't too often, and quarterly is even better. Include a brief assessment in each discussion of the employee's development needs. Ask your employee what he or she can do to fulfill them. If those needs require additional support, determine what form of support the employee needs and when the support should be scheduled. Career development plans are adjusted and resources are redirected as necessary.

The Top Ten Ways To Develop Employees

1. Provide employees opportunities to learn and grow.
2. Be a mentor to an employee.
3. Let an employee fill in for you in staff meetings.
4. Assign your employees to teams.
5. Allow employees to pursue and develop any idea they have.
6. Provide employees with a choice of assignments.
7. Send your employees to seminars on new topics.
8. Bring an employee along with you when you call on customers.
9. Introduce your employees to top managers in your organization and arrange to have them perform special assignments for the managers.
10. Allow an employee to shadow you during your workday.

SELF-CHECK

1. How often should you meet with employees to discuss their careers?
2. Why is it important to stick to the development plan agreement?
3. Why is it important to assess where employees are in their careers before beginning the development process?

FOR EXAMPLE

Development and Downsizing

Career planning and development provide employees in organizations undergoing rapid change with the tools that they need to regain control of their careers. For example, IBM overhauled the career plans of thousands of employees who transitioned from staff positions to sales positions as a result of a massive corporate reorganization.

8.4 Finding a Mentor, Being a Mentor

When you're an inexperienced employee working your way up an organization's hierarchy, having someone with more experience to help guide you along the way is invaluable. Someone who's already seen what it takes to get to the top can advise you about the things that you must do and the things that you shouldn't do as you work your way up. This someone is called a **mentor.**

Isn't a manager supposed to be a mentor? No. A mentor is most typically an individual high up in the organization who isn't your boss. A manager's job is clearly to coach and help guide employees. Although managers certainly can act as mentors for their own employees, mentors most often act as confidential advisers and sounding boards to their chosen employees and therefore aren't typically in the employee's direct chain of command.

The day that a mentor finds you and takes you under his or her wing is a day for you to celebrate. Why? Celebrate because not everyone is lucky enough to find a mentor. And don't forget that someday you'll be in the position to be a mentor to someone else. When that day comes, don't be so caught up in your busy business life to neglect to reach out and help someone else find his or her way up the organization.

Mentors provide definite benefits to the employees they mentor, and they further benefit the organization by providing needed guidance to employees who may not otherwise get it. The following reasons are why mentors are a real benefit, both to your employees and to your organization:

▲ **Explain how the organization really works.** Mentors are a great way to find out what's really going on in an organization. You've probably noticed that a big difference exists between what's formally announced to employees and what really goes on in the organization—particularly within the ranks of upper management. Your mentor quite likely has intimate knowledge behind the formal pronouncements, and he or she can convey that knowledge to you (at least, the knowledge that isn't confidential) without your having to find it out the hard way.

▲ **Teach by example.** By watching how your mentor gets tasks done in the organization, you can discover a lot. Your mentor has likely already seen it all, and he or she can help you discover the most effective and efficient ways to get things done. Why reinvent the wheel or get beaten up by the powers that be when you don't have to?

▲ **Provide growth experiences.** A mentor can help guide you to activities above and beyond your formal career development plans that are helpful to your growth as an employee. For example, though your official development plan doesn't identify a specific activity, your mentor may strongly suggest that you join a group, such as Toastmasters, to improve your public-speaking skills. Your mentor makes this suggestion because he or she knows that public-speaking skills are very important to your future career growth.

▲ **Provide career guidance and discussion.** Your mentor has probably seen more than a few employees and careers come and go over the years. He or she knows which career paths in your organization are dead ends and which offer the most rapid advancement. This knowledge can be incredibly important to your future as you make career choices within an organization. The advice your mentor gives you can be invaluable.

The mentoring process often happens when a more experienced employee takes a professional interest in a new or inexperienced employee. Employees can also initiate the mentoring process by engaging the interest of potential mentors while seeking advice or working on projects together. However, recognizing the potential benefits for the development of their employees, many organizations—including Merrill Lynch, Federal Express, and the Internal Revenue Service—have formalized the mentoring process and made it available to a wider range of employees than the old informal process ever could. If a formal mentoring program isn't already in place in your organization, why don't you recommend starting one?

You, as a manager, can create a supportive workplace in the following ways:

▲ **Build and maintain trust and respect.** Employees who are trusted and respected by their managers are motivated to perform their best. By including employees in the decision-making process, today's managers get better ideas (that are easier to implement), and at the same time, they improve employee morale, loyalty, and commitment. "I'll bet our sales clerks can come up with the best way to handle this problem."

▲ **Open the channels of communication.** The ability of all your employees to communicate openly and honestly with one another is critical to the ultimate success of your organization and has a major role in employee motivation. Today, quick and efficient communication of information throughout your organization can be what differentiates you from your competition. Encourage your employees to speak up, to make suggestions, and to break down the organizational barriers—the rampant departmentalization, protecting one's turf, and similar roadblocks—that separate them from one another, where and whenever they find them.

▲ **Make your employees feel safe.** Are your employees as comfortable telling you the bad news as they are telling you the good news? If the answer is no, you haven't created a safe environment for your employees. Everyone makes mistakes; people discover valuable lessons from their mistakes. If you want employees who are motivated, make it safe for them to take chances and to let you know the bad along with the good. Avoid the urge to punish them when they make a mistake. At least be thankful that they are doing something!

▲ **Develop your greatest asset—your employees.** By helping meet your employees' needs, you are also achieving your organization's needs. Challenge your employees to improve their skills and knowledge and provide them with the support and training that they need to do so. Concentrate on the positive progress that they make and recognize and reward it whenever possible.

SELF-CHECK

1. What is a **mentor**?
2. A manager is always a mentor. True or false?
3. List and describe two ways managers can support employees.

8.5 Getting What You Reward

Another way to develop employees is to guide them in their job by giving them habits that will make them successful both in their current job and throughout their career. How do you do this? The answer is that you get what you reward. Now don't let the seeming simplicity of the statement fool you—great depth is hiding behind the two dimensions of this printed page. You may think that you're rewarding your employees to do what you want them to do; but are you really?

Consider the following example. You have two employees: Employee A is incredibly talented and Employee B is a marginal performer. You give similar assignments to both employees. Employee A completes the assignment before the due date and turns it in with no errors. Because Employee A is already done, you give her two additional assignments. Meanwhile, Employee B is not only late, but when he finally turns in the report you requested, it is full of errors. Because you're now under a time crunch, you accept Employee B's report and then correct it yourself.

What's wrong with this picture? Who's actually being rewarded: Employee A or Employee B?

If you answered Employee B, you're right! This employee has discovered that submitting work that is substandard and late is okay. Furthermore, he also sees that you'll personally fix it! That's quite a nice reward for an employee who clearly doesn't deserve one. (Another way to put it is Employee B certainly has you well trained!)

On the other hand, by giving Employee A more work for being a diligent, outstanding worker, you're actually punishing her. Even though you may think nothing of assigning more work to Employee A, she knows the score. When Employee A sees that all she gets for being an outstanding performer is more work (while you let Employee B get away with doing less work), she's not going to like it one bit. And if you end up giving both employees basically the same raise (and don't think they won't find out), you make the problem even worse. You will lose Employee A, either literally, as she takes another job, or in spirit, as she stops working so hard.

If you let the situation continue, all your top performers eventually realize that doing their best work is not in their best interest. As a result, they leave their position to find an organization that values their contribution, or they simply kick back and forget about doing their best work. Why bother? No one (that means you, the manager) seems to care anyway!

After you put your employee-reward system into place, you need to check periodically to see that the system has the results that you want. Check with those you're trying to motivate and see if the program is still working. If it isn't, change it!

Most managers reward the wrong things, if they reward their employees at all. This tendency has led to a crisis of epic proportions in the traditional system of incentives and motivation in business. Consider these statistics quoted in the *Management Accounting* journal:

▲ Only 3 percent of base salary separates average from outstanding employees in American companies.
▲ Eighty-one percent of American workers report that they would not receive rewards for increasing their productivity.
▲ Sixty percent of American managers say that they would not receive increases in their compensation for increasing their performance.

If managers and workers aren't being rewarded for increasing their productivity and performance, what are they being rewarded for?

For an incentive program to have meaningful and lasting effects, it must be contingent, that is, it must focus on performance—nothing less and nothing more.

"But wait a second," you say, "that isn't fair to the employees who aren't as talented as my top performers." If that's what you think, we'll straighten out that misunderstanding right now. Everyone, regardless of how smart, talented, or productive they are, has the potential to be a top performer.

Suppose that Employee A produces 100 widgets an hour and stays at that level of performance day in and day out. On the other hand, Employee B produces 75 widgets an hour but improves output to 85 widgets an hour. Whom should you reward? Employee B! This example embodies what you want to reward: the efforts that your employees make to improve their performance, not just to maintain a certain level (no matter how good that level is).

The following are examples of performance-based measures that any manager must recognize and reward. What measures should you be monitoring, measuring, and rewarding in your organization? Don't forget, just showing up for work doesn't count!

▲ Defects decrease from 25 per 1000 to 10 per 1000.

▲ Annual sales increase by 20 percent.

▲ The department records system is reorganized and color-coded to make filing and retrieval more efficient.

▲ Administrative expenses are held to 90 percent of the authorized budget.

▲ The organization's mail is distributed in one hour instead of one and one-half hours.

You must have a plan to reinforce the behavior that you want. In general, employees are more strongly motivated by the potential to earn rewards than they are by the fear of punishment. Clearly, a well-thought-out and planned rewards system is important to creating a motivated, effective workforce. Here are some simple guidelines for setting up a system of low-cost rewards in your organization:

▲ **Link rewards to organizational goals.** To be effective, rewards need to reinforce the behavior that leads to an organization's goals. Use rewards to increase the frequency of desired behavior and decrease the frequency of undesired behavior.

▲ **Define parameters and mechanics.** After you identify the behaviors that you want to reinforce, develop the specifics of your reward system and create rules that are clear and easily understood by all employees. Make sure that targets are attainable and that all employees have a chance to obtain rewards. For example, your clerks also should have a shot at the rewards, not just salespeople or assemblers.

▲ **Obtain commitment and support.** Of course, communicate your new rewards program to your employees. Many organizations publicize their programs in group meetings. They present the programs as positive and fun activities that benefit both the employees and the companies. To get the best results, plan and implement your rewards program with your employees' direct involvement.

▲ **Monitor effectiveness**. Is your rewards system getting the results that you want? If not, take another look at the behaviors you want to reinforce and make sure that your rewards are closely linked. Even the most successful rewards programs tend to lose their effectiveness over time as employees begin to take them for granted. Keep your program fresh by discontinuing rewards that have lost their luster and bringing in new ones from time to time.

SELF-CHECK

1. Why is it important for managers to remember the statement, "you get what you reward"?

2. Are employees more motivated by positive reinforces or by negative consequences such as punishment?

3. Which employees should be eligible for rewards?

8.6 Figuring Out What Employees Want

The new business realities of the twenty-first century bring a need to find different ways to motivate employees. Motivation is no longer an absolute, my-way-or-the-highway proposition. The incredible acceleration of change in business and technology today is coupled with greatly expanded global competitive forces. With these forces pressing in from all sides, managers can have difficulty keeping up with what employees need to do, much less figure out what to tell them to do. In fact, a growing trend is for managers to manage individuals who are doing work that the managers themselves have never done.

Inspiring managers must embrace these changing business forces and management trends. Instead of using the power of their positions to motivate workers, managers must use the power of their ideas. Instead of using threats and intimidation to get things done, managers must create environments that support their employees and allow creativity to flourish.

In today's tight, stressful, changing times, what things are most important to employees? Bob Nelson conducted a survey of about 1500 employees from across seven industries to answer that question.[1] The top ten items he found employees said were most important are listed, along with some thoughts on how you can better provide each of these things to your own employees.

▲ **A learning activity (No. 1) and choice of assignment (No. 9):** Today's employees most value learning opportunities in which they can gain skills that can enhance their worth and marketability in their current job as well as future positions. Find out what your employees want to find out, how they want to grow and develop, and where they want to be in five years. Give them opportunities as opportunities arise and the ability to choose work assignments whenever possible. When you give employees the choice, more often than not they'll rise to meet or exceed your expectations.

▲ **Flexible working hours (No. 2) and time off work (No. 7):** Today's employees value their time—and their time off. Be sensitive to their off-schedule needs, whether they involve family or friends, charity or church, education or hobbies, and provide flexibility whenever you can so they can meet those obligations. Time off may range from an occasional afternoon off to attend a child's play at school or the ability to start the workday an hour early so they can leave an hour early. By allowing work to fit best with your employees' life schedules, you increase the chances that they will be motivated to work harder while at work, and to do their best to make their schedules work. As long as the job gets done, what difference does it matter what hours they work?

▲ **Personal praise—verbal (No. 3), public (No. 8), or written (No. 10):** Although you can thank someone in ten to fifteen seconds, most employees report that they're never thanked for the job they do—especially not by their manager. Systematically start to thank your employees when they do good work, whether one-on-one in person, in the hallway, in a group meeting, on voice mail, in a written thank-you note, in an e-mail, or at the end of each day at work. Better yet, go out of your way to act on and share and amplify good news when it occurs—even if it means interrupting someone to thank him or her for a job well done. By taking the time to say you noticed and appreciate your employees' efforts, those efforts—and results—will continue.

▲ **Increased autonomy (No. 5) and authority (No. 4) in their job:** The ultimate form of recognition for many employees is to have increased autonomy and authority to get their job done, including the ability to spend or allocate resources, make decisions, or manage others. Greater autonomy and authority means, "I trust you to act in the best interests of the company, to do so independently and without approval of myself or others." Increased autonomy and authority should be awarded to employees as a form of recognition itself for the past results they have achieved. Autonomy and authority are privileges, not rights, which should be granted to those employees who have most earned them, based on past performance, and not based on tenure or seniority.

▲ **Time with their manager (No. 6):** In today's fast-paced world of work in which everyone is expected to get more done faster, personal time with one's manager is in itself also a form of recognition. As managers are busier, taking time with employees is even more important. The action says: "Of all the things I have to do, one of the most important is to take time to be with you, the person or persons I most depend upon for us to be successful." Especially for younger employees, time spent with one's manager is a valued form of validation and inspiration, as well as serving a practical purpose of learning and communication, answering questions, discussing possibilities, or just listening to an employee's ideas, concerns, and opinions.

By the way, you may wonder where money ranked in importance in this survey. A "cash reward" ranked thirteenth in importance to employees. Everyone needs money to live, but work today involves more than what anyone gets paid.

Employees report that the most important aspects at work today are primarily the intangible aspects of the job that any manager can easily provide—if the manager makes it a priority to do so. Now you're going to learn a big secret. This secret is the key to motivating your employees. You don't need to attend an all-day seminar or join the management-video-of-the-week club to discover this secret: You are learning it right now at no extra charge!

The simplest way to find out how to motivate your employees is to *ask them*. Often managers assume that their employees want only money. These same managers are surprised when their employees tell them that other things— such as being recognized for doing a good job, being allowed greater autonomy in decision making, or having a more flexible work schedule—may be much more motivating than cash. Regardless of what preferences your employees have, you'll be much better off knowing those preferences explicitly rather than guessing or ignoring them. So, knowing this secret, managers should:

▲ **Plan to provide employees more of what they value.** Look for opportunities to recognize employees for having done good work and act on those opportunities as they arise, realizing that what motivates some employees doesn't motivate other employees.

▲ **Stick with it over time.** Motivation is a moving target and you need to constantly be looking to meet your employees' needs to motivate them to help you meet your needs.

Consider the following as you begin setting the stage for your efforts:

1. Create a supportive environment for your employees by first finding out what they most value.
2. Design ways to implement recognition to thank and acknowledge them when they do good work.
3. Be prepared to make changes to your plan, based on what works and what doesn't.

8.6.1 Starting with the Positive

You're more likely to lead your employees to greater results by focusing on their positive accomplishments rather than by finding fault with and punishing their negative outcomes. Despite this fact, many managers' primary mode of operation is correcting their employees' mistakes instead of complimenting their successes.

In a recent study, 58 percent of employees reported that they seldom received a personal thank-you from their managers for doing a good job even though they ranked such recognition as their most motivating incentive. They ranked a written thank-you for doing a good job as motivating incentive No. 2, whereas 76 percent said that they seldom received thanks from their managers. Perhaps these statistics show why a lack of praise and recognition is one of the leading reasons for people leaving their jobs.

Years of psychological research have clearly shown that positive reinforcement works better than negative reinforcement for several reasons. Without getting too technical, the reasons are that positive reinforcement:

▲ Increases the frequency of the desired behavior.
▲ Creates good feelings within employees.

On the other hand, negative reinforcement may decrease the frequency of undesired behavior, but doesn't necessarily result in the expression of desired behavior. Instead of being motivated to do better, employees who receive only criticism from their managers eventually come to avoid their managers whenever possible. Furthermore, negative reinforcement can create tremendously bad feelings with employees. And employees who are unhappy with their employers have a much more difficult time doing a good job than employees who are happy with their employers.

The following ideas can help you seek out the positive in your employees and reinforce the behaviors that you want:

▲ **Have high expectations for your employees' abilities.** If you believe that your employees can be outstanding, soon they will believe it, too.
▲ **Give your employees the benefit of the doubt.** Do you really think that your employees want to do a bad job? Unless they are consciously

trying to sabotage your firm, no one wants to do a bad job. Your job is to figure out what you can do to help them do a good job. Additional training, encouragement, and support should be among your first choices—not reprimands and punishment.

▲ **Catch your employees doing things right.** Although most employees do a good job in most of their work, managers naturally tend to focus on what employees do wrong. Instead of constantly catching your employees doing things wrong, catch them doing things right. Not only can you reinforce the behaviors that you want, but you can also make your employees feel good about working for you and for your firm.

8.6.2 Making a Big Deal about Something Little

Okay, here's a question for you: "Should you reward your employees for their little day-to-day successes, or should you save up rewards for when they accomplish something really major?" The answer to this question lies in the way that most people get their work done on a daily basis.

The simple fact is for most people in business, work is not a string of dazzling successes that come one after another without fail. Instead, the majority of work consists of routine, daily activities; employees perform most of these duties quietly and with little fanfare. A manager's typical workday, for example, may consist of an hour or two of reading memos and e-mail messages, listening to voice-mail messages, and talking to others on the phone. The manager spends another couple of hours in meetings and perhaps another hour in one-on-one discussions with staff members and coworkers, much of which involves dealing with problems as they occur. With additional time spent on preparing reports or filling out forms, the manager actually devotes precious little time to decision making—the activity that has the greatest impact on an organization.

For a line worker, this dearth of opportunities for dazzling success is even more pronounced. If the employee's job is assembling lawnmower engines all day (and she does a good, steady job), when does she have an opportunity to be outstanding in the eyes of her supervisor?

Major accomplishments are usually few and far between, regardless of your place in the organization chart. Work is a series of small accomplishments that eventually add up to big ones. If you wait to reward your employees for their big successes, you may be waiting a long time.

Therefore, reward your employees for their small successes as well as for their big successes. You may set a lofty goal for your employees to achieve—one that stretches their abilities and tests their resolve—but remember that praising your employees' progress toward the goal is perhaps even more important than praising them when they finally reach it.

Praising Guidelines

A basic foundation for a positive relationship is the ability to give a good praising.

▲ **As soon.** Timing is very important when using positive reinforcement. Give praise as soon as the desired behavior is displayed.

▲ **As sincere.** Words alone can fall flat if you're not sincere in why you're praising someone. Praise someone because you are truly appreciative and excited about the other person's success. Otherwise, it may come across as a manipulative tactic.

▲ **As specific.** Avoid generalities in favor of details of the achievement. For example, "You really turned that angry customer around by focusing on what you could do for him, not on what you could not do for him."

▲ **As personal.** A key to conveying your message is praising in person, face-to-face. This shows that the activity is important enough to you to put aside everything else you have to do and just focus on the other person.

▲ **As positive.** Too many managers undercut praise with a concluding note of criticism. When you say something like "You did a great job on this report, but there were quite a few typos," the *but* becomes a verbal erasure of all that came before.

▲ **As proactive.** Lead with praising and "catch people doing things right" or else you will tend to be reactive—typically about mistakes—in your interactions with others.

A good praising is given directly with the employee, in front of another person (in public), or when the person isn't around (via letter, e-mail, voice mail, and so forth). Praising employees takes only a moment, but the benefits—to your employees and to your organization—will last for years.

SELF-CHECK

1. Should you reward employees' small accomplishments or big accomplishments?
2. List and describe three guidelines for giving praise.
3. List and describe three top motivators for employees.
4. Poor-performing employees usually fail to perform well because they do not want to do a good job. True or false?

FOR EXAMPLE

American Express Recognizes Great Performers

If you could increase your organization's net income by 500 percent in a decade's time, would you take the time to recognize your great performers? The Travel Related Services division of American Express did it by creating its Great Performers program to recognize and reward exceptional employee performance. The program accepted nominations from employees, supervisors, and even customers. Winners of the Great Performers award were eligible for selection by a worldwide governing committee to become Grand Award recipients. In addition to an all-expenses-paid trip for two to New York City, Grand award winners received $4,000 in American Express traveler's checks, a platinum award pin, and a certificate.[2]

8.7 Rewarding Employees

There are many ways to reward employees. Although money, in the form of a raise or bonus, may be the most obvious choice it is not always the best choice. In addition, you may work for a company that does not have the cash to spare. Let's look at all the choices.

8.7.1 Money

You may think that money is the ultimate incentive for your employees. After all, who isn't excited when they receive a cash bonus or pay raise? The problem is that money really isn't the top motivator for employees—at least not in the way that most managers think. And it can be a huge demotivator if you manage it badly!

Money is clearly important to your employees. They need money to pay bills, buy food and clothes, put gas in their cars, and afford the other necessities of life.

Most employees consider the money that they receive on the job (whether it comes in the form of pay or cash bonuses) to be a fair exchange for the labor that they contribute to their organizations. Today's employees view compensation as a right. Recognition, on the other hand, is a gift. Using recognition, however, helps you get the best effort from each employee.

In particular, employees who receive annual bonuses and other periodic, money-based rewards quickly come to consider them part of their basic pay. Employees quickly include the amount of their bonus into their annual salary and treat as an entitlement. And if a year goes by and the annual bonus is not paid, open hostility is the result.

Management expert Peter Drucker hit the nail on the head when he pointed out in his book *Management: Tasks, Responsibilities, Practices,* "Economic incentives are becoming rights rather than rewards. Merit raises are always introduced as rewards for exceptional performance. In no time at all, they become a right. To deny a merit raise or to grant only a small one becomes punishment. The increasing demand for material rewards is rapidly destroying their usefulness as incentives and managerial tools."[3] In other words, money becomes an expectation, then an entitlement, for many if not most workers.

The ineffectiveness of money as a motivator for employees is a good news/bad news kind of thing. We start with the bad news first. Many managers have thrown lots of money into cash-reward programs, and for the most part, these programs didn't have the positive effect on motivation that the managers expected.

That's not to say that you waste your money on these programs, but that you can use it more effectively. In fact, with other programs you may achieve better results with far fewer dollars!

Now you get the good news: Because you know that money is not the most effective motivation tool, you can focus on using tools that are more effective—and the best forms of recognition cost little or no money!

According to Dr. Gerald Graham of Wichita State University, the most motivating incentives (as reported by employees today) are as follows:

▲ **Manager-initiated incentives:** Instead of coming from some nebulous ad hoc committee, corporate bigwig, or completely out of the blue, the most valuable recognition comes directly from one's supervisor or manager.

▲ **Performance-based incentives:** Employees want to be recognized for the jobs they are hired to do. The most effective incentives are therefore based on job performance and not on nonperformance-related things such as attendance, attire, or drawing the lucky number out of a hat at the monthly sales meeting.

So you're a busy manager. Cash rewards are convenient because you simply fill out a check request once a year to take care of all your motivation for the year. This manager-initiated, based-on-performance stuff sounds like a lot of work! To be frank, running an effective rewards program does take more work on your part than running a simple, but ineffective one. But as you will see, the best rewards can be quite simple. After you get the hang of using them, you can easily integrate them into your daily routine. Doing so is part of managing today.

Don't save up recognition for special occasions only—and don't just use them with the top performers! Every employee needs to be recognized when they do good work in their job. Your employees are doing good things, things that you want them to do every day. Catch them doing something right and recognize their successes regularly and often!

8.7.2 Ten Other Ways to Recognize Employees

Bob Nelson's book *1001 Ways to Reward Employees*[4] lists thousands of real-life positive rewards, most of which cost little or nothing. Following is a list of what Nelson found out from thousands of employees across industries about what they consider most important in terms to recognition. The findings are categorized and prioritized in order of greatest importance from a list of fifty specific possibilities.

Support and Involvement

Your employees need information and support in order to do their jobs. Give them what they need when they need it, to do their best work. And if they make a mistake in the process, support them and help them learn from that mistake. Mistakes are to be expected in any job, but how you handle mistakes when they occur can be critical to building ongoing trust, knowledge, and performance.

Every employee wants his or her manager's support after making a mistake. Furthermore, involve your employees when you're making key decisions—especially when those decisions affect your employees and their work. You can also involve employees by, when possible, asking them for their opinions and ideas. Doing so further shows that you respect and trust them—and that they actually have ideas worth sharing!

Personal Praise

Nearly 60 percent of employees report they never get a simple thank-you from their manager for doing a good job—even though employees have reported this top motivator for many years.

Taking the time to thank employees personally shows them that no matter how busy you are and no matter what else you have to do, nothing is more important to you than them. By thanking them, you're saying that your employees are more important than everything else in your work life. Isn't that why employees are called "the organization's greatest asset"?

Remember to make your praise as timely, as sincere, and as specific as possible to have the greatest impact. Actively seek out employees when you have something to commend them for and don't be shy about acknowledging them in front of others—management, peers, or even customers.

Autonomy and Authority

Employees highly value being given the latitude to perform their work the way they see fit. No one likes a supervisor or manager who always hovers, micromanaging every move, reminding the employees of the exact way everything should be done and making corrections every time they make a slight deviation. Guess what? Your employees actually may come up with a better way to do the task than your way if you give them a chance!

When you tell employees what you want done, provide them with the necessary training, and then give them the room to do the job. When you give them the training, you increase the likelihood that they will perform to—or even beyond—your expectations.

Flexible Working Hours

Another great, no-cost way to reward your employees is to give them flexibility in their working hours, which includes when they start work and when they finish, the ability to leave work early when needed, and time off. Because most of them are trying to balance multiple priorities on both the work and home fronts, time is very important. As such, flexibility and time off work has become an increasingly valuable commodity.

People want to spend more time with their families and friends and less time in the office. Of course, with downsizing and reengineering, employees have more work to do, not less. Giving your employees flexible working hours can help them keep fresh and focused while on the job!

Learning and Development

Guaranteed employment may be gone for everybody, but guaranteed employability is still very much alive in today's job market. As a result, employees are increasingly interested in learning new skills where they work. They can enhance their abilities and the value they offer the organization. Remember, too, that most employee development happens on the job, not in the classroom. New work challenges and responsibilities and the chance to represent one's manager or group are ways to develop, grow, and master new skills.

Giving your employees new opportunities to perform is very motivating. You aren't going to motivate your employees by building a fire under them. Instead, find ways to build a fire within them to make work a place where they want and are able to do their best as they learn and grow. Talking with employees about their long-term hopes and career plans is also important. You develop an emotional bond and trust with each employee. If you know where someone wants to be in five years, you can think about aspects of their current job and circumstances that can help them prepare for the future.

Manager Availability and Time

Having access to one's manager is a big motivator. Access is different from being located physically near where your manager works. Access and accessibility today have less to do with physical proximity than with a manager's responsiveness in taking employees' questions and concerns seriously and in getting information, resources, or assistance back to employees in a timely manner.

In one executive position Nelson held, he made a personal commitment that within twenty-four hours of any management or executive meeting he was a part of, he would communicate what was discussed and decided in those meetings with his immediate staff and get back to them if they had questions he couldn't answer. As a result, trust, respect, and teamwork flourished and his department attained higher levels of performance. Employees also report that they like their managers to take time to get to know them and spend time with them.

Written Praise

Employees also desire written praise as a form of recognition. Whether it comes in the form of letters of praise added to an employee's personnel file, a written note of thanks from one's manager or peers, or a simple thank-you card, written praise has a sense of permanence about it that can last for quite some time as the employee saves the communication.

Written praise also has a multiplier effect as employees refer to previous written thanks time and time again, perhaps posting a note at their work station or creating a "victory file" specifically for that purpose. They also may decide to share the written information with their families or friends.

Electronic Praise

Similar to written praise, electronic praise enables you to leverage positive communication as it occurs in your daily work. Use today's communication technologies not just to process information, but also to connect with others and to commend them when they've done good work.

In a recent Internet survey Bob Nelson conducted, some 28 percent of employees report it is "extremely important" to them to have positive e-mail messages forwarded to them and 65 percent say it's "extremely or very important" to be copied on positive e-mail messages.

Don't forget the use of voice mail as a way to leave a positive word of thanks—without rolling into another work assignment or project!

Public Praise

Most employees value being publicly praised. You have a nearly endless variety of ways to acknowledge employees publicly. Sharing positive letters from customers or posting them on a "Good News Bulletin Board" or even bringing some key customers in-house to acknowledge employees sends an important message to everybody in the organization that their work is important and valued.

Taking time at the beginning or end of department or companywide meetings to thank performers or allowing employees to acknowledge one another at group meetings can also be very effective. Or using the company newsletter to post positive information, name top performers, or thank project teams are a few other possibilities that can work well to make people feel important and special when they've achieved.

Cash or Cash Substitutes

A manager can give an employee a nominal on-the-spot cash award when he or she "catches" an employee doing something right. The award can motivate and help remind employees what's truly important about their work. But cash has its drawbacks as well, having very little memory impact or "trophy value." Often when employees get extra money, they end up spending it on an immediate need or bill, quickly forgetting the reason for the award. **Cash substitutes,** however, such as gift certificates, vouchers, or entertainment tickets, provide variety, flexibility, and a chance to share a reward with a friend or family member, thus increasing the emotional impact and memory potential of the reward.

You don't have to spend a lot of time or money to show your employees how you feel about them and their work. Use the previous proven recognition strategies to create the most motivating work environment in which every employee feels valued, trusted, and respected!

SELF-CHECK

1. Does money motivate employees? Why or why not?
2. A gift certificate is an example of a(n) _____ _____.
3. What are manager-initiated incentives?
4. Why is flexibility important to employees?

SUMMARY

As you have seen in this chapter, developing and mentoring employees not only gives them the skills they need to be excellent at their current job but also prepares them for future jobs in their career. Additionally, employees are more motivated to do a good job when they are able to spend quality time with their manager. In this chapter, you evaluated how to best develop employees and why it is important. You assessed a career development plan and identified its key elements. You also examined the difference between a manager and a mentor. In addition to development, rewards and praise also motivate employees. You examined how to reward employees, what to base the rewards on, and different methods for rewarding employees. Using these skills will increase the efficiency and productivity of your staff as well as improve employees' morale.

KEY TERMS

Cash substitute	Gift with a monetary value that can be redeemed such as gift certificates.
Development	Teaching employees the kinds of long-term skills that they'll need in the future as they progress in their careers.
Mentors	Confidential advisers high up in the organization who develop and support employees. They are usually not in the employee's chain of command.
Stretch assignments	Assignments that are not too hard or too easy and require some learning.
Training	Teaching employees the short-term skills that they need to know to do their jobs.

ASSESS YOUR UNDERSTANDING

Go to www.wiley.com/college/nelson to evaluate your knowledge of inspiring employees.
Measure your learning by comparing pre-test and post-test results.

Summary Questions

1. Assignments that challenge employees and are given for career development are _____ _____.

2. You get what you reward. True or false?

3. Managers need to discuss career development with employees only once a year during their annual review. True or false?

4. Career development focuses on:
   (a) short-term skills.
   (b) training.
   (c) long-term skills.
   (d) both long-term and short-term skills.

5. According to surveys, average employees are separated from outstanding employees by:
   (a) a high percentage of money in terms of salary and raises.
   (b) verbal recognition only.
   (c) a small percentage of money in terms of salary and raises.
   (d) nothing at all.

6. Most Americans do not receive recognition in any way for increased performance. True or false?

7. An example of a cash substitute is:
   (a) written praise.
   (b) flexible hours.
   (c) greater autonomy.
   (d) a gift certificate to a local mall.

8. According to surveys, employees are more motivated by:
   (a) money.
   (b) a learning activity.
   (c) praise.
   (d) greater authority.

9. Of the following rewards, which one do employees prefer more?
   (a) Flexibility
   (b) Money

(c) Praise

(d) Time off work

10. It is fair to reward every employee in the same way. True or false?

11. Additional money such as a raise or bonus quickly becomes an entitlement for employees. True or false?

Applying This Chapter

1. You open a small consulting firm and hire two employees. One employee works extra hours and brings in three times her salary in revenue for the firm. The other employee does not work any extra hours and brings in twice his salary in revenue for the firm. Do you reward both employees? If not, why not? What kinds of rewards do you give?

2. You own a fast-food restaurant with many employees. Why is it cost-effective for you to develop your employees and lower turnover?

3. You own a health care company and you have four managers. None of them have ever done a career development plan with their employees before. What key elements do you ask them to include in their career development plans?

4. You work at a manufacturing company and you learn that the managers are not spending time with their employees or guiding their careers. You decide to choose a few of them and become their mentor. What types of interactions do you have with the employees that you mentor?

5. You work at a large city newspaper and you have three hundred paper route drivers. What qualities do you measure the paper route drivers on and how do you reward them?

6. You work for a sales and marketing firm and one of your fellow managers gives praise to employees but then follows it up immediately with a list of what they did incorrectly. Is this a good or bad approach? Why? What are the guidelines for praising employees?

Career Development Plan

You work in a public relations firm and have just hired Steve Thomas right out of college. Steve has a journalism degree and wants a long-term career in public relations. His current job is entry level, but the job he wants is that of account manager. An account manager works with two or three clients and writes all their press releases, works with them on all their marketing efforts, trains their representatives on how to give good interviews and interact with the press, and keeps a tally of how many times their company is in the news. Write a sample career development plan for Steve that will guide him in the direction of the job he wants.

Rewards Program

You are the CEO for a large textbook publisher. The previous CEO did not have any kind of rewards or recognition program in place nor were the managers very good at recognizing their employees. What types of rewards program do you establish? What types of behavior do you want to reward? What company rewards would you like to see implemented? What type of rewards would you like your managers to use on a regular basis? Write a paper and outline your motivation strategy.

9

EVALUATING THE TEAM MEMBERS
Measuring Projects and Performance

Starting Point

Go to www.wiley.com/college/nelson to assess your knowledge of measuring projects and performance.
Determine where you need to concentrate your effort.

What You'll Learn in This Chapter

▲ How to measure progress
▲ How to track the steps and success of a project
▲ The importance of performance-related feedback
▲ How to provide continuous feedback to employees
▲ What mistakes to avoid when conducting performance evaluations

After Studying This Chapter, You'll Be Able To

▲ Quantify your goals
▲ Develop a performance-feedback system
▲ Chart your results graphically
▲ Use data to improve performance
▲ Conduct performance evaluations

INTRODUCTION

Measuring and monitoring the performance of individuals in your organization is like walking a tightrope: You don't want to overmeasure or overmonitor your employees. Doing so only leads to needless bureaucracy and red tape, which can negatively affect your employees' ability to perform their tasks. Neither do you want to undermeasure nor undermonitor your employees. This lack of watchfulness can lead to nasty surprises when a task is completed late, overbudget, or not at all.

As a manager, your primary goal in measuring and monitoring your employees' performance is not to punish them for making a mistake or missing a milestone. Instead you help your employees stay on schedule and find out whether they need additional assistance or resources to do so. Few employees like to admit that they need help getting an assignment done—whatever the reason. Because of their reluctance, you must systematically check on the progress of your employees and regularly give them feedback on how they're doing.

If you don't monitor desired performance, you won't achieve desired performance. Don't leave achieving your goals to chance; develop systems to monitor progress and ensure that your goals are achieved.

In addition to tracking the progress of projects, timely and accurate performance evaluations are an extremely important tool for every business manager or supervisor. So if performance evaluations are so important to the successful management of employees, why do most managers and supervisors dread doing them, and why do so many employees dread receiving them? According to studies on the topic, an estimated 40 percent of all workers never receive performance evaluations. And for the 60 percent of the workers who do receive performance evaluations, most are poorly done. Very few employees actually receive regular, formal performance evaluations that are thoughtful, complete, and beneficial to the employee.

Ask any human resources manager: Are formal performance evaluations really necessary? The answer you get will likely be a resounding yes! However, if you look a little below the surface, the reality may echo something quite different. Although most managers consider performance evaluations a necessary tool in developing their employees, reinforcing good performance, and correcting poor performance, these evaluations are often too little, too late. They often miss the mark as tools for developing employees. If performance evaluations are done poorly, managers are better off not doing them at all—especially if by not doing evaluations, the alternative is more frequent coaching.

In this chapter, we consider the benefits of measuring performance, tracking progress, and conducting performance evaluations and explore the right and wrong ways to do them.

9.1 Measuring Progress

The first step in checking your employees' progress is to determine the key indicators of a goal's success. If you follow the advice in Chapter 3, you set goals with your employees that are few in number and *SMART* (specific, measurable, attainable, relevant, and time-bound).

When you quantify a goal in precise numerical terms, your employees have no confusion over how their performance is measured and when their job performance is adequate (or less than adequate). If you measure performance in terms of the quantity of sprockets produced per hour, your workers know exactly what you mean. If the goal is to produce 100 sprockets per hour, with a reject rate of one or less, your employees clearly understand that producing only 75 sprockets per hour with 10 rejects is unacceptable performance. Nothing is left to the imagination, and the goals aren't subject to individual interpretation or to the whims of individual supervisors or managers.

How you measure and monitor the progress of your employees toward completion of their goals depends on the nature of the goals. You can measure some goals, for example, in terms of time, others in terms of units of production, and others in terms of delivery of a particular work product (such as a report or a sales proposal).

The following are examples of different goals and the ways you can measure them:

▲ **Goal:** Plan and implement a company newsletter before the end of the second quarter of the current fiscal year.
Measurement: The specific date (for example, June 30) that the newsletter is mailed out (time).

▲ **Goal:** Increase the number of mountain bike frames produced by each employee from twenty to twenty-five per day.
Measurement: The exact number of mountain bike frames produced by the employee each day (quantity).

▲ **Goal:** Increase profit on the project by 20 percent in fiscal year 2009.
Measurement: The total percentage increase in profit from January 1 through December 31, 2009 (percentage increase).

Although noting when your employees attain their goals is obviously important, recognizing your employees' incremental progress toward attaining their goals is just as important. For example:

▲ The goal for your drivers is to maintain an accident-free record. This goal is ongoing with no deadline. To encourage them in their efforts, you prominently post a huge banner in the middle of the garage that reads "153 Accident-Free Days," and you increase the number for each day of accident-free driving.

▲ The goal of your fiscal clerks is to increase the average number of transactions from 150 per day to 175 per day. To track their progress, you publicly post a summary of each employee's daily production counts at the end of each week. As production increases, you praise the progress of your employees toward the final goal.

▲ The goal set for your reception staff is to improve the percentage of "excellent" responses on customer feedback cards by 10 percent. You tabulate the monthly counts for each receptionist and announce the results at department staff meetings. The department manager buys lunch for the receptionist with the highest total each month.

The secret to performance measuring and monitoring is the power of positive feedback. When you give positive feedback (increased number of units produced, percentage increase in sales, and so on), you encourage the behavior that you want. However, when you give negative feedback (number of errors, number of work days lost, and so on), you aren't encouraging the behavior you want; you're only discouraging the behavior that you don't want. Consider the following examples:

▲ **Instead of measuring this:** Number of defective cartridges.
Measure this: Number of correctly assembled cartridges.

▲ **Instead of measuring this:** Number of days late.
Measure this: Number of days on time.

▲ **Instead of measuring this:** Quantity of backlogged transactions.
Measure this: Quantity of completed transactions.

You're much more likely to get the results you want when you put group performance measures (total revenues, average days sick, and so on) out in the open for everyone to see, but keep individual performance measures (sales performance by employee, tardiness rankings by employee, and so on) private. The intent is to get a team to work together to improve its performance—tracking and publicizing group measures, and then rewarding improvement can lead to dramatic advances in the performance you seek. What you do not want to do is to embarrass your employees or subject them to ridicule by other employees when their individual performance is not up to par. Instead, counsel them privately, and coach them (and provide additional training and support, as necessary) to improve performance.

9.2 Developing a System for Providing Immediate Performance Feedback

You can measure an infinite number of behaviors or performance characteristics. What you measure and the values that you measure against are up to you and your employees. In any case, keep certain points in mind when you design a system for measuring and monitoring your employees' performance. Build your system on the *MARS* system. MARS is an acronym for *milestones, actions, relationships,* and *schedules.* We describe each element of the MARS system in the following sections.

9.2.1 Setting Your Checkpoints: The Milestones

Every goal needs a starting point, an ending point, and points in between to measure progress along the continuum. **Milestones** are the checkpoints, events, and markers that tell you and your employees how far along you are on the road to reaching the goals that you've set together.

For example, suppose that you establish a goal of finalizing corporate budgets in three months time. The third milestone along the way to your ultimate goal is that draft department budgets be submitted to division managers no later than June 1. If you check with the division managers on June 1 and they haven't submitted the draft budgets, you quickly and unambiguously know that the project is behind schedule. If, however, all the budgets are in on May 15, you know that the project is ahead of schedule and that you may reach the final goal of completing the corporate budgets sooner than you originally estimated.

9.2.2 Reaching Your Checkpoints: The Actions

Actions are the individual activities that your employees perform to get from one milestone to the next. To reach the third milestone in your budgeting project, your employees must undertake and complete several actions after they reach the second milestone in the project. In this example, these actions may include the following:

▲ Review prior year expenditure reports and determine the relationship, if any, to current activities.

▲ Review current year-to-date expenditure reports and project final, year-end numbers.

▲ Meet with department staff to determine their training, travel, and capital equipment requirements for the new fiscal year.

▲ Review possible new hires, terminations, and pay raises to determine the impact on payroll cost.

▲ Create a computerized draft budget spreadsheet using numbers developed in the preceding actions.

▲ Print the draft budget and manually double-check the results. Correct entries and reprint if necessary.

▲ Submit the draft budget to the division manager.

Each action gets your employees a little farther along the way toward reaching the third milestone in the project—completion of draft corporate budgets by June 1—and is therefore a critical element in your employees' performance. When developing a plan for completion of a project, note each action in writing. By taking notes, you make focusing easier for your employees because they know exactly what they must do to reach a milestone, how far they have gone, and how much farther they have to go.

9.2.3 Sequencing Your Activity: The Relationships

Relationships are how milestones and actions interact with one another. Relationships shape the proper sequencing of activities that lead you to the successful, effective accomplishment of your goals. Although sequence doesn't always matter, it usually can be more effective to perform certain actions before others and to attain certain milestones before others.

For example, in the prior list of actions needed to achieve the third project milestone, trying to perform the fifth action before the first, second, third, or fourth is not going to work! If you haven't figured out the right numbers to put into your spreadsheet before you fill in the blanks, your results will be meaningless.

However, keep in mind that you may have more than one way to reach a milestone and give your employees the latitude to find their own ways to reach their goals. Doing so empowers your employees to take responsibility for their work and to learn from their mistakes and successes. The results are successful performance and happy, productive employees.

9.2.4 Establishing Your Time Frame: The Schedules

How do you determine how far apart your milestones should be and how long project completion should take? You can plan better by estimating the **schedule** of each individual action in your project plan. How long does it take to review current year-to-date expenditure reports and project final, year-end numbers? A day? A week? How long does it take you to meet with all your staff members to assess their needs?

Using your experience and training to develop schedules that are realistic and useful is important. For example, you may know that if everything goes perfectly, meeting with all your employees will take exactly four days. However, you also know that if you run into problems, the process can take as long as six days. Therefore, for planning purposes, you decide that five days is an appropriate schedule to apply to this particular action. This schedule allows for some variability in performance while ensuring that you meet the milestone on time.

Application of each characteristic—milestones, actions, relationships, and schedules—results in goals that you can measure and monitor. If you can't measure and monitor your goals, chances are that your employees will never achieve them and you won't know the difference.

FOR EXAMPLE

Learning to Measure Instead of Count

According to management guru Peter Drucker, most business people spend too much time counting and too little time actually measuring the performance of their organizations. What does Drucker mean by this? Drucker is talking about the tendency of managers to be shortsighted in their application of management controls such as budgets. For example, most budgets are meant to ensure that company funds are spent only where authorized. They are control mechanisms that prevent spending from going out of control unnoticed by counting the number of dollars spent for a particular activity. However, Drucker suggests that, instead of using budgets only to count, managers can use them to measure things that are even more important to the future of the business. Managers can relate proposed expenditures to future results, for example, and provide follow-up information to show whether the desired results were achieved.

Drucker likens counting to a doctor using an X-ray machine to diagnose an ill patient. Although some ailments—broken bones, pneumonia, and such—show up on an X-ray, other more life-threatening illnesses such as leukemia, hypertension, and AIDS don't. Similarly, most managers use accounting systems to X-ray their organization's financial performance. However, accounting systems don't measure a catastrophic loss of market share or a failure of the firm to innovate until it's already too late and the "patient" has been damaged—perhaps irretrievably.

9.2.5 Putting Performance Measuring and Monitoring into Practice: Case Study

You may not always measure the results you want for your organization in terms of the number of widgets produced or the percentage increase in an employee's contributions to profitability. Sometimes you simply want your employees to show up on time and to at least seem to enjoy the eight or nine hours that they spend at work each day. If your employees' morale is poor, their productivity is likely to be poor, too.

A survey of employees at Cascades Diamond, Inc., that's cited in Bob Nelson's *1001 Ways to Reward Employees* showed that 79 percent of employees felt they weren't being rewarded for a job well done, 65 percent felt that management treated them disrespectfully, and 56 percent were pessimistic about their work.[1] Not exactly the formula for a great company! Fortunately, company managers recognized that they had a problem and what follows is what they did to fix it.

Step 1: Create a Program Based on the Behaviors You Want

The first step the management of Cascades Diamond took was to create a brand-new club in the company. They developed the 100 Club to reinforce the behaviors that management wanted to promote throughout the organization. These behaviors were as follows:

▲ Attendance
▲ Punctuality
▲ Safety

The plan was to award points to employees based on certain measurable criteria related to these behaviors. Any employee who attained a total of 100 points received an award—in this case, a nylon jacket with the Diamond Fiber logo and the words "The 100 Club" imprinted on it.

Step 2: Assign Points to the Desired Behaviors

The next step was to assign points to each desired behavior. Depending on whether employees exhibit the desired behavior (or not), they can either receive points or have them taken away. For example, employees receive 25 points for a year of perfect attendance. However, for each full or partial day of absence, they have points deducted from their totals. Employees who go an entire year without formal disciplinary actions receive 20 points, and employees who work for a year without injuries resulting in lost time receive 15 points. Employees can also receive points for making cost-saving suggestions, safety suggestions, or participating in community service projects such as Red Cross blood drives or the United Way.

In assigning points to each behavior, management made sure that the number of points was proportionate to the behavior's importance to the organization. Furthermore, management ensured that, although the numeric goals weren't too easy to attain—that is, employees had to stretch themselves to reach them—they weren't impossible to reach and thereby weren't demotivating.

Step 3: Measure and Reward Employee Performance

Measurement and reward of the desired employee behavior are the heart of Diamond Fiber's program. Supervisors and managers closely track the performance of their employees and assign points for each of the factors. When employees reach the coveted 100-point level, they're inducted into the 100 Club, and the jacket—and all the pride that goes along with it—is theirs.

You may think that this program is trivial; who really cares about getting a jacket with a company logo and three words "The 100 Club" printed on it? Your employees, that's who! A local bank teller tells a story about a Diamond Fiber employee who once visited the bank to proudly model her new 100 Club jacket to bank customers and employees. According to the woman, "My employer gave this to me for doing a good job. It's the first time in the 18 years that I've been there that they've recognized the things I do every day."

Even more telling, in the first year of the program, Diamond Fiber saved $5.2 million, increased productivity by nearly 15 percent, and reduced quality-related mistakes by 40 percent. Not only that, but also 79 percent of employees said that their work quality concerned them more now than before the program started; 73 percent reported that the company showed concern for them as people; and an amazing 86 percent of employees said that the company and management considered them to be either "important" or "very important." Not bad results at all for a $40 baby blue jacket!

SELF-CHECK

1. What does *MARS* stand for?

2. _____ are how **milestones** and **actions** interact with one another.

3. Checkpoints in a project are also referred to as:

   (a) milestones.

   (b) actions.

   (c) results.

   (d) performance.

4. Each action in a project action plan should have a **schedule**. True or false?

5. In the case study of Cascades Diamond, why did its program work to change employee performance?

9.3 Charting Progress

In some cases, measuring your employees' progress toward achieving a goal doesn't really take much. For example, if the goal is to increase the number of widgets produced from 100 per hour to 125 per hour, a simple count can tell you whether your employees have achieved that goal. However, if the goal is to fabricate a prototype electric-powered vehicle in six months' time, the job of measuring and monitoring individual performance gets much more complicated and confusing.

Although you may decide to write out all the different milestones and actions, reading and understanding a graphical representation of the project is often much easier for complex projects.

9.3.1 Bar Charts

Bar charts, also known as **Gantt charts,** are probably one of the simplest and most common means for illustrating and monitoring project progress. With a quick glance, a manager can easily see exactly where the project is at any given date and can compare actual progress against planned progress.

The three key elements of bar charts are the following:

▲ **Timeline:** The timeline provides a scale with which you measure progress. You can express the timeline in any units you want: Days, weeks, months, or whatever is most useful for managing the project. In most bar charts, the timeline appears along the horizontal axis (the x axis).

▲ **Actions:** Actions are the individual activities that your employees perform to get from one milestone to the next. In a bar chart, each action is listed—usually in chronological order—vertically along the left side of the chart (the y axis).

▲ **Bars:** Now, what would a bar chart be without bars? An "unbar" chart perhaps? Bars are the open blocks that you draw on your bar chart to indicate the length of time that a particular action is estimated to take. Short bars mean short periods of time; long bars mean long periods of time. What's really neat about bars is that, as an action is completed, you can fill in the bar—providing a quick visual reference of complete and incomplete actions.

Let's use our prior example again to illustrate the use of a bar chart. Figure 9-1 shows a typical bar chart; in this case, the chart illustrates the actions that lead up to the third milestone in the corporate budgeting example.

As Figure 9-1 shows, the timeline is along the top of the bar chart—just as we expected it would be. In this example, the timeline stretches from April 15 to June 1, with each increment representing one week. The six actions necessary to reach the third milestone are listed vertically along the left side of the bar chart. Finally, you see those neat little bars that are really the heart and soul

Figure 9-1

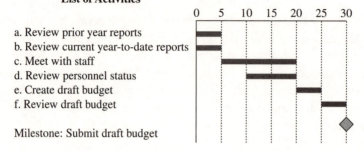

Third Milestone: Submit Draft Budget

List of Activities

A bar chart illustrating actions leading up to the third milestone.

of the bar chart. Leave the bars unfilled until an action is completed; you may color them in now if you'd like.

If all actions are completed according to the bar chart, the third milestone will be reached on June 1. If some actions take longer to complete than estimated, you may not reach the milestone on time and someone may end up in hot water. Conversely, if some actions take less time than estimated, the milestone can be reached early.

9.3.2 Flowcharts

When the going gets tough, the tough get going—and they reach for their **flow-charts** (see Figure 9-2). Flowcharts are graphical representations of the sequential flow of projects. Although flowcharts look completely different than bar charts, they also have three key elements:

▲ **Actions:** In the case of flowcharts, arrows indicate actions. Arrows lead from one event to the next on a flowchart until the project is completed. The length of the arrows doesn't necessarily indicate the duration of an action. The arrows' primary purpose in a flow chart is to illustrate the sequential relationship of actions to one another.

▲ **Events:** Events, represented in flowcharts by circles, signify the completion of a particular action.

▲ **Time:** Time estimates are inserted alongside each action (arrow) in the flowchart. By adding the number of time units along a particular path, you can estimate the total time for the completion of an action.

By following the longest path in terms of time, you can determine the **critical path** of the project. This kind of analysis is called the critical path method (CPM) and assumes that the time to complete individual actions can be estimated

Figure 9-2

Third Milestone: Submit Draft Budget

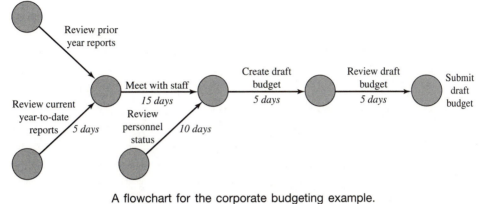

A flowchart for the corporate budgeting example.

with a high degree of certainty. The CPM highlights the actions that determine the soonest that a project can be completed—in this case, thirty days.

9.3.3 Software

Microsoft Project, one of the foremost project-planning software packages on the market today, enables you to create and revise project schedules quickly and easily. Setting up a project with Microsoft Project requires taking the following steps.

Step 1: Enter the actions to be completed.

Step 2: Enter the sequence of the actions and their dependencies on other actions.

Step 3: Enter the resources (people and money) required to complete the action.

As a project progresses, you can input data such as actual start and completion dates, actual expenditures, and more to get a realistic picture of where the project is at any time. You can print out these results in the form of tables, charts, or graphs—whatever your preference—and then save them for future reference.

9.3.4 You Have Their Number: Now What?

You've set up your goals, you've set performance measures, and you've obtained pages of data for each of your employees. Now what? Now you determine whether the expected results were achieved, as follows.

Step 1: Compare results to expectations. What is the expected goal? Suppose that the goal is to complete the budget by June 1. When was the budget completed? It was completed on May 17—well ahead of the deadline. Terrific! The mission was accomplished with time to spare.

Step 2: Record the results. Make note of the results—perhaps put them in the files that you maintain for each employee or print them out on your computer and post them in the work area.

Step 3: Praise, coach, or counsel your employees. If the job was done right, on time, and within budget, congratulate your employees for a job well done and reward them appropriately: A written note of appreciation, a day off with pay, a formal awards presentation—whatever you decide.

However, if the expected results were not achieved, find out why and what you can do to ensure that the expected results are achieved the next time. If the employees need only additional support or encouragement, coach them for a better performance. You can listen to your employees, refer them to other employees, or provide your own personal examples. If the poor results stem from a more serious shortcoming, counsel or discipline your employees.

SELF-CHECK

1. The three key elements in a **flowchart** are:
   (a) milestones, action, and results.
   (b) actions, events, and time.
   (c) timeline, actions, and bars.
   (d) schedule, actions, and results.

2. The three key elements in a bar chart are:
   (a) milestones, action, and results.
   (b) actions, events, and time.
   (c) timeline, actions, and bars.
   (d) schedule, actions, and results.

3. It is easier to create bar charts and flowcharts with software. True or false?

4. If employees do not meet their goals, what is the best way to proceed?

9.4 Evaluating Performance

You can find many good reasons for conducting regular formal performance evaluations with your employees. Formal performance evaluations are just one part of an organization's system of delegation, goal setting, coaching, motivating, and ongoing informal and formal feedback on employee performance. There are positive elements of performance evaluations:

▲ **A chance to summarize past performance and establish new performance goals:** All employees want to know whether they're doing a good job. Formal performance evaluations force managers to communicate performance results—both good and bad—to their employees and to set new goals. In many organizations, the annual performance evaluation is the only occasion when supervisors and managers speak to their employees about performance expectations and the results of employee efforts for the preceding evaluation period.

▲ **An opportunity for clarification and communication:** You need to constantly compare expectations. In fact, try this exercise with your manager. List your ten most important activities. Then ask your manager to list what he or she considers to be your ten most important activities. Chances are, your lists are quite different. On average, business people who do this exercise find that their lists overlap only 40 percent at best. Performance evaluations help the employer and employee compare notes and make sure that assignments and priorities are in order.

▲ **A forum for learning goals and career development:** In many organizations, career development takes place as a part of the formal performance evaluation process. Managers and employees are busy and often have difficulty setting aside the time to sit down and chart out the steps that they must take to progress in an organization or career. Although career development discussions should generally take place in a forum separate from the performance evaluation process, combining the activities does afford the opportunity to kill both birds with the same stone, or something like that.

▲ **A formal documentation to promote advancement or dismissal:** Most employees get plenty of informal performance feedback—at least of the negative kind. Most informal feedback is verbal and, as such, undocumented. If you're trying to build a case to give your employee a promotion, you can support your case much easier if you have plenty of written documentation (including formal performance evaluations) to justify your decision.

The preceding list gives very important reasons for conducting regular formal performance evaluations. However, consider this statement: Many companies have paid a lot of money to employees and former employees who have successfully sued them for wrongful termination or for other, biased employment decisions.

One of the most important things you can do as a manager is conduct accurate and timely performance evaluations of your employees.

Many managers, however, tend to see the performance evaluation process in very narrow terms: How can I get this thing done as quickly as possible so I can get back to my real job? (Whatever their "real" job is as managers.) In their haste to get the evaluation done and behind them, many managers merely consider a few examples of recent performance and base their entire evaluation on them. And because few managers give their employees the kind of meaningful, ongoing performance feedback that they need to do their jobs better, the performance evaluation can become a dreaded event—full of surprises and dismay. Or it can be so sugarcoated that it becomes a meaningless exercise in management. This scenario isn't the right way to evaluate your employees!

The performance appraisal process is much broader than just the formal, written part of it. Here are five steps that help you encompass the broader scope of the process. Follow them when you evaluate your employees' performance:

Step 1: **Set goals, expectations, and standards.** Before your employees can achieve your goals, or perform to your expectations, you have to set goals and expectations with them and develop standards to measure their performance. And after you've done all this, you have to communicate the goals and expectations before you evaluate your employees—not after. In fact, the performance review really starts on the first day of work! Tell your employees right then how you evaluate them, show them the forms to be used, and explain the process. Make sure that job descriptions are clear and unambiguous, and that you and your employees understand and agree to the standards you've set for them. This is a two-way process. Make sure that employees have a voice in setting their goals and standards.

Step 2: **Give continuous and specific feedback.** Catch your employees doing things right—every day of the week—and tell them about it then and there. And if you catch them doing wrong, then let them know about that, too. Feedback is much more effective when you give it regularly and often than when you save it up for a special occasion. The best formal performance evaluations contain the fewest surprises.

Step 3: **Prepare a formal, written performance evaluation with your employee.** Every organization has different requirements for the formal performance evaluation. Some evaluations are simple, one-page forms that only require checking off a few boxes—others are multipage extravaganzas that require extensive narrative support. The form often varies by organization, and by the level of the employee being evaluated. Regardless of the requirements of your particular organization, the formal performance evaluation should be a summary of the goals and expectations for the evaluation period: events that you have discussed previously (and frequently!) with your employees. Support your words with examples and make evaluations meaningful to your employees by keeping your discussion relevant to the goals, expectations, and standards that you developed in Step 1. As a collaborative process, have the employee complete his or her own performance evaluation. Then compare your (the manager's) comments with the employee's comments; the differences that you find become topics of discussion and mutual goal setting.

Step 4: Meet personally with your employees to discuss the performance evaluation. Most employees appreciate the personal touch when you give the evaluation. Set aside some quality time to meet with them to discuss their performance evaluation. This doesn't mean five or ten minutes, but at least an hour or maybe more. When you plan performance appraisal meetings, less is definitely not more. Pick a place that's comfortable and free of distractions. Make the meeting positive and upbeat. Even when you have to discuss performance problems, center your discussions on ways that you and your employees can work together to solve them. Often performance appraisals and discussions can become defensive as negative elements are raised and the employee starts to feel that he or she will get little or no raise. Start with letting the employee share how his or her job is going, what's working—and what's not; then share your version, starting with the positive.

FOR EXAMPLE

Turning the Tables: Upward and 360-Degree Evaluations

In recent years, a new kind of performance evaluation has emerged. Instead of the typical downward evaluation where managers review their workers' performance, the upward evaluation process stands this convention on its head by requiring workers to evaluate their managers' performance. If you think that getting a performance evaluation from your manager is uncomfortable, you haven't seen anything yet. There's nothing quite like the feeling you get when a group of your employees gives you direct and honest feedback about the things you do that make it hard for them to do a good job. Ouch!

However, despite the discomfort that you may feel, the upward evaluation is invaluable—who better to assess your real impact on the organization than your employees? The system works so well that Fortune 500 companies such as Federal Express and others have institutionalized the upward evaluation and made it a part of their corporate cultures. In a recent survey, almost 15 percent of American firms are using some form of the upward performance evaluation to assess the performance of their managers.

Also popular is the 360-degree evaluation, which companies such as Levi Strauss & Co. and Boeing Co use. Levi's 360-degree evaluation process dictates that all employees are evaluated by their supervisors and by their underlings and peers. The results can be quite a surprise to the lucky employee who is the subject of the evaluation who may find that other employees see him or her as less caring and visionary than he or she thought.

Step 5: Set new goals, expectations, and standards. The performance evaluation meeting gives you and your employees the opportunity to step back from the inevitable daily issues for a moment and to take a look at the big picture. You both have an opportunity to review and discuss the things that worked well and the things that, perhaps, didn't work so well. Based on this assessment, you can then set new goals, expectations, and standards for the next review period. The last step of the performance evaluation process becomes the first step, and you start all over again.

SELF-CHECK

1. List two reasons why supervisors should give employees a performance evaluation.
2. What should occur in performance appraisal meetings?
3. Why is it important to provide employees written feedback?

9.5 Avoiding Common Mistakes That Evaluators Make

Evaluators can easily fall into certain traps in the evaluation process. The mistakes include:

▲ **The halo effect:** This happens when an employee is so good in a particular area of his or her performance that you ignore problems in other areas of performance. For example, you may give your star salesperson (whom your firm desperately needs to ensure continued revenue growth) a high rating (a halo) despite the fact that she refuses to complete and submit paperwork within required time limits.

▲ **The recency effect:** The opposite of the halo effect, the recency effect happens when you allow an instance of poor performance to adversely affect your assessment of an employee's overall performance. For example, your administrative assistant has done a very good job for you in the months preceding his evaluation, but last week he missed a customer's deadline for submission of a proposal to continue with their advertising account. Your firm lost the account and you gave your assistant a scathing performance evaluation as a result.

▲ **Stereotyping:** This occurs when you allow preconceived notions about your employees to dictate how you rate them. For example, you may be convinced that women make better electronic parts assemblers than do men. As a result, your stereotyping automatically gives female employees the benefit of the doubt and higher ratings, whereas men have to prove themselves before you take them seriously.

▲ **Comparing:** Often, when you rate two employees at the same time, you can be tempted to compare their performances. If one of the employees is a particularly high performer, your other employee may look bad in comparison—despite his or her individual level of performance. Conversely, if one of the employees is a particularly low performer, the other employee may look really good in comparison. Make your assessment of an individual employee's performance and allow it to stand on its own two feet and not be subject to how good or bad your other employees are.

▲ **Mirroring:** Everyone naturally likes people who are most like themselves. That's why you can easily fall into the trap of rating highly those employees who are most like you (same likes, dislikes, interests, hobbies, and so forth) and rating lowly those employees who are least like you. Although this is great for the employees whom you favor, the employees you don't favor won't like it. Take some advice: don't do it.

▲ **Nice guy/gal role:** One reason that many managers dread doing performance evaluations is that it forces them to acknowledge the failings of their employees and then talk to their employees about them. Few managers enjoy giving their employees bad news, but employees need to receive the bad news as well as the good. Otherwise, they won't know where they need to improve. And if they don't know where they need to improve, you can bet they won't.

9.5.1 Realizing Why Evaluations Go Bad

Few employee evaluations are done well. Not only do managers write evaluations that lack any meaningful examples and insights, but they also fail to give the main process of the performance evaluation—the discussion—the time and attention that it deserves. Furthermore, performance evaluation meetings often become one-way presentations from manager to employee, rather than two-way discussions or conversations. As a result, performance evaluations often fail to have the kind of impact that the managers and supervisors who gave them intended.

Real apprehension can surround the evaluation process from both sides of the equation. Often, managers don't feel adequate to the task, and workers don't get the kind of timely and quality feedback that they need to do the best job possible. In addition, an underlying tension often accompanies the performance evaluation process and comes from the fact that most companies tie money and pay raises to performance evaluations. Evaluations that focus on the pay instead of on the performance, or the lack thereof, are not uncommon.

Why do so many performance evaluations go bad? To begin, although the performance evaluation process itself is pretty simple, a lot more goes into it than filling out a three-page form you get once a year to justify a salary action and then meeting with your employees for fifteen minutes to give them the results of your assessment. The performance evaluation process begins on the day that your employees are hired, continues each and every day that they report to you, and doesn't end until, through transfer, promotion, or termination, they move out of your sphere of responsibility.

The entire process consists of setting goals with your employees, monitoring their performance, coaching them, supporting them, counseling them, and providing continuous feedback on their performance—both good and bad. If you've been doing these things before you sit down for your annual or semiannual performance evaluation session with your employees, you're going to find reviews a pleasant wrap-up and look at the past accomplishments instead of a disappointment for both you and your employees.

Don't be among the many managers who fail to give their employees ongoing performance feedback and, instead, wait for the scheduled review. Despite your best intentions, and the best efforts of your employees, assignments can easily go astray. Schedules can stretch, roadblocks can stop progress, and confusion can wrap its ugly tentacles around a project. However, if you haven't set up systems to track the progress of your employees, you may not figure out this oversight until it's too late.

9.5.2 Preparing for the No-Surprises Evaluation

If you're doing your job as a manager, the evaluation holds no surprises for your employees. Follow the lead of the best managers: Keep in touch with your employees and give them continuous feedback on their progress. Then, when you do sit down with them for their formal performance evaluation, the session is a recap of the things that you've already discussed during the evaluation period, instead of an ambush. Keeping up a continuous dialog lets you use the formal evaluation to focus on the positive things that you and your employees can work on together to get the best possible performance.

Like interviews, many managers leave their preparation for performance evaluation meetings for the last possible minute. The average manager spends about one hour preparing for an employee review that required an entire year of performance.

Performance evaluation is a year-round job. Whenever you recognize a problem with your employees' performance, mention it to them, make a note of it, and drop it in your employees' files. Similarly, whenever your employees do something great, mention it to them, make a note of it, and drop it in their files. Then, when you're ready to do your employees' periodic performance evaluations, you can pull their files and have plenty of documentation available on which to base the evaluations. Not only does this practice make the process easier for you, but also it makes the evaluation a lot more meaningful and productive for your employees.

FOR EXAMPLE

Why Evaluations Go Wrong

In the following comments, conducted within the Managing People board of *Inc.* magazine's service on America Online, participants consider the pluses and minuses of different kinds of performance evaluations.

MWEISBURGH (Mitchell Weisburgh, President, Personal Computer Learning Centers): "A few things to watch out for, though, are that sometimes there is a popularity contest. A manager may go out of the way to get employees to give him or her a good rating. Also, no matter how well you spell things out, each person grades on their own scale, so one group of people may think a 3 is really good, while another may regard anything less than a 4 as being poor. Finally, we tried having managers evaluated by other managers. This was a disaster. The responses indicated a real hidden agenda. More like, 'How will my career benefit if I rate this person well, or how if I rate this person poorly?'"

SELF-CHECK

1. What is it called when an employee is so good in a particular area of performance that the supervisor ignores problems in other areas of performance?

    (a) The recency effect

    (b) The halo effect

    (c) Stereotyping

    (d) Comparing

2. Everyone naturally likes people who are most like _____.

3. Performance evaluation should:

    (a) occur once a year.

    (b) occur after every project.

    (c) occur year-round.

    (d) occur from the moment the employee is hired and continue throughout his or her career.

SUMMARY

As you have learned, project and performance evaluations can greatly impact an organization. If they are done poorly, they have a negative impact leading to lower employee morale and poor performance. If they are done well, the positive impact can translate into high employee morale and improved financial performance. In this chapter, you quantified goals and assessed different ways of tracking projects that were designed to accomplish your goals. You evaluated data and how they can be used to improve performance. You also assessed how to develop a performance-feedback system. Finally, you learned how a performance evaluation should be conducted and how to avoid the common mistakes managers make when evaluating others.

KEY TERMS

Actions	Individual activities performed between milestones.
Critical path	The longest period of time associated with one task in a project. If it is not completed on time, then it will affect the rest of the project.
Flowcharts	Graphical representations of the sequential flow of projects.
Gantt charts	Graphical representation of projects using bars, also known as bar charts.
Milestones	The checkpoints, events, and markers that show progress toward goals.
Relationships	How milestones and actions interact with one another.
Schedule	The time it takes to complete a task.

ASSESS YOUR UNDERSTANDING

Go to www.wiley.com/college/nelson to evaluate your knowledge of measuring projects and performance.
Measure your learning by comparing pre-test and post-test results.

Summary Questions

1. The first step in determining an employee's progress is to determine what goals the organization has for the employee. True or false?
2. If you measure goals in terms of _____ then employees will have no confusion over how their performance is measured.
3. A Gantt chart is not the same thing as a bar chart. True or false?
4. _____ are the graphical representations of the sequential flow of projects.
5. Employees' progress toward their goals should be noted in their file. True or false?
6. _____ are the checkpoints or events that demonstrate progress toward goals.
7. If you have to complete task one before starting on task two, then there is a(n) _____ between the projects:
   (a) Gantt
   (b) relationship
   (c) action
   (d) milestone
8. When an employer gives a good evaluation to someone who is like them, this is known as _____.
9. What are the checkpoints or events that demonstrate progress toward goals?
   (a) Actions
   (b) Relationships
   (c) Milestones
   (d) Gantts
10. When managers allow one recent negative incident to color the entire annual review of an employee, this is known as:
    (a) the halo effect.
    (b) stereotyping.
    (c) the recency effect.
    (d) comparing.

11. Evaluations should be based on an employee's _____ performance and not compared to others.

12. Evaluation should be given to employees throughout the year. True or false?

13. Evaluations should include only constructive criticism. True or false?

14. When you have preconceived notions about an employee, this is called _____.

Applying This Chapter

1. You work for an Internet service provider in the sales department. Your department has a goal that no prospective customer will be on hold for more than five minutes. How do you measure this and make this measurement public?

2. You work in a manufacturing facility that makes shampoo bottles. You usually make 5000 bottles every ten days. You are told by management that your group must increase production and make 10,000 bottles in twelve days. What milestones do you establish and why? You spend some time setting milestones, actions, relationships, and a schedule. Unfortunately, the team fell short and made only 9000 bottles in twelve days. Now what do you do?

3. You work at a marketing firm and hire two new employees. What can you do to ensure that their ninety-day review and annual performance review do not contain any surprises?

4. You are the editorial director at a daily newspaper. Your company gives evaluations to all employees on the same day of the year. So you have ten evaluations due on June 10. What common evaluation pitfalls do you need to work hard to avoid?

Changing Behaviors

You are the CEO of a hospital. You have taken a survey and 80 percent of the janitorial staff members dislike their jobs, 60 percent think that management does not care about them, and 50 percent are looking for new jobs. Obviously, employee morale is low. You can also see it in performance as many of the rooms are not cleaned quickly or thoroughly. Develop a plan with steps that will help you increase morale.

Measuring Progress

You decide that you want to get a new job within the next six months. Write out the milestones, actions, relationships, and schedule for this goal.

10

LEADING CHANGE
Managing Change and Employee Expectations

Starting Point

Go to www.wiley.com/college/nelson to assess your knowledge of leading change.
Determine where you need to concentrate your effort.

What You'll Learn in This Chapter

▲ How to deal with a crisis
▲ Common roadblocks to change that managers and employees put up
▲ How to help others with change
▲ How to inspire initiative in others
▲ How to help employees through layoffs

After Studying This Chapter, You'll Be Able To

▲ Assess change and overcome the common mental roadblocks to change
▲ Evaluate the four stages of change
▲ Evaluate employees' reactions to change and assist them through the change
▲ Prepare for layoffs

INTRODUCTION

Nothing stays the same, in business or in life. Change is all around us—it always has been, and it always will be. Although many people consider change something to be feared and avoided at any cost, the reality is that change brings with it excitement, new opportunities, and growth.

So what does change mean to you as a manager? The world of business is constantly changing, and the pressures on managers to perform are greater than they've ever been before. In addition, most organizations have gone from being bastions of stability and status quo in the stormy seas of change to being agile ships, navigating the fluid and ever-changing seas in which they float.

The words *business* and *change* are quickly becoming synonymous. And the more things change, the more everyone in an organization is affected. This chapter is about managing and thriving on change and about helping your employees find ways to take advantage of it (instead of change taking advantage of them!). In the chapter, you will define what it means to manage crises, identify roadblocks to change, and assess how to become a leader in change. In addition, you will examine one of most difficult changes to handle: employee layoffs.

10.1 Managing Urgency and Crises

Managers have many different responsibilities and tasks to juggle on a daily basis. A manager may have two employees who need to talk privately, a request from the vice president to complete a report within a couple of hours, and potential applicants to interview all in one day. All these matters seem urgent. Urgency has its place in an organization. The rate of change in the global business environment demands it. The revolutions in computer use, telecommunications systems, and information technology demand it. The need to be more responsive to customers than ever before demands it. In these urgent times, companies that provide the best solutions faster than anyone else are the winners. The losers are the companies that wonder what happened as they watch their competitors gain market share.

However, an organization has a real problem when its managers fall into the behavior of managing by crisis and the trap of reacting to change instead of leading change. When every problem in an organization becomes a drop-everything-else-that-you-are-doing crisis, the organization isn't showing signs of responsiveness to its business environment. Instead, the business is showing signs of poor planning and lousy execution. Someone isn't doing his or her job.

Sometimes outside forces beyond your control as a manager cause crises. For example, suppose that a vital customer requests that all project designs be submitted by this Friday instead of next Friday. Or perhaps the city sends you a notice that a maintenance crew plans to cut off the power to your plant for three days while the crew performs needed maintenance on switching equipment.

Or a huge snowstorm in the Northeast cuts off all flights, in and out, for the rest of the week.

On the other hand, many crises occur because someone in your organization drops the ball, and now you have to fix everything. The following are avoidable crisis situations:

▲ Hoping that the need will go away, you avoid making a necessary decision. The need won't go away, and now you have a crisis to deal with.

▲ An employee forgets to relay an important message from your customer, and you're about to lose the account as a result—another crisis.

▲ A coworker decides that informing you about a major change to a manufacturing process isn't important. Because of your experience, you would have quickly seen that the change would lead to quality problems in the finished product. When manufacturing grinds to a halt, you come in after the fact to clean up the mess; one more crisis to add to your list.

You have to be prepared to deal with externally generated crises. You have to be flexible, you have to work smart, and you have to work hard. But your organization can't afford to become a slave to internally generated crises. Managing by crisis forgoes one of the most important elements in business management. That element is planning.

You establish plans and goals for a reason—to make your company as successful as possible. However, if you continually set your plans and goals on a back burner because of today's crisis, why waste your time making the plans? Where does your organization go then? When you, as a manager, allow everything to become a crisis through your own inaction or failure to anticipate change, not only do you sap the energy of your employees, but also eventually, they lose the ability to recognize when a real crisis is upon them. Remember the old fable about the boy who cried "Wolf"? After the boy issued several false alarms in jest, the villagers didn't bother to respond to his cries when some wolves really appeared to attack his sheep. After responding to several manufactured crises, your employees begin to see the crises as routine, and they may not be there for you when you really need them.

SELF-CHECK

1. The best managers react to crises. True or false?

2. Due to global changes and information technology, companies must act _____ to keep up with the competition.

3. If managers spend time only managing crises, they can't fulfill their ____ or plans.

10.2 Identifying the Four Stages of Change

Change happens, and you can't do anything about it. You can try to ignore it, but does that stop change? No, you only blind yourself to what is really happening in your organization. You can try to stop it, but does that keep change from happening? No, you're only fooling yourself if you think that you can stop change—even for a moment. You can try to insulate yourself and those employees around you from the effects of change, but can you really afford to ignore it? No, to ignore change is to sign a death warrant for your organization and, quite possibly, for your career.

Unfortunately, most managers seem to spend their entire careers trying to fight change—to predict, control, and harness change and its effects on the organization. But why? Change is what allows organizations to progress, products to get better, and people to advance, both personally and in their careers. Change is not easy. Despite the excitement that change can bring to your working life—both good and bad—you've probably had about all the change you can handle. But as change continues, you go through four distinct phases in response to change:

1. **Deny change.** When change happens, the first response you have (if you're like most people) is one of immediate denial. "Whose dumb idea was that? That idea is never going to work here. Don't worry, they'll see their mistake and go back to the old way of doing things!" Operating with this attitude is like an ostrich sticking its head in the sand: If you can't see it, it'll go away. The ideas of change usually go away.

2. **Resist change.** At some point, you realize that the change isn't just a clerical error; however, this realization doesn't mean that you have to accept the change lying down! "Nope, I'm sticking with the old way of doing that job. If that way was good enough then, why isn't it good enough now?" Resistance is a normal response to change—everyone goes through it. The key isn't to let your resistance get you stuck. The quicker you get with the program, the better for your organization and the better for your career.

3. **Explore change.** By now, you know that further resistance is futile and the new way just may have some pluses. "Well, maybe that change actually does make sense. I'll see what opportunities can make the change work for me instead of against me." During this stage, you examine both the good and bad that come from the change, and you decide on a strategy for managing the change.

4. **Accept change.** The final stage of change is acceptance. At this point, you have successfully integrated the change into your routine. "Wow, this new system really works well. It beats the heck out of the old way of doing things!" Now, the change that you so vigorously denied and resisted is part of your everyday routine; the change is now the status quo.

FOR EXAMPLE

Resisting Change

Many companies had a difficult time adjusting to how the Internet changed the way of doing business. For example, the video rental giant Blockbuster lost many customers to the online rental site Netflix. Although Blockbuster had a limited online presence, charged late fees for its movies, and did not expand its collections at stores, Netflix came in and had a very different business model. Netflix does not have any late fees, has over 50,000 titles, and had a very strong online presence. Blockbuster is now reacting to the competition instead of acting in a proactive way to anticipate the changes the Internet would bring. Resisting change can do immense damage to a company's bottom line.

At the end of your change responses, you come full circle, and you're ready to face your next change.

You may be fighting change and not even know it. Besides watching the number of gray hairs on your head multiply, how can you tell? Look out for these seven warning signs of resistance to change:

▲ **You're still using the old rules to play a new game.** The steady, secure work environment that our parents knew is gone. The pressures of global competition have created a brand-new game with a brand-new set of rules. For example, if you're one of those increasingly rare managers who refuses to find out how to use a new computer system, you're playing by the old rules. Computer literacy and information proficiency are the new rules. If you're not playing with the new rules, not only is this a warning sign that you're resisting change, but you can bet on being left behind as the rest of your organization moves along the path to the future.

▲ **You're ducking new assignments.** Usually, two basic reasons cause you to avoid new assignments. First, you may be overwhelmed with your current job and can't imagine taking on any more duties. If you're in this situation, try to remember that new ways often make your work more efficient or even wipe out many outdated ways of doing things. Second, you may simply be uneasy with the unknown, and so you resist change. Ducking new assignments to resist change is a definite no-no. Not only are you interfering with the progress of the organization, but also you're effectively putting your own career on hold.

▲ **You're trying to slow things down.** Trying to slow down is a normal reaction for most people. When something new comes along—a new way of doing business, a new assignment, or a new wrinkle in the market-place—most people tend to want to slow down, take the time to examine and analyze, and then decide how to react. The problem is that the newer something gets, the slower some people go.

As a manager, you want to remain competitive in the future. You don't have the luxury of slowing down every time something new comes along. Instead of resisting innovation by slowing down (and risking an uncompetitive and obsolete organization), you need to keep up your pace. How? When you're forced to do more with less, focus on less.

▲ **You're working hard to control the uncontrollable.** Are you resisting change by trying to control the uncontrollable at work? Perhaps you want to try to head off a planned corporate reorganization or stop your foreign competitors from accessing your domestic markets or delay the acquisition of your firm by a much larger company. The world of business is changing all around you, and you can't do anything about it. You have a choice: You can continue to resist change by pretending that you're controlling it (you can't), or you can concentrate on figuring out how to most effectively respond to change to leverage it to your advantage.

▲ **You're playing the role of victim.** Oh, woe is me! This response is the ultimate cop-out. Instead of accepting change and finding out how to respond to it (and using it to your own advantage as well as your organization's), you choose to become a victim of change. Playing the role of victim and hoping that your coworkers feel sorry for you is easy to do, but today's successful businesses can't afford to waste their time or money employing victims. If you're not giving 110 percent each day that you go to work, your organization will find someone who can.

▲ **You're hoping someone else can make things better for you.** In the old-style hierarchical organization, top management almost always took responsibility for making the decisions that made things better (or worse) for workers. The old-style organization is changing, and the new-style organization that is taking its place has empowered every employee to take responsibility for decision making.

The pressures of global competition and the information age require that decisions be made quicker than ever. In other words, the employees closest to the issues must make the decisions; a manager who is seven layers up from the frontline and 3000 miles away can't do it. You hold the keys to your future. You have the power to make things better for yourself. If you wait until someone else makes things better for you, then you're going to be waiting a long time.

▲ **You're absolutely paralyzed, like a deer in the headlights.** This condition is the ultimate sign of resistance to change and is almost always terminal. Sometimes change seems so overwhelming that the only choice is to give up. When change paralyzes you, not only do you fail to respond to change, but also you can no longer perform your current duties. In today's organization, such resistance is certain failure.

SELF-CHECK

1. List and define the first stage of change.
2. List and define two signs of resistance to change.
3. The final stage of change is _____.
4. Resisting change is usually futile. True or false?

10.3 Becoming a Leader of Change

Instead of allowing change to paralyze you, become a leader of change. Here are some ways to do that:

▲ Embrace the change. Become its friend and its biggest cheerleader.
▲ Be flexible and be responsive to the changes that swirl all around you and through your organization.
▲ Be a model to those employees around you who continue to resist change. Show them that they can make change work for them instead of against them.
▲ Focus on what you can do—not what you can't do.
▲ Recognize and reward employees who have accepted the change and who have succeeded as a result.

If you notice any of the seven warning signs of resistance to change in yourself or in your coworkers, you can do something about it. As long as you're willing to embrace change instead of fighting it, you hold incredible value for your organization, and you can take advantage of change rather than fall victim to it. Make responsiveness to change your personal mission: be a leader of change, not a follower of resistance.

10.3.1 Change Affects Everyone

When your organization finds itself in the midst of change—whether because of fast-moving markets, changing technology, rapidly shifting customer needs, or some other reason—you need to remember that change affects everyone, not just you as a manager. And, although some of your employees can cope well with these changes, others may have a difficult time adjusting to their new environment and the expectations that come along with it. Be on the alert for employees who are resisting or having a hard time dealing with change, and then help them transition through the process.

The following tips can help your employees cope with change on the job:

▲ **Show that you care.** Managers are very busy people, but never be too busy to show your employees that you care—especially when they're having difficulties on the job. Take a personal interest in your employees and offer to help them in any way you can.

▲ **Widely communicate the potential for change.** Nothing is more disconcerting to employees than being surprised by changes that they didn't expect. As much as possible, give your employees a heads-up on potential changes in the business environment, and keep them up-to-date on the status of the changes as time goes on.

▲ **Seek feedback.** Let your employees know that you want their feedback and suggestions on how to deal with potential problems resulting from change, or how to capitalize on any opportunities that may result.

▲ **Be a good listener.** When your employees are in a stressful situation, they naturally are going to want to talk about it—this part of the process helps them cope with change. Set aside time to chat informally with employees, and encourage them to voice their concerns about the changes that they and the organization are going through.

▲ **Don't give false assurances.** Although you don't want to needlessly frighten your employees with tales of impending doom and gloom, also avoid sugarcoating the truth. Be frank and honest with your employees and treat them like the adults they are.

▲ **Involve employees.** Involve employees in planning for upcoming changes, and delegate the responsibility and authority for making decisions to them whenever practicable.

▲ **Look to the future.** Paint a vision for your employees that emphasizes the many ways that the organization will be a better place as everyone adapts to change and begins to use it to their benefit.

Change can be traumatic for those people who go through it. Stay alert to the impact of change on your employees, and help them work their way through it. Not only will your employees appreciate your support—showing their appreciation with loyalty to you and your organization—but also morale will improve and your employees will be more productive as a result.

10.3.2 Encouraging Employee Initiative

One of the most effective ways to help employees make it through the change process in one piece is to give them permission to take charge of their own work.

You can encourage your employees to take the initiative to come up with ideas to improve the way they do their work, and then to implement those ideas.

The most successful organizations are the ones that actively encourage employees to take initiative, and the least successful ones are those organizations that stifle initiative.

Consider how these companies reward employee initiative:

▲ **Above and beyond:** Employees who take the initiative to help others by going beyond what's expected at CIC Pharmaceuticals Group in Wilmington, Delaware, receive the Performance Excellence Award and $300. Peers, supervisors, or anyone else who knows of someone's special work can nominate an employee.

▲ **They add up:** At El Torito Restaurants, based in Irvine, California, employees receive a "Be a Star" award for going above and beyond their job description. Winners receive Star Bucks, which are entered for a monthly drawing for up to $1,000 worth of merchandise.

As a manager, you need to make your employees safe to take initiative in their jobs. Not only will your employees better weather the change that swirls all around them, but they also will create a more effective organization and provide better service to customers in the process. Ask your employees to take the following suggestions and put them to use:

▲ Look for ways to make improvements to the status quo, and follow through with an action plan.

▲ Focus suggestions on areas that have the greatest impact on the organization.

▲ Follow up suggestions with action. Volunteer to help implement your suggestions.

▲ Step outside your box. Look for areas of improvement throughout the organization, not just within your department or business unit.

▲ Don't make frivolous suggestions. They degrade your credibility and distract you from more important areas of improvement.

FOR EXAMPLE

Encouraging Employees

Federal Express, based in Memphis, Tennessee, awards the Golden Falcon to employees who go above and beyond to serve their customers. For example, one winner took the initiative to order new shipping forms for a regular customer after noticing that the customer had not thought to change his area code on a return address.

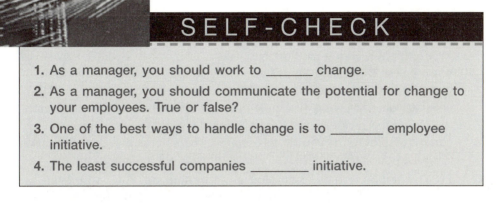

SELF-CHECK

1. As a manager, you should work to _____ change.
2. As a manager, you should communicate the potential for change to your employees. True or false?
3. One of the best ways to handle change is to _____ employee initiative.
4. The least successful companies _____ initiative.

10.4 Handling Mergers and Layoffs

For better or worse, mergers and layoffs are two of the biggest causes for change in the work environment.

▲ **Layoffs** occur when the size of a workforce has to be reduced to external factors such as shrinking profits, duplication of positions resulting from a merger, or a shift in a company's strategy.

▲ **Mergers** take place when one company buys another one and the two companies form one new company.

When two companies merge to form a new company, there are often more employees than are needed for the new company. For example, there may now be two human resource departments, two accounting departments, and so on. When this happens, there are likely to be company rumors as to who is and who isn't getting laid off. As a manager, you will have to handle the layoffs. Call it what you like: a reduction in force, a downsizing, a rightsizing, a reengineering, or whatever. The causes and results are still the same. Your organization needs to reorganize its operations, or cut payroll and related personnel and facilities costs, and some of your employees need to go.

Although understandably traumatic for those employees involved, layoffs are different from firings because the employees who are terminated generally aren't at direct fault. They're usually good employees who follow the rules. They're productive and do their jobs. They're loyal and dedicated workers. They may even be your friends. The real culprits are usually external factors, such as changes in markets, mergers and acquisitions, and pressures of a more competitive global marketplace.

When it's time to conduct a layoff, use the following step-by-step guide to help you through the process:

1. **Determine the extent of the problem and figure out what departments will be affected.** How deep is the financial hole that your organization finds itself in? Does the possibility exist that fortunes will change anytime

soon? If certain products or services aren't selling, what departments are affected?

2. **Freeze hiring.** Hiring employees during a layoff process doesn't make sense unless the position is critical. For example, if a receptionist quits, you still need someone to answer the phones and receive visitors. Not only do you risk laying off a new hire, but also hiring at this time sends the wrong message to your employees that you don't care about your current employees. If you do have to hire, be sure to first consider previously laid-off employees before you go outside the organization.

3. **Prepare tentative lists of employees to be laid off.** After you determine the extent of the problem and the affected departments, the next step is to determine which employees to lay off. Determine which employees have the most skill and experience in the areas that the organization needs, and which employees have the least. The first employees to go in a layoff are usually those employees whose skills and experience don't mesh with the organization's needs.

4. **Notify all employees of planned layoffs in advance.** When the need for a layoff seems certain, get the word out to all employees immediately and well in advance of the planned layoff. Fully disclose the financial and other problems that your organization faces and solicit employee suggestions for ways to cut costs or improve efficiency. Sometimes employee suggestions can save you enough money to avert the layoff or at least soften its blow on the organization. Err on the side of overcommunication.

5. **Prepare a final list of employees to be laid off.** After you turn the organization upside down to find potential savings, you need to prepare a list of employees to be laid off. Write the list in rank order in the event of a change that may allow you to remove employees from the list. Most companies have standard procedures for ranking employees for layoff—especially if a union represents workers. These procedures generally give preference to permanent employees over temporary ones and include seniority and/or performance in the formula for determining who stays and who goes. If you don't have a policy, you need to determine the basis for laying off employees. In this case, you want to consider your employees' experience and how long they've been with the organization. Be careful not to discriminate against protected workers—older employees, for example—who are good performers.

6. **Notify affected employees.** By now, many employees are probably paralyzed with the fear that they'll be let go. As soon as you finish developing the layoff list—updating it to account for employees who may have already found new jobs on their own—notify the affected employees. Private, one-on-one meetings are the best way to handle notification.

7. **Provide outplacement services to terminated employees.** If time and money permit, provide outplacement and counseling support to the

employees being terminated. Your organization can provide training in subjects, such as résumé writing, financial planning, interviewing, and networking, and allow the employees to use company-owned computers, fax machines, and telephones in their job searches. If you can help your employees by providing job leads or contacts, by all means do so.

8. **Terminate.** Conduct one-on-one termination meetings with employees to finalize arrangements and complete termination paperwork. Explain the severance package, continuation of benefits, and any other company-sponsored termination programs as appropriate. Collect keys, identification badges, and any company-owned equipment and property. Escort (you can do this personally, or have a security guard or human resources representative fill the role) your newly terminated, former employees out of the facility and wish them well.

9. **Rally the "survivors."** Rally your remaining employees together in an "all-hands" meeting to let them know that, now that the layoffs are completed, the firm is back on the road to good financial health. Tell the team that, to avoid future layoffs, you have to pull together to overcome this momentary downturn in the business cycle.

FOR EXAMPLE

Layoffs in 2006

Unfortunately, layoffs are common. In October 2006, 110,996 people were laid off; 45,378 of these jobs were in the auto industry. The best thing you can do as a manager is help your employees get the education, training, and experience they need to be valuable in the workplace. If employees have the skills they need to be successful, then they can be successful anywhere and they have a much better chance of finding a new job.[1]

SELF-CHECK

1. **Mergers** always result in **layoffs**. True or false?

2. List and describe two steps managers can take to help them through the layoff process.

3. Mergers often result in the new company having two departments performing the same functions, one department from each of the two companies. True or false?

4. Only the weakest workers get laid off. True or false?

SUMMARY

As you have learned, change can greatly impact an organization. The way employees react to change can either help the organization improve or lead the organization in decline. In this chapter, you learned that managers must be proactive and manage change while at the same time pursuing their goals for growth in their departments. Managers must also identify common obstacles to change, identify ways to deal with change, and help employees adapt to change. You also assessed in this chapter how to handle one of the biggest and most disruptive changes to a company—employee layoffs.

KEY TERMS

Layoffs	When the size of a workforce has to be reduced to external factors such as shrinking profits, duplication of positions resulting from a merger, or a shift in a company's strategy.
Mergers	When one company buys another one and the two companies form one new company.

ASSESS YOUR UNDERSTANDING

Go to www.wiley.com/college/nelson to evaluate your knowledge of leading change and performance.
Measure your learning by comparing pre-test and post-test results.

Summary Questions

1. Urgency has a place in an organization. True or false?
2. If managers are constantly being reactive, they cannot be _____.
3. When change occurs, some people have a tendency of playing the role of a victim. True or false?
4. You cannot use the old rules to play a(n) ____ game when it comes to change.
5. Change affects only managers. True or false?
6. During times of change, it is important that managers _____ employees.
7. The first stage of change is:
   (a) exploring change.
   (b) denying change.
   (c) accepting change.
   (d) resisting change.
8. When an employee loses his or her job due to external factors, this is called:
   (a) getting fired.
   (b) getting laid off.
   (c) being merged.
   (d) none of the above.
9. When two companies become one, this is a(n):
   (a) layoff.
   (b) merger.
   (c) downsizing.
   (d) alliance.
10. The third stage of change is:
   (a) exploring change.
   (b) denying change.
   (c) accepting change.
   (d) resisting change.

Applying This Chapter

1. You work for a book publisher and you manage twenty editors. You have just been told that you will no longer be publishing hard-copy books, but rather will be putting all the content online. By doing this, you will be asking the editors to learn and use different skills than they have now. You know there will be resistance to the change. How do you help employees overcome their resistance to change?

2. You work in a retail store that has gone through four owners in two years. As a result, employee morale is low because their goals and compensation package are constantly changing. What are some ways you can improve employee morale?

3. You work in a marketing department and you have one superior employee who does a great job. Her only fault is that she is resistant to change. She denies change, will not take on new projects, and plays the role of victim. Worse yet, her attitude is rubbing off on the other employees. What can you do to help her through the various changes that the company and department have to make to remain competitive?

Changing Behaviors

You bought a large marketing firm that has over 100 employees. Within this firm, there are 10 managers. The managers had a personal, friendly relationship with the previous owner. In addition, the managers were never held accountable to goals and the company lost its competitve focus. You need to institute goals and a performance appraisal procedure so employee performance improves. You know the managers will be resistant to this. Write a paper outlining five to six ways you can make these changes so that managers will embrace them.

Conducting Layoffs

You work in a manufacturing facility that makes auto parts. You manage twenty employees who range from new hires to those who have been there for twenty years. The employees also range in skill level and competence. You have to lay off ten of them. Write down the criteria you would use to conduct the layoffs and your reasoning behind the criteria.

11

MANAGING DIVERSITY
Supervising Employees from Different Cultures

Starting Point

Go to www.wiley.com/college/nelson to assess your knowledge of managing diversity.
Determine where you need to concentrate your effort.

What You'll Learn in This Chapter

▲ Tips to keep in mind for managing people from different cultures, different generations, and different races
▲ How organizations have distinct and unique cultures
▲ Different cultural attributes
▲ Diversity trends that impact the global workforce

After Studying This Chapter, You'll Be Able To

▲ Manage employees who are from different cultures and have different attributes in terms of age, gender, and ability
▲ Predict clashes between employees and the organizational culture
▲ Evaluate global trends and how they will affect your business
▲ Evaluate ways to embrace differences in employees and how to use those differences to the advantage of your company

INTRODUCTION

Modern management theory considers that what a person is should not be important; it is what they do and contribute to an organization that matters. Employees are different in many ways; they come from diverse backgrounds, have different abilities, and are of all different ages. This is increasingly true in the global business environment. For example, managers in the United States could end up managing local employees as well as employees in India and Mexico. It is not only the United States that has outsourcing and a diverse workforce. Europe also outsources operations and has an increasingly large minority workforce, workers who have migrated from other countries. Germany, for example, has a large Turkish workforce.

Successful managers prize diversity and recognize that diversity contributes to the success of an organization. In this chapter, you will learn how organizations have their own unique culture. You will assess different cultures and reasons why some cultures clash. You will also evaluate trends in the global workforce. Finally, you will assess ways you can improve your own management skills when it comes to working with employees from diverse backgrounds.

11.1 Managing Cultural Diversity

The word *culture* is often used to mean different things. A formal definition of **culture** is how a group of people or a distinct geographic region operates in terms of laws, mores, and customs. In organizational terms, the simple definition is "the way things are done around here." From this definition, which is also useful for defining national cultures, it can be discerned that there may well be different ways of doing the same thing. It is important to note that, in many cases, a particular way is not better than that chosen by another organization or even another national group—it is just different. Different does not imply a judgment; it is purely a statement of fact. One culture is not better than the other. They are just different, and have adopted different procedures and laws to suit their national cultures and attitudes. Culture is something that develops over long periods of time and is transmitted from one generation to the next. In the context of national cultures, this is done within the family structure, from parents to children, and within schools, through the education system. Organizational culture is transmitted from longer-serving staff to new employees and through induction programs, corporate events, publications, and other techniques. Modern methods of managing cultural diversity seek not so much to impose one way of doing things, but to combine the best of the organization with the best of the host, whether the host is an actual country, or just those employees with a different background who have come into the organization.

Managers must effectively relate to employees from diverse backgrounds. In addition to cultural diversity, social changes have increased the scale of diversity even within relatively homogeneous work groups by the increasing employment of women, older people, and the disabled. All these groups are able to add to the organization. **Contingency theory** suggests that there is no single best method of managing—each manager should use the techniques best suited to each particular situation and to the people involved, and should recognize that there may be different methods of achieving objectives, depending on the organization, the people and the culture that he or she is working with.

11.1.1 Organizational Culture

Organizational culture is a reflection of the way an organization operates and it often reflects the core values of the organization. Organizational cultures may be bureaucratic and role-related, as they are in many government and public sector organizations. They may be related more to power and to the influence of the most prominent individual within the organization, a situation often found in entrepreneurial organizations. There may be little formal structure, as in a partnership of lawyers or physicians, or there may be a matrix approach, in which knowledge and expertise are the most valued assets of the organization and bureaucracy is kept to a minimum. It is not difficult to imagine the frustration that a rule-driven bureaucratic culture might experience when dealing with an entrepreneurial one where the influence and wishes of the owner or CEO take precedence over everything else. The former's rules may well be totally alien to the latter. It is perfectly possible for there to be different cultures operating within the same organization. An accounting department may resemble a bureaucratic culture, whereas research and development, with a more free-thinking head, may operate in a matrix mode. Nevertheless, especially within the same organization, it is important that the cultures "get on with each other," and this requires all the staff to have knowledge of the organizational culture.

It may well be that huge organizations actually have divisions or controlled subsidiaries that operate with different cultural norms, especially when they are situated in another country. Here again, understanding is the key to effective cooperation. Although an organization may be able to control the cultural behavior within itself to a degree, that of outside organizations may be completely beyond its control. Again, knowledge and a willingness to work together to overcome any cultural differences for mutual benefit are required. It is true throughout humanity that, however different we are, our similarities are normally much greater: This is also true of organizations. A willingness by all concerned to bend a little when necessary works wonders.

11.1.2 Cultural Change

It was stated earlier that there is a generational aspect to the transfer of culture. Cultural change too is often generational. It is easy for a senior management to announce that the culture of an organization is to change, but much less easy to achieve it in anything other than the long term. Values, attitudes and beliefs, whether personal, national or organizational, are deeply held—indeed, wars are often fought over them and people may be willing to lay down their lives for them—so they can be changed only gradually, hence the concept of generational change. It is particularly important to realize that those who enter an organization from a different cultural background, whether it is from another national culture or just that they are coming from another organization, will be expected to undergo an overnight transformation into a new set of values. This process requires understanding, time, and patience from managers. One very important step in the process is not only to tell people "the way we do things around here," but also to explain why things are done that way.

SELF-CHECK

1. The theory that there is no single best way to manage is:
   (a) contingency theory.
   (b) modern management theory.
   (c) matrix theory.
   (d) cultural diversity theory.
2. Too often, cultural change is _____.
3. It is possible for there to be different cultures within the same organization. True or false?
4. Organization culture reflects the core _____ of an organization.

11.2 Understanding National Culture

As the world, especially the world of business, becomes smaller through improved communications, so paradoxically does the importance of understanding cultural diversity. It has already been observed that cultural change is generational and responds at a much slower rate than technological change. Thus, whereas communications between different cultural groups is quicker and easier, the differences between those groups still remain. Only perhaps in the fields of popular culture such as pop music and international sports is there rapid global convergence on a single issue. It stands to reason, therefore, that as organizations undertake their operations on an increasingly global basis and/or employ a more culturally diverse workforce, the need for cultural understanding becomes greater and greater. Cultural diversity can be described as a series of differing attitudes held by various national groups. It should be noted that such attitudes are always just a general tendency—not all Americans will react in one way to a particular set of circumstances and not all Germans another—but research reveals a consistent series of national tendencies. The attitudes most critical were

▲ Attitude toward time
▲ Universal vs. particular
▲ Individualism vs. collectivism
▲ Emotional vs. neutral
▲ Specific vs. diffuse
▲ Achievement vs. ascription
▲ Attitude toward the environment

To these should be added attitudes toward gender, age, and disability. None of these concepts is absolute: national tendencies lie on a continuum between the two extremes. In the following section, the various factors are described and, where appropriate, the cultures lying at each end and in the middle are given. Dutch researcher Fons Trompenaars spent many hours researching this, often by asking multiple-choice questions requiring a response to a certain set of circumstances. For example, how much right does a friend have to expect you to lie for him or her in a certain set of circumstances? The replies he received to this particular question were interesting, since it was clear that in some cultures it is expected that friends will support one another come what may (a particular response), whereas in others, if a friend breaks the rules then those rules should apply whatever the circumstances (a universal response).

11.2.1 Attitude toward Time

It might be thought that time is a universal constant, as an hour is an hour is an hour whether in Los Angeles or Shanghai or Oxford. In looking at the cultural effect of time, however, it is not the absolute nature of time that is important, but the different attitudes toward it. Eastern cultures often have a reverence for ancestors and historical precedent. The United States, according to the research, was less interested in the past and much more concerned about the future. In many Western cultures, punctuality is prized and the lack of it is considered bad manners, thoughtless, and insulting. In other cultures, punctuality is given far less importance. This difference of attitude can immediately lead to a cultural clash in the workplace. If employees come to work in a culture where punctuality is important, say in the United States, then they must respect that and be on time. It may be necessary to help them develop that respect by pointing out how lateness can impact on schedules, upset work patterns, and cause colleagues to waste time. Explanation often goes a long way to achieving the desired result. A U.S. manager working in a culture where punctuality is less critical may well have to learn not to be stressed by it, but to adjust working practices to allow for it. Frustration on both sides is inevitable until the compromise is reached.

11.2.2 Universal vs. Particular

In some cultures, a set of rules or laws is universally applied (or so perceived wisdom tells us, despite the fact that there is sometimes one law for certain members of society and another for others). In other cultures, rules and norms may be applied depending on the circumstances. Writers on culture have pointed out that relationships such as friendship may confer special rights and obligations in a particular culture, but are less welcome in a universal one. In a universal culture, an individual has much less right to expect a friend to cover up for him or her than in a culture where particularism is the accepted norm. In general, the United States and Japan display high levels of universalism when tested, whereas the former constituents of Yugoslavia and certain Far Eastern countries (excluding Japan) tended toward the particularism, although even in these countries it must be stressed that the overall tendency was that there should be universal rules applicable to everybody.

This is perhaps a change that is having a global impact. Certain countries, such as the United States, have strict rules against bribery, and anyone attempting to offer or accept bribes can expect to receive heavy punishment when caught. In many parts of the world such behavior is the norm, and those who do not indulge in it do not receive good service or treatment. They can also become objects of derision because of their unawareness of local practice. In dealing with a culture at the particularism end of the spectrum, organizations need to know exactly which rules are being applied, by whom, and to whom.

11.2.3 Individualism vs. Collectivism

Basically, people regard themselves either as members of a group first and as individuals second, or vice versa. Not surprisingly, the United States is an individualism-oriented culture, whereas the Japanese came out, together with countries such as Nepal, East Germany under the communist regime, and other Far Eastern groupings, as tending toward a more collectivist approach. This should not be surprising given the political and social creeds of many Eastern areas and of communism.

For those conducting business in other cultures, it is important to realize that it may be a group rather than a key individual that needs to be satisfied in a collectivist-oriented culture, and that the building of collective relationships will be of great importance.

11.2.4 Emotional vs. Neutral

To what degree is it culturally acceptable to show personal feelings, especially in business relationships? In the United States, United Kingdom, and Japan such revelations may be frowned on; less so in Italy and France. Latin cultures tend to accept displays of emotion more readily than those designated as

FOR EXAMPLE

Mitsubishi and Boeing: Keeping Emotions in Check

The Japanese company Mitsubishi Heavy Industries works with Boeing on the 777. Mitsubishi makes the doors for the airliners as well as some other parts. In the case of the 777 passenger doors, there were delays to the doors. In Japanese society, the manner in which the rebuke is delivered can be very important, since it may cause the recipient to lose face. The emphasis given to the correct degree of respect for individuals within the hierarchy is very important in Japan. In the United States, an executive could lose his temper, apologize, and the meeting would move on. Such behavior is highly offensive in a meeting with Japanese colleagues. The relationship between Boeing and Mitsubishi was such that both sides had taken care to understand the cultural backgrounds of the others. Boeing executives were able to express their concerns with sufficient force to get the point across, but with enough tact to remain polite.

Anglo-Saxon. Emotion is a good psychological safety valve; maybe this is part of the explanation for the apparently lower incidence of heart disease and other stress-related illnesses in Latin areas. Whereas a display of emotion, and even temper, may be acceptable as a means of showing true feelings in Latin cultures, it is far less likely to produce effective results in North America, Northern Europe, and the Far East, where the whole issue of "face" can be very important. The British "stiff upper lip" and Japanese inscrutability are examples of such concealed emotion.

11.2.5 Specific vs. Diffuse

In many cultures, it is accepted, and expected, that there will be a personal relationship between those involved in business transactions, whereas in others the relationship is more between organizations than individuals, who are mere representatives of the organization. Position within the hierarchy may also be important in this respect in cultures where the hierarchy is itself important.

In some cultures, work and home are closely related; in others, employees are not expected to bring domestic issues into their workplace. This begs the question of how an individual is supposed to leave a problem at home—it is the belief that the two should not mix, and not the actual reality of the situation, that is important here. Fons Trompenaars quotes China as a very diffuse culture, using the example of asking how many respondents would refuse to help their manager paint his home. In China 72 percent would help, whereas in the much more specific culture of the United Kingdom only 8 percent would agree to give up their own time this way (the U.S. figure was 11 percent). Similarly, in China

89 percent of employees believed that the organization had a responsibility to help house its employees, compared to 55 percent of Japanese, but only 18 percent in the United Kingdom and 15 percent in the United States. There has been a change of attitude on this issue in the United States and the United Kingdom, since during the late nineteenth and early twentieth centuries many organizations provided housing for staff. An organization in a specific culture may appear, to those adopting that culture as in-comers, to be much more focused on its objectives, whereas in a diffuse culture time may be spent talking about nonorganizational-related issues. Neither is right or wrong; both attitudes suit their cultures. It is again a matter of knowing, understanding, and reacting in a culturally acceptable manner.

11.2.6 Achievement vs. Ascription

Different cultures also reward status to people based on differing criteria:

▲ An **achievement-oriented culture** confers status according to what people have done.
▲ An **ascription-oriented culture** rewards people for their position, connections, and even birth.

The United States is the best example of an achievement-oriented culture, where it is believed that, with hard work and education, anybody can rise to the top. The careers of many early immigrants and their immediate descendants showed just what was possible. Achievement societies are more interested in what somebody studied, whereas ascription societies may be more concerned with where the studies occurred. In that respect, even the United States, with its Ivy League of universities (Harvard, Yale, and others), is not completely an achievement culture. Titles and qualifications are much more important in ascription-oriented cultures, and great offense can be caused by omitting them or even by listing them incorrectly.

11.2.7 Attitude toward the Environment

The extent that members of a culture believe that it is right and proper for humankind to try to control nature may well influence behavior and strategy at work. The developments in genetic engineering in the United States and Europe suggest that these cultures believe that this research is acceptable. Fons Trompenaars claimed that 35 percent in the United Kingdom and 38 percent in the United States believed that it is worth trying to control nature, compared with only 10 percent in Japan.

Environmental issues are now taken very seriously, and people are beginning to realize that interfering with nature can have potentially disastrous consequences, as global warming has shown. Countries that ignore internationally agreed limits on chemical emissions are increasingly finding themselves under internal and external pressure to comply, as the United States is now discovering. There is also a related issue in the extent to which people feel they are the masters or mistresses of their own destinies. In the developed world, people believe this far more than those living under communist regimes did. Controlling one's own destiny and controlling nature are closely linked, as is the concept of individualism vs. collectivism. Fate, so important in many Eastern cultures, plays a much smaller role in the cultural psychology of the West.

SELF-CHECK

1. Employees from which country are more likely to be collectivist?

    (a) United Kingdom

    (b) United States

    (c) Japan

    (d) None of the above

2. People who are prized because of their connections, position, and birth live in a(n) _____ culture.

3. More people in Japan believe it is worth trying to control the environment than do in the United States. True or false?

4. In the United States, laws are universally applied. True or false?

5. In China, the problems of work and home are closely related. True or false?

6. Punctuality is valued in all countries and cultures. True or false?

11.3 Understanding Diversity Trends

Discrimination is the result of the actions of someone who is prejudiced. Most jurisdictions in the developed world have legislation in place dealing with discrimination on the grounds of gender or race. The United States has also age discrimination legislation that provides a degree of protection for older workers. Governments can legislate to prevent discrimination, and can punish those who discriminate against diversity. They cannot, however, legislate against prejudice. Prejudice can be removed only by understanding, educating, and working with others in circumstances that will demonstrate that similarities are much greater than differences. Discrimination and prejudice can exist for a variety of reasons including race, gender, age, and disability.

11.3.1 Migration

Since the end of World War II, there has been considerable migration in order to seek a better economic life from the less-developed parts of the world into North America and Europe, and also from former communist regimes in Eastern Europe to the West. To these so-called economic refugees must be added those who have fled their own country as a consequence of war, famine, and persecution. In the 1960s and 1970s, both Kenya and Uganda expelled large numbers of their citizens of Asian origin, many of whom were relocated, with U.K. government assistance, in the United Kingdom. Many of these East African Asians met an initially hostile reception from some parts of British society, which were fearful of the social and economic impact of such an influx. In fact, the East African Asians brought excellent commercial skills with them, and Kenya's and Uganda's losses were Britain's gain, as many of them prospered and set up their own businesses. They brought a positive addition to the commercial and cultural diversity of the United Kingdom. At the same time, the Kenyan and Ugandan economies suffered as a result of the removal of some of their more entrepreneurial elements.

In the developed world, most governments have legislation in place to protect people entering a new society from discrimination. It is important for organizations to recognize that diversity may simply mean doing things differently. Different cultural groups may need special facilities for religious observance (although most of the world's major religions are pragmatic when it comes to balancing religious observance and work) and there may be the need for different food to be available—some cultures demand that food is slaughtered and prepared in a particular manner, *halal* and *kosher* for example. Body language and customs differ between groups, and mutual knowledge can save misunderstanding, embarrassment, and offense.

FOR EXAMPLE

Commercials and Diversity

In 1971, Coca-Cola became a truly global organization with the famous advertisement "I'd like to buy the world a Coke . . ." Using thirty young people of all races and colors, the advertisement was sung to the tune "I'd like to teach the world to sing in perfect harmony . . ." This struck a chord with many young people; it expressed the ideals of peace and love—and all brought about by Coca-Cola! The advertisement was so memorable that it is consistently voted as one of the top advertisements ever in polls both for the United States and the United Kingdom. Interestingly, the advertisement was the first positive use of nonwhite faces in a U.K. television advertisement.

If an organization is dealing with an ethnically diverse workforce, or is operating abroad, it must remember that just because people have migrated does not mean that they have lost interest in their homeland. Political events and natural tragedies in the homeland may cause distress thousands of miles away; an empathetic approach from an employer will go a long way toward building respect. People may also bring their prejudices with them, and this needs to be taken into account when setting up teams and work groups, although every attempt must be made to defuse potentially damaging attitudes.

11.3.2 Women in the Workplace

It is widely believed that it was the loss of a large proportion of the male population into the armies of the World War I that brought women into the workplace. This is a misconception; the war may have increased the number of women in employment and increased their skill base, but women had formed an important part of employment statistics long before 1914. Although the women in the upper echelons of medieval society may have lived lives of luxury and idleness, the lot of ordinary women was very different, and women formed an important and integral part of the economy. Long-established industries, such as coal mining and the cotton industry, had made considerable use of women and children, although public outcry led to the passing of a number of legislative measures to restrict this. For example, in the United Kingdom throughout the nineteenth century laws were passed banning the use of women and children in coal mines, outlawing the use of children as chimney sweeps, and eventually raising the age at which children could begin work. Whereas child labor is virtually unknown in the West, it has by no means been eradicated in less-developed areas (as some global manufacturers have discovered), and it is an issue that attracts increasing concern from United Nations agencies and international children's charities.

In a number of cultures, the role of women is restricted to domestic duties and the caring professions. In extreme cases, such as the Taliban regime in contemporary Afghanistan, women are forbidden to take any form of employment. The Taliban and their supporters claim that this is for religious reasons connected with modesty, although it may have a great deal to do with the males in that culture protecting their power base. There are no logical reasons for the reluctance of many organizations to promote women to senior positions. The concept of a "glass ceiling" inhibiting the progress of women has been postulated by a number of writers, particularly Davidson and Cooper in *Shattering the Glass Ceiling* and Morrison and others in *Breaking the Glass Ceiling*.[1] The progress toward sexual equality was painfully slow at times during the twentieth century; women in the United States did not gain full suffrage until 1920. One of the major developments in managing diversity has been the number of additional women entering employment through part-time jobs and the growth of the concept of job sharing. Originally developed in connection with lower-paid work, even some of the most high-powered jobs can be undertaken in this manner and this provides an antidote to often-quoted but erroneous ideas that childcare may inhibit effective performance by female workers. In the developed world, little gender differentiation exists in education and training, and it is in those areas that equality begins to have a marked and unalterable effect.

It is important that men and women have equal treatment in pay and conditions at work, but women should be employed in roles that are best suited both to the gender and to the individual. Many of the old ideas that women could not do "male" jobs have been proved fallacious, or removed by technology. There are now many female airline pilots and truck drivers. At one time both these jobs needed a degree of physical strength better provided by a man, but fly-by-wire and power steering/automatic transmissions have meant that strength is no longer a factor. The armed forces, particularly in Europe and North America, are still one area where there is considerable debate over the deployment of women in combat conditions. The Israeli armed forces, however, have used women as proactively and as effectively as men, especially when the country has been threatened by invasion. The key to managing the diversity between male and female employees is to consider them not as opposites but as complementary to one another.

11.3.3 Age and Disability

Two other types of diversity have become more common in the workplace through the increasing employment of those with disabilities and of those who have retired or been laid off from their original career. Although employing a worker with a disability may require some ergonomic adjustments, the motivation that people with disabilities often bring to their work can more than compensate for this. Many tasks can be performed just as competently by somebody who is disabled as by someone who is fully able and mobile. From a socially selfish point of view, every person with a disability who is employed is a relief to a government in terms of the need to supply care provision and financial allowances. It is always psychologically better for people to be as self-sufficient as possible. It keeps their self-esteem high, and their work benefits as a result.

Older workers have been shown to be more reliable and more productive than younger employees. They generally have fewer potential distractions in their social lives and more highly developed attitudes to loyalty and teamwork. Eastern culture places more reverence on age and experience than is found in the Western culture. Many Western executives laid off in their late forties have come to feel that their working lives are at an end and that younger successors are in greater demand than they are. There has, however, been a slow but growing trend for organizations to hire older workers in order to tap into their experience and motivation. Many of those taking early retirement now seek new careers, perhaps part time, and they provide valuable diversity to their new employers, together with a deeper understanding of the world and the way it works.

SELF-CHECK

1. Older workers are less productive than younger workers. True or false?

2. Women were brought into the workforce because of the death of men during war. True or false?

3. The United States has laws against discrimination. True or false?

4. Western culture places more reverence on age than Eastern cultures do. True or false?

5. As a manager, you may need to make workplace modifications for an employee that is _____.

11.4 Taking Ten Steps to Make Diversity Work

In the modern world, even the smallest organization will be dealing with diversity. Diversity of staff, diversity of suppliers, and diversity of customers is now the norm in any business. From the smallest gas station to an international oil company, from a small car lot to an international manufacturer, from a real estate agent to a construction conglomerate, from a wayside diner to a global burger chain, managing an organization means managing diversity. The organizations, large or small, that will be successful in the fast-changing commercial, economic, and political world of the twenty-first century will be those that can use diversity to their advantage and can see in diversity an opportunity and not a threat.

This chapter offers ten steps to assist organizations and individuals in the process of managing diversity. It might be thought that the steps are just common sense. That is half right. They do make sense, but unfortunately they are not always a common phenomenon when common sense is most needed.

11.4.1 Step 1: Know the Culture of the Organization

Every manager should have considered the culture of his or her own organization, and the impact that this might have on other organizations and individuals who may operate to a different set of norms. There is little point in analyzing the outside world unless a manager has a clear idea of how his or her own organization works and, equally critically, why it works in that way. Why do certain organizations have complex rules and others are more laid back? The answer will lie at the cultural level and may well be linked to the beliefs and philosophies of the organization's founder.

11.4.2 Step 2: Find Out about the Culture of the Area, Region, or Country

The importance of the culture of an outside environment, especially where the organization is moving into a new area, has been a theme throughout this book. All managers working in a new region must equip themselves with knowledge of the cultural and social attitudes of that area.

11.4.3 Step 3: Understand the Culture of the Individual or Group of Employees

The culture of an individual, or of a culturally similar group of employees, is likely to be composed of factors connected with the culture of their place of origin (whether they were born there or not) and the culture of where they live now. Even people not born in a place may be brought up in its cultural traditions; second- and third-generation citizens of an adopted country can often retain their true native culture far more fiercely that their emigrant ancestors did. However, the longer people live away from what might be called their birth culture, the more the two cultures will become intertwined. Many people operate within two or even three cultures: a culture at home, a culture when they are out socially, and yet a third at work. This presents problems only when aspects of one culture conflict with those of another. This conflict presents a major dilemma—which culture to follow. Someone from a culture where honesty is highly valued may have problems if asked by an employer to mislead a customer (it should not happen, but it does).

11.4.4 Step 4: Understand the Nature of the Business

Different sectors of business have different ways of doing things. Cooperation between competitors may be encouraged or actively discouraged, the amount of credit allowed may differ, and working practices may vary widely. All managers should have a good working knowledge of all sectors that interface with their organization. They are likely to meet diverse working practices, some of which may be alien to their own way of doing things. This does not make them wrong, just different. What works in one sector may be totally inappropriate in another.

11.4.5 Step 5: Understand Yourself

Imagine a scenario where three U.S. managers are working with a group of employees in a U.S.-based organization in Brazil. Who is dealing with diversity? The answer, of course, is that both sets of people are. It is all too easy to regard others as different without remembering that they will see you and your colleagues as different. This situation does not just happen to different national groups; it can happen between members of different departments working on the same site. To be sensitive, the next step in this chapter, it is necessary to understand one's own prejudices and feelings. An analysis of them may point out irrationalities that need to be addressed. The more comfortable a person is with himself or herself, the more effectively he or she will be able to manage diversity.

11.4.6 Step 6: Be Sensitive

Arrogance and assumed superiority are two great enemies of managing diversity. The belief that one's way of doing things is superior may, in fact, be true or it may not be true at all, but the method by which this belief is communicated is all-important. Sensitive handling of diversity and a willingness to listen and take new ideas on board is a critical skill for all managers, especially those who have to manage diversity.

11.4.7 Step 7: Encourage Diversity

Meredith Belbin in the United Kingdom has pioneered the concept of team roles. This concept states that teams should be composed of a series of diverse roles if they are to be effective. Team roles are described by Belbin as "a pattern of behavior characteristic of the way in which one team member interacts with another where his performance serves to facilitate the progress of the team as a whole." The work of Belbin on team roles has shown the importance of encouraging diversity. Belbin's research demonstrated that homogeneous teams (i.e., those composed of similar personalities) were less successful than those that were diverse. Despite the problems that diversity in teams might cause, correct management of the allowable weaknesses creates a considerable degree of synergy. Whatever the type of diversity, whether it is based on gender, race, culture, personality, or anything else, the diverse experiences and ideas can, if managed effectively, produce results that are better than those from a homogeneous situation. It is worth remembering that every problem raised by diversity is not only a challenge, it is also an opportunity.

11.4.8 Step 8: Treat People as Equals

Semantically, *equality* means treating everybody the same, whereas *equity* means providing different experiences but to the same standard and level. Current management practice recognizes diversity and thus stresses equity. Organizations working in a global environment may not be in a position to treat people equally. For instance, wage rates and the cost of living differ widely throughout the world. Giving U.S.-level wages to employees in a country where the cost of living is lower than that in the United States, but where wage rates are also lower, would make them relatively better off than their U.S. colleagues. Equity involves taking local conditions and culture into account. If a large number of staff members in a U.S. organization's U.S. plant speak Spanish, should all communication be in English? The answer may well be yes, because the plant deals with outsiders too—suppliers, customers, neighbors, competitors. Customer communications should be in the language used by the customer, but a wise management will recognize that for purely internal use, dual language notices can be employed. In this way everybody's sensitivities will be addressed. Equality is a simple solution to diversity, whereas equity is more effective but more complex. To ensure equity involves an understanding of the nature of the diversity and a desire to treat people as individuals with their own unique needs.

11.4.9 Step 9: Educate against Prejudice

Prejudice, however irrational, exists in the mind, and it is not possible to legislate against it. Discrimination (see step 10) can and should be legislated against. Discrimination is prejudice in action. The way to deal with prejudice is through education. Education is not something only for the young. All people learn throughout their lives. A preparedness to continue learning may well contribute to a longer life. The type of education that combats prejudice involves learning about others and gaining an understanding of the reasons they do things the way they do. Although this may take time and effort, it is worth reflecting that one definition of *learning* is "a permanent change in behavior." It is that permanence of knowledge and understanding that can remove prejudice. Managers should take every opportunity to improve both their own knowledge of diversity and the knowledge of those for whom they have managerial responsibility.

11.4.10 Step 10: Act against Discrimination

Many countries have enacted antidiscriminatory legislation. Managers should ensure that no discriminatory practices (even casual comments and humor which can cause offense) are allowed. Part of equity is respect, and discrimination is not only illegal, but it is also disrespectful. It is highly demotivating to all parties and thus impacts widely on organizational efficiency. Sensitivity is important. A first offense can provide the initial step in educating against prejudice, but if it is ignored, it is likely to lead to an escalation in inappropriate behavior.

SELF-CHECK

1. Teams should be comprised of people who play _____ roles.

2. It is possible to legislate against prejudice. True or false?

3. Arrogance and _____ are two great enemies of managing diversity.

4. The more comfortable you are with _____, the more effectively you will be able to manage diversity.

5. As a manager you should _____ the culture of your organization.

6. If you are sent on an international assignment, you should become familiar with the culture of that area. True or false?

SUMMARY

As you have learned, diversity is a key strength of any organization. You are likely to find yourself working not only with those of different ages, genders, and work experience, but also with those who are from a different part of the world, who have a different culture, and who speak a different language. Harnessing the potential of such diversity requires a reappraisal of managerial skills. In this chapter, you assessed the different types of diversity, attributes of different countries, and the trends affecting diversity. You also evaluated ways to improve your skills managing a diverse workforce.

KEY TERMS

Achievement-oriented culture	A culture that confers status according to what people have done.
Ascription-oriented culture	A culture that rewards people for their position, connections, and even birth.
Contingency theory	Belief that there is no single best way to manage others. Under this theory, each manager should use the techniques best suited to each individual situation and to the people involved.
Culture	How a group of people or a distinct geographic region operates in terms of laws, mores, and customs.
Organizational culture	A reflection of the way an organization operates and a reflection of an organization's core values.

ASSESS YOUR UNDERSTANDING

Go to www.wiley.com/college/nelson to evaluate your knowledge of managing diversity.
Measure your learning by comparing pre-test and post-test results.

Summary Questions

1. An organization's core values are reflected in its organizational culture. True or false?
2. Values, attitudes, and beliefs are _____ held.
3. _____ _____ can be described as a series of differing attitudes held by various national groups.
4. The United States is a(n) _____-oriented culture, unlike the collectivist culture of the former communist countries.
5. Discrimination is the result of the actions of someone who is prejudiced. True or false?
6. When people migrate, they lose interest in their homeland. True or false?
7. In some Middle Eastern countries women still have few legal rights. True or false?
8. It is important for managers to explain to employees:
   (a) the way things are done.
   (b) why things are done the way they are.
   (c) expectations of employees.
   (d) all of the above.
9. Different cultures have different attitudes toward:
   (a) achievement.
   (b) time.
   (c) bribes.
   (d) all of the above.
10. Many people operate within two or three cultures. True or false?
11. If you are working with someone from Japan, only the Japanese worker is dealing with issues of diversity. True or false?

Applying This Chapter

1. You are sent to London for a meeting where you get lost and are twenty minutes late. The executives you are meeting with are very angry that you are late. Why are they angry?

2. You are the manager of a large IT department and you hire five people from Calcutta, India. What do you do to prepare for your new employees?

3. You work in a marketing department with three people who are over sixty years old. What are the advantages, in general, of older employees?

4. You work in a restaurant that has employees from seven different nations. The majority of the employees, however, are from the United States and a large number shun the international workers. What do you do to help the situation?

YOU TRY IT

Merging Cultures

You are the CEO of a large oil company that just merged with several Middle Eastern companies. You are in charge of the cultural change for the entire organization. Write a paper on what you think the challenges will be in terms of clashes of cultural attributes for this merger.

Changing Cultures

You work for an automobile manufacturer that was just bought out by the Japanese. Write a paper on the changes you expect will be made in the organizational culture and why. What are some ways a Japanese CEO will differ from an American CEO?

12

ETHICS AND OFFICE POLITICS
Setting an Example

Starting Point

Go to www.wiley.com/college/nelson to assess your knowledge of ethics and office politics.
Determine where you need to concentrate your effort.

What You'll Learn in This Chapter

▲ How to define ethics
▲ What a code of ethics consists of
▲ How to evaluate your political environment
▲ How to read the hidden meanings behind corporate communications
▲ How to manage your managers
▲ Why it is important to document business transactions

After Studying This Chapter, You'll Be Able To

▲ Create a code of ethics
▲ Assess who the key players are in an organization and determine their role
▲ Create an accurate organization chart
▲ Assess the real meaning behind corporate communications
▲ Manage your managers and their expectations
▲ Document important business transactions, meetings, and achievements

INTRODUCTION

Ethics and office politics are very powerful forces in any organization. **Ethics** is the framework of values that employees use to guide their behavior. You've seen the devastation that poor ethical standards can lead to—witness the string of business failures attributed to less than sterling ethics in more than a few large, seemingly upstanding businesses. Today, more than ever, managers are expected to model ethical behavior and to ensure that their employees follow in their footsteps—and to purge the organization of employees who refuse to align their own standards with that of their employer.

At its best, **office politics** means the relationships that you develop with your coworkers—both up and down the chain of command—that allow you to get tasks done, to be informed about the latest goings-on in the business, and to form a personal network of business associates for support throughout your career. Office politics help ensure that everyone works in the best interests of the organization and their coworkers. At its worst, office politics can degenerate into a competition, where employees concentrate their efforts on trying to increase their personal power at the expense of other employees—and their organizations.

This chapter is about building an ethical organization, determining the nature and boundaries of your political environment, understanding the unspoken side of office communication, unearthing the unwritten rules of your organization, and, in the worst-case scenario, becoming adept at defending yourself against political attack.

12.1 Defining Ethics

With an endless parade of business scandals—overstated revenues, mistaken earnings, and misplaced decimals—hitting the daily news, rocking the stock market, and shaking the foundations of the global economic system, you often wonder whether those in charge know the difference between right and wrong. Or, if they do know the difference, whether they really care.

Of course, the reality is that many business leaders do know the difference between right and wrong, despite appearances to the contrary. Now more than ever, businesses and the leaders who run them are trying to do the right thing, not just because the right thing is politically correct, but also because it's good for the bottom line. Ethics are in—and that's good for all of us.

Do you know what ethics are? Ethics are standards of beliefs and values that guide conduct, behavior, and activities; in other words, ethics are a way of thinking that provides boundaries for our actions. Ethics are simply doing the right thing. And, not just *talking* about doing the right thing, but really *doing* it!

Although each of you comes to a job with your own sense of ethical values—based on your own upbringing and your own life experiences—organizations and leaders for which you work are responsible for setting clear ethical standards.

When you have high ethical standards on the job, you generally exhibit some or all of the following personal qualities and behaviors:

- ▲ Honesty
- ▲ Integrity
- ▲ Impartiality
- ▲ Fairness
- ▲ Loyalty
- ▲ Dedication
- ▲ Responsibility
- ▲ Accountability

Ethical behavior starts with you. As a manager, you're a leader in your organization, and you set an example—both for other managers, and for the many workers who are watching your every move. When others see you behaving unethically, you're sending the message loud and clear that ethics don't matter. The result? Ethics won't matter to them, either.

However, when you behave ethically, others follow your example and behave ethically, too. And, if you practice ethical conduct, it also reinforces and perhaps improves your own ethical standards. As managers, we have a responsibility to try to define, live up to, and improve our own set of personal ethics.

We all make ethical choices on the job every day—how do you make yours? According to Trainingscape, you have six keys to make better ethical choices:

- ▲ **E—Evaluate** circumstances through the appropriate filters (filters include culture, laws, policies, circumstances, relationships, politics, perceptions, emotions, values, biases, and religion).
- ▲ **T—Treat** people and issues fairly within the established boundaries. Fair doesn't always mean equal.
- ▲ **H—Hesitate** before making critical decisions.
- ▲ **I—Inform** those affected of the standard or decision that has been set or made.
- ▲ **C—Create** an environment of consistency for yourself and your working group.
- ▲ **S—Seek** counsel when you have any doubt (but from those who are honest and whom you respect).

12.1.1 Creating a Code of Ethics

Although most people have a pretty good idea about what kinds of behavior are ethical and what kinds of behavior aren't, ethics are—to some degree—subjective and a matter of interpretation to the individual employee. One worker may, for

> ## FOR EXAMPLE
>
> ### Enron
>
> The bankruptcy of Enron, a Houston-based energy company, was due to one of the largest systemic ethical lapses in recent years. Not only did executives at Enron act unethically, those organizations that supported Enron such as banks and financial analysts were complicit in their support of Enron and acted unethically as well. For example, financial analysts overvalued the stock and listed it as a "buy" just days before its collapse. It is now believed that these analysts were co-opted by banks like JPMorgan Chase and Citigroup who pressured rating agencies to delay their downgrade of Enron stock so Enron could find a buyer.
>
> One of the tragedies of the Enron story was the fact that Enron employees were continually told to buy as much Enron stock as possible for their 401k plan. As the troubles at Enron began, top executives sold their stock while they kept telling employees to buy. Many employees lost their life savings when the stock went to pennies per share.[1]

example, think that making unlimited personal phone calls from the office is okay, whereas another worker may consider that to be inappropriate.

So, what's the solution to ethics that vary from person to person in an organization? By creating and implementing a **code of ethics,** a document that explicitly states your organization's ethical expectations clearly and unambiguously, you avoid misunderstandings. A code of ethics isn't a substitute for company policies and procedures; the code complements them. Instead of leaving your employees' definition of ethics on the job to chance—or someone's upbringing—you clearly spell out that stealing, sharing trade secrets, sexually harassing a coworker, and other unethical behavior are unacceptable and may be grounds for dismissal. And, when you require your employees to read and sign a copy acknowledging their acceptance of the code, then your employees can't very well claim that they didn't know what you expected of them.

Four key areas form the foundation of a good code of ethics:

▲ Compliance with internal policies and procedures
▲ Compliance with external laws and regulations
▲ Direction from organizational values
▲ Direction from individual values

Of course, a code of ethics isn't worth the paper it's printed on if it doesn't address some very specific issues, as well as the more generic ones listed previously. The following are some of the most common issues addressed by typical codes of ethics:

▲ Equal opportunity

▲ Sexual harassment

▲ Diversity

▲ Privacy and confidentiality

▲ Conflicts of interest

▲ Gifts and gratuities

▲ Employee health and safety

In addition to working within an organization, a well-crafted code of ethics can be a powerful tool for publicizing your company's standards and values to people outside your organization, including vendors, clients, customers, investors, potential job applicants, the media, and the public at large. Your code of ethics tells others that you value ethical behavior and that it guides the way you and your employees do business.

Of course, simply having a code of ethics isn't enough. You and your employees must also live it. Even the world's best code of ethics does you no good if you file it away and never use it.

What's in a comprehensive code of ethics? According to the Ethics Resource Center Web site, a comprehensive code of ethics has seven parts.[2] These parts include:

1. **Memorable title.** Examples include Price Waterhouse's *The Way We Do Business* and the World Bank Group's *Living Our Values*.

2. **Leadership letter.** A cover letter that briefly outlines the content of the code of ethics and clearly demonstrates commitment from the very top of the organization to ethical principles of behavior.

3. **Table of contents.** The main parts within the code, listed by page number.

4. **Introduction-prologue.** Explains why the code is important, the scope of the code, and to whom it applies.

5. **Statement of core values.** The organization lists and describes its primary values in detail.

6. **Code provisions.** This part is the meat of the code, the organization's position on a wide variety of issues including such topics as sexual harassment, privacy, conflicts of interest, gratuities, and so forth.

7. **Information and resources.** Places that employees can go for further information or for specific advice or counsel.

12.1.2 A Sample Code of Ethics

Because of the nature of the public trust that they are charged with, government workers have long been held to a higher standard of ethical behavior than those in private industry. Here is the Code of Ethics for Government Service, adopted by the U.S. Congress on July 11, 1958 (and still just as valid today).

Any person in government service should:

1. Put loyalty to the highest moral principals and to country above loyalty to Government persons, party, or department.

2. Uphold the Constitution, laws, and legal regulations of the United States and of all governments therein and never be a party to their evasion.

3. Give a full day's labor for a full day's pay; giving to the performance of his duties his earnest effort and best thought.

4. Seek to find and employ more efficient and economical ways of getting tasks accomplished.

5. Never discriminate unfairly by the dispensing of special favors or privileges to anyone, whether for remuneration or not; and never accept for himself or his family, favors or benefits under circumstances which might be construed by reasonable persons as influencing the performance of his governmental duties.

6. Make no private promises of any kind binding upon the duties of office, since a Government employee has no private word, which can be binding on public duty.

7. Engage in no business with the Government, either directly or indirectly, which is inconsistent with the conscientious performance of his governmental duties.

8. Never use any information coming to him confidentially in the performance of governmental duties as a means for making private profit.

9. Expose corruption wherever discovered.

10. Uphold these principles, ever conscious that public office is a public trust.

SELF-CHECK

1. How does a **code of ethics** resolve disputes between employees as to what is acceptable behavior and what is not?

2. Name two common issues addressed by typical codes of ethics.

3. Name and define three sections of a comprehensive code of ethics.

12.2 Evaluating Your Political Environment

How political is your office or workplace? As a manager, having your finger on the political pulse of the organization is particularly important. Otherwise, the next time you're in a management meeting, you may blurt out, "Why is it so difficult to get an employment requisition through human resources? You'd think it was their money!" only to find out that the owner's daughter-in-law heads the human resources department.

With just a little bit of advance information and forethought, you could have approached this issue much more tactfully than you did. Getting in touch with your political environment can help you be more effective, and it can help your department and your employees have a greater impact within the organization.

Asking insightful questions of your coworkers is one of the best ways to assess your organization's political environment. Such questions show you to be the polite, mature, and ambitious employee that you are, and the questions are a sure sign of your well-developed political instincts. Why don't you give these questions a try?

▲ "What's the best way to get a nonbudget item approved?"
▲ "How can I get a product from the warehouse that my client needs today when I don't have time to do the paperwork?"
▲ "Can I do anything else for you before I go home for the day?"

Although asking politically savvy questions gives you an initial indication of the political lay of the land in your organization, you can do more to assess the political environment. Watch out for the following signs while you're getting a sense for how your organization really works:

▲ **Find out how others who seem to be effective get tasks done.** How much time do they spend preparing before sending through a formal request for a budget increase? Which items do they delegate and to whose subordinates? When you find people who are particularly effective at getting tasks done in your organization's political environment, model their behavior.

▲ **Observe how others are rewarded for the jobs they do.** Does management swiftly and enthusiastically give warm and personal rewards in a sincere manner to make it clear what behavior is considered important? Is credit given to everyone who helped make a project successful, or does only the manager get his or her picture in the company newsletter? By observing your company's rewards, you can tell what behavior is expected of employees in your organization. Practice this behavior.

▲ **Observe how others are disciplined for the jobs they do.** Does your management come down hard on employees for relatively small mistakes? Are employees criticized in public or in front of coworkers? Is everyone held accountable for decisions, actions, and mistakes even if they had no prior involvement? Such behavior on the part of management indicates that it doesn't encourage risk taking. If your management doesn't encourage risk taking, make your political style outwardly reserved as you work behind the scenes.

▲ **Consider how formal the people in the organization are.** When you are in a staff meeting, for example, you definitely show poor form if you blurt out, "That's a dumb idea. Why would we even consider doing such a thing?" Instead, buffer and finesse your opinions like so: "That's an interesting possibility. Could we explore the pros and cons of implementing such a possibility?" The degree of formality you find in your company indicates how you need to act to conform to the expectations of others.

12.2.1 Identifying Key Players

Now that you've discovered that you work in a political environment, you need to determine who the key players are. Why? Because they are the individuals who can help make your department more effective and who can provide positive role models to you and your employees.

Key players are those politically astute individuals who make things happen in an organization. You can identify them by their tendency to make instant decisions without having to refer people "upstairs," their use of the latest corporate slang, such as Six Sigma, and their affinity for always speaking up in meetings if only to ask "What's our objective here?"

Sometimes influential people don't hold influential positions. For example, Jack, as the department head's assistant, may initially appear to be nothing more than a gofer. However, you may later find out that Jack is responsible for scheduling all his boss's appointments, setting agendas for department meetings, and vetoing actions on his own authority. Jack is an informal leader in the organization and, because you can't get to your boss without going through Jack, you know that Jack has much more power in the organization than his title may indicate.

All the following factors are indicators that can help you identify the key players in your organization:

▲ Which employees are sought for advice in your organization?

▲ Which employees are considered by others to be indispensable?

▲ Whose office is located closest to those of the organization's top management and whose are located miles away?

▲ Who eats lunch with the president, the vice presidents, and other members of the upper management team?

As you figure out who the key players in your organization are, you start to notice that they have different office personalities. Use the following categories to help you figure out how to work with the different personality types of your organization's key players. Do you recognize any of these players in your organization?

▲ **Movers and shakers:** These individuals usually far exceed the boundaries of their office positions. For example, you may find a mover and shaker in charge of purchasing, helping negotiate a merger. Someone in charge of the physical plant may have the power to designate a wing of the building to the group of his or her choosing. Nonpolitical individuals, on the other hand, tend to be bogged down by responsibilities—such as getting their own work done.

▲ **Corporate citizens:** These employees are diligent, hardworking, company-loving individuals who seek slow but steady, long-term advancement through dedication and hard work. Corporate citizens are great resources for getting information and advice about the organization. You can count on them for help and support, especially if your ideas seem to be in the best interest of the organization.

▲ **The town gossip:** These employees always seem to know what's going on in the organization—usually before those individuals who are actually affected by the news know it. Assume that anything you say to them will get back to the person about whom you say it. Therefore, always speak well of your bosses coworkers when you are in the presence of town gossips.

▲ **Firefighters:** These individuals relish stepping into a potential problem with great fanfare at the last conceivable moment to save a project, client, deadline, or whatever. Keep them well informed of your activities so that you aren't the subject of the next "fire."

▲ **The vetoer:** This person in your organization has the authority to kill your best ideas and ambitions with a simple comment such as "We tried that and it didn't work." In response to any new ideas that you may have, the favorite line of a vetoer is "If your idea is so good, then why aren't we already doing it?" The best way to deal with vetoers is to keep them out of your decision loop. Try to find other individuals who can get your ideas approved or rework the idea until you hit upon an approach that satisfies the vetoer.

▲ **Techies:** Every organization has technically competent workers who legitimately have a high value of their own opinions. Experts can take charge of a situation without taking over. Get to know your experts well—you can trust their judgments and opinions.

▲ **Whiners:** A few employees are never satisfied with whatever is done for them. Associating with them inevitably leads to a pessimistic outlook, which is not easily turned around. Or worse, your boss may think that you're a whiner, too. In addition, pessimistic people tend to be promoted less often than optimists. Be an optimist: your optimism makes a big difference in your career and in your life.

12.2.2 Redrawing Your Organization Chart

Your company's organization chart may be useful for determining who's who in the formal organization, but it really has no bearing on who's who in the informal political organization. What you need is the real organization chart. Figure 12-1 illustrates a typical official organization chart.

Figure 12-1

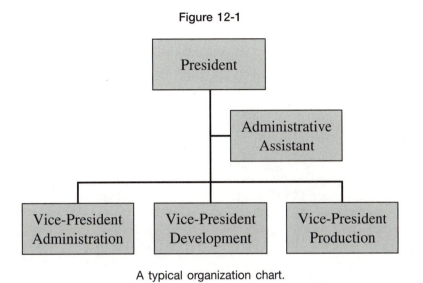

A typical organization chart.

Start by finding your organization's official organization chart—the one that looks like a big pyramid. Now, from your impressions and observations, start outlining the real relationships in your organization in your mind. Begin with the key players whom you've already identified. Indicate their relative power by level and relationships by approximation. Use the following questions as a guideline:

▲ **Whom do these influential people associate with?** Draw the associations on your chart and connect them with solid lines. Also connect friends and relatives.

▲ **Who makes up the office cliques?** Be sure that all members are connected, because talking to one is like talking to them all.

▲ **Who are the office gossips?** Use dotted lines to represent communication without influence and solid lines for communication with influence.

▲ **Who's your competition?** Circle those employees likely to be considered for your next promotion. Target them for special attention.

▲ **Who's left off the chart?** Don't forget about these individuals. The way that today's organizations seem to change every other day, someone who is off the chart on Friday may be on the chart on Monday. Always maintain positive relationships with all your coworkers and never burn bridges between you and others within and throughout the company. Otherwise, you may find yourself left off the chart someday.

The result of this exercise is a chart of who really has political power in your organization and who doesn't. Figure 12-2 shows how the organization really

Figure 12-2

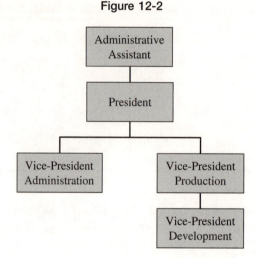

How the organization really works.

SELF-CHECK

1. Why is it important to be politically savvy in the office environment?

2. Before you speak up in a meeting, it's a good idea to have an understanding of how formal your colleagues are. True or false?

3. These employees are diligent, hardworking, company-loving individuals who seek slow but steady, long-term advancement through dedication and hard work.

   (a) Corporate citizens

   (b) Movers and shakers

   (c) Firefighters

   (d) Whiners

works. Update your organization chart as you find out more information about people. Take note of any behavior that gives away a relationship—such as your boss cutting off a coworker in midsentence—and factor this observation into your overall political analysis. Of course, understand that you may be wrong. You can't possibly know the inner power relationships of every department. Sometimes, individuals who seem to have power may have far less of it than people who have discovered how to exhibit their power more quietly.

12.3 Scrutinizing Communication: What's Real and What's Not?

One of the best ways to determine how well you fit into an organization is to see how well you communicate. But, deciphering the real meaning of communication in an organization takes some practice. So how do you determine the real meaning of words in your organization? You can best get to the underlying meanings by observing behavior, reading between the lines, and, when necessary, knowing how to obtain sensitive information.

One way to decipher the real meaning of communication is to pay close attention to the corresponding behavior of the communicator. The values and priorities (that is, the ethics) of others tend to come through more clearly in what they do rather than in what they say.

So, for example, if your manager repeatedly says he is trying to get approval for a raise for you, look at what actions he has taken toward that end. Did he make a call to his boss or hold a meeting? Did he submit the necessary paperwork or establish a deadline to accomplish this goal? If the answers to these questions are no, or if he is continually waiting to hear, the action is probably going nowhere fast. To counter this situation, try to get higher up on your boss's list of priorities by suggesting actions that he can take to get you your raise. You may find that you need to do some or all of the footwork yourself. Alternatively, your manager's actions may indicate that your boss is not a power player in the organization. If that's the case, then make a point to attract the attention of the power players in your organization who can help you get the raise you deserve.

12.3.1 Reading between the Lines

In business, don't take the written word at face value. Probe to find out the real reasons behind what is written. For example, here's a typical notice in a company newsletter announcing the reorganization of several departments:

> *With the departure of J. R. McNeil, the Marketing Support and Customer Service department will now be a part of the Sales and Administration division under Elizabeth Olsen, acting vice president. The unit will eventually be moved under the direct supervision of the sales director, Tom Hutton.*

Such an announcement in the company newsletter may seem to be straightforward on the surface, but if you read between the lines, you may be able to conclude:

> *J. R. McNeil, who never did seem to get along with the director of sales, finally did something bad enough to justify getting fired. Tom Hutton apparently made a successful bid with the board of directors to add the area to his empire, probably because his sales were up 30 percent from*

FOR EXAMPLE

Resignations

Many companies force out people by telling them that they can either resign or quit. After the employees resign, then a corporate press release is issued detailing all the employee's accomplishments without mentioning the reason why they left the company. For example, Hewlett-Packard admitted in 2006 that it read employees' e-mails, listened to the private phone calls of employees and board members, and violated other laws in an effort to see who was leaking information to a reporter. Ann Baskins, the company lawyer, allegedly approved these practices. Just hours before she was to testify in front of Congress, she resigned from Hewlett-Packard. The press release quoted Mark Hurd, the CEO, as follows: "I want to thank Ann for 24 years of outstanding service and devotion to HP. She began her career here shortly after law school and worked her way up to serve as the company's top lawyer, earning along the way a reputation for hard work and integrity."[3]

last year. Elizabeth Olsen will be assigned as acting vice president for an interim period to do some of Tom's dirty work by clearing out some of the deadwood. Tom will thus start with a clean slate, 20 percent lower expenses, and an almost guaranteed increase in profits for his first year in the job. This all fits very nicely with Tom's personal strategy for advancement.

Announcements like these have been reworked dozens of times by so many people that they appear to be logical and valid when you initially read them. By reading between the lines, however, you can often determine what is really going on. Of course, you have to be careful not to jump to the wrong conclusions. McNeil may have simply gone on to better opportunities and the company has taken advantage of that event to reorganize. Make sure to validate your conclusions with others in the company to get the real story.

12.3.2 Probing for Information

In general, you can get ongoing information about your organization by being a trusted listener to as many people as possible. Show sincere interest in the affairs of others, and they'll talk about themselves openly. After they begin talking, you can shift the topic to work, work problems, and eventually more sensitive topics. Ask encouraging questions and volunteer information as necessary to keep the exchange equitable.

Even after you've developed such trusted relationships, you need to know how to probe to uncover the facts about rumors, decisions, and hidden agendas. Start by adhering to the following guidelines:

▲ Have at least three ways of obtaining the information.

▲ Check the information through two sources.

▲ Promise anonymity whenever possible.

▲ Generally know the answers to the questions you ask.

▲ Be casual and nonthreatening in your approach.

▲ Assume that the initial answer is superficial.

▲ Ask the same question in different ways.

▲ Be receptive to whatever information you're given.

One more thing: If you find yourself in an organization rife with political intrigue, where you're always looking over your shoulder and are worried when the next rumor is going to be about you, seriously consider changing jobs! Although every organization has its share of politics, spending too much time worrying about it is certainly counterproductive, and it can't be good for your well-being.

SELF-CHECK

1. It is ideal to have at least _____ sources of information and to check your story with _____ sources.

2. Official corporate communications often do not tell the complete story. True or false?

3. You should not volunteer information to others in exchange for information. True or false?

12.4 Uncovering the Unwritten Rules of Organizational Politics

Every organization has rules that are never written down and seldom discussed. Such unwritten rules pertaining to the expectations and behavior of employees in the organization can play a major role in your success or failure. Because unwritten rules aren't explicit, you have to piece them together by observation, insightful questioning, or simply through trial and error.

12.4.1 Interpreting the Company Policy Manual

Even when written in black and white, an organization's policies are rarely what they appear to be. Most policies came about as a directive from the top to solve a particular problem. For example, if the company employed a single employee who preferred to wear gaudy jewelry, the individual could be confronted in a two- to three-minute discussion that would probably settle the matter. What is more often the case, however, is that management appoints a task force to develop a dress code and company plan for personal hygiene. Even after the policy is enacted, the targeted individual is likely to be oblivious to any perceived problem and may even wholeheartedly endorse the new code "for all those who need it"—that is, seemingly everyone except her.

A similar explanation can be made for most policies, and you should be alert to the following ways in which some employees try to skirt their responsibilities:

▲ Refer to the policy only when it clearly supports exactly what they want to do.

▲ Always assume that a policy that doesn't support what they want was intended for others.

▲ Claim an inability to equitably enforce policies they don't like by citing a rumored abuse or possible misinterpretation.

▲ When a conflict arises about policy implementation, argue that the policy is too specific (for general application) or too general (for specific circumstances).

▲ Argue that all policies should be considered flexible guidelines.

The point is that sometimes policies don't work. Your job is to recognize that some policies don't work and to try to change those policies. For example, if you want to give your employees the flexibility to set their own work schedules, but company policy prohibits that, do whatever you can to get management to sign off on a new policy that accomplishes your goal.

Never underestimate the power of the unwritten rules of organizational politics. In many companies, the unwritten rules carry just as much importance, if not more, than the written rules contained in the company's policy manuals.

The more individuals you have as friends in an organization, the better off you are. If you haven't already done so, start cultivating friends in your immediate work group and then extend your efforts to making contacts and developing friendships in other parts of the organization. The more favorably your coworkers view you, the greater your chances of becoming their manager in the future. Cultivate their support by seeking advice or by offering assistance.

Build a network by routinely helping new employees who enter your organization. As they join, be the person who takes them aside to explain how the organization really works. As the new employees establish themselves and move on to other jobs in other parts of the organization, you have a well-entrenched network for obtaining information and assistance.

Knowing others throughout the organization can be invaluable for clarifying rumors, obtaining information, and indirectly feeding information back to others. An astute manager maintains a large number of diverse contacts throughout the organization, all on friendly terms. The following are excellent ways to enlarge your network:

▲ **Walk around:** Those managers who walk the halls tend to be better known than those managers who don't. Return telephone and e-mail messages in person whenever possible. Not only do you have the opportunity for one-on-one communication with the individual who left you the message, but also you can stop in to see everyone else you know along the way.

▲ **Play company sports or games:** You can meet employees from a wide range of functions and locations by joining a company sports league. Whether bowling, golf, or softball is your cup of tea, surely something catches your fancy. If you prefer, start or join a lunchtime bridge or chess group.

▲ **Join committees:** Whether the committee has been formed to address employee security or simply to determine who cleans out the refrigerator in the employee lounge, take part. You get to meet new people in an informal and relaxed setting.

12.4.2 Helping Others Get What They Want

A fundamental, unwritten rule of office politics is: Getting what you want is easier when you give others what they want. Win the assistance of others by showing them what they stand to gain by helping you. When a benefit isn't readily apparent, create or allude to one that may occur if they offer to help. Such benefits can include:

▲ **A favor returned in kind:** Surely, you can provide some kind of favor to your counterparts in exchange for their assistance. Lunch or the temporary loan of an employee is always a popular option.

▲ **Information:** Don't forget: Information is power. You may find that many of your coworkers crave the latest and greatest information in an organization. Perhaps you can be the one to give it to them.

▲ **Money:** Perhaps you have a little extra money in your equipment budget that you can allocate to someone's project in exchange for that person's help.

▲ **A recommendation:** The higher-ups trust your judgment. Your willingness to recommend a coworker for promotion to a higher position or for recognition for extraordinary performance is a valuable commodity. The right words to the right people can make all the difference to someone's success in an organization.

This is not to suggest that you do anything unethical or illegal. When you provide these kinds of benefits to others in your organization, make sure that you are within your company's rules and policies. And, as a side benefit, you may actually find satisfaction in giving. Don't violate your personal set of ethics or company policy to get ahead.

12.4.3 Not Partying at Company Parties

Social affairs are a serious time for those employees seeking to advance within a company. Social events offer one of the few times when everyone in the company is supposed to be on equal footing. Don't believe it. Although social functions provide those managers at the top a chance to show that they're regular people and give those employees below a chance to ask questions and laugh at their bosses' jokes, they are also a time to be extremely cautious.

Beware of whom you talk to and, of course, what you say. Social functions, such as holiday parties and company picnics, are neither the time nor the place to sink your career by making some injudicious comment or by making a fool of yourself. Managing most social encounters involves art and skill, especially those encounters that involve coworkers. Proper poise begins with proper mingling techniques. Use these techniques at your next company party:

▲ Use the middle of the room to intercept individuals that you especially want to speak with. As an alternative strategy for getting their attention, watch the hors d'oeuvres table or the punch bowl. Go for refills when the person you are seeking does so.

▲ Keep discussions loose and light and avoid discussing work topics with anyone other than your boss. Try to move on before the person you're speaking to runs out of topics to discuss and is overcome with a blank expression. Don't fawn or brownnose. These behaviors are more likely to lose respect for you than to gain it.

▲ Leave the social function only after the departure of the highest-ranking company official. If you're forced to leave before, let him or her know why.

FOR EXAMPLE

Alcohol and Employees

Companies that serve alcohol at parties or dinners can be held liable for actions of employees who become intoxicated. For example, if an employee drives while intoxicated and gets into an accident, the victim and the employee can sue the company. For this reason, when you are out with employees do not buy them or serve them alcohol.

12.4.4 Managing Your Manager

Successful managers know the importance of managing not just their employees, but their manager as well. The idea is to encourage your manager to do what most directly benefits you and your staff. The following tried-and-true techniques for manager management have evolved through the ages:

▲ **Keep your manager informed of your successes:** "That last sale puts me over quota for the month."

▲ **Support your manager in meetings:** "Gadsby is right on this. We really do have to consider the implications of this change on our customers."

▲ **Praise your manager publicly:** "Ms. Gadsby is probably the best manager I have ever worked for."

Although a well-controlled relationship with your manager is important, you need connections to those above your manager, too. A key relationship to develop is with your manager's manager—an individual who is likely to have a very big influence on your future career.

Volunteer for an assignment that happens to be a pet project of your manager's boss. If you do a good job, you'll more than likely be asked to do another project. If you don't have an opportunity like a pet project, try to find an area of common interest with your manager's boss. Bring up the topic in casual conversation and agree to meet later to discuss it in more detail. But be careful not to press your boss too hard. You don't want to appear overly anxious or like you're stalking your boss.

12.4.5 Working with a Mentor

A **mentor** is an individual—usually higher up in the organization—who provides advice and helps guide your progress. Mentors are necessary because they can offer you important career advice, as well as become your advocate in higher levels of the organization—the levels that you don't have direct access to.

Make sure the person whom you select as your mentor (or who selects you, as is more often the case) has organizational clout and is vocal about touting your merits. If possible, get the support of several powerful people throughout the organization. Sponsorships (your relationships with your mentors) develop informally over an extended period of time.

Seek out a mentor by finding an occasion to ask for advice. If you find the advice extremely helpful, frequently seek more advice from the same person. Initially, ask for advice related to your work, but as time goes on, you can ask for advice about business in general and your career advancement specifically. Proceed slowly, or your intentions may be suspect. Always display tact and discretion in your approach to your mentor:

▲ **The wrong approach:** "Mr. Fairmont, I've been thinking. In the marketing department, a lot of bad rumors have been going around about you and Suzy. I could try to squelch some of them if I see something in it for me. You know: You take care of me, and I take care of you. What do you say?"

▲ **The right approach:** "Here's that special report you asked for, Ms. Smith. Correlating customer color preferences with the size of orders in the Eastern region was fascinating. You seem to be one of the forward-looking people in this organization."

Similar to having a mentor is being a loyal follower of an exceptional performer within the organization. Finding good people to trust can be difficult, so if you're trustworthy, you're likely to become a valued associate of a bright peer. As that person rises quickly through the organization, he or she can bring you along. However, whenever possible, hitch your wagon to more than one star: You never know when a star may fall and leave you all alone in the stardust.

SELF-CHECK

1. What are three techniques you can use to manage your manager?
2. Why is it important to have a **mentor**?
3. How would it help you to join committees at work?
4. You can let your guard down at social functions. True or false?

12.5 Protecting Yourself

Inevitably, you may find yourself on the receiving end of someone else's political aspirations. Astute managers take precautions to protect themselves—and their employees—against the political maneuverings of others. These precautions can also help if your own strategies go wrong. What can you do to protect yourself?

12.5.1 Documenting for Protection

Document the progress of your department's projects and activities, especially when expected changes in plans or temporary setbacks affect your project. Documenting the changes or setbacks gives you an accurate record of your projects' history and ensures that individuals who don't have your best interest at heart don't forget (or inappropriately use them against you). The form of the documentation can vary, but the following are most common:

> ## FOR EXAMPLE
>
> ### Keep Your E-mails
>
> It is best to keep all e-mails relating to a project or a disagreement with a co-worker, employee, or boss. If you ever need to retrace the steps of a disastrous outcome, then you have the e-mails to back up your side of the story. In addition, if someone is asking you to do something that you feel is unethical an e-mail can be proof that you can take to the department of human resources.

▲ Confirmation memos
▲ Activity reports
▲ Project folders
▲ Correspondence files
▲ Notes
▲ E-mails

12.5.2 Making Promises

Avoid making promises or firm commitments for your employees when you don't want to or you can't follow through. Don't offer a deadline, final price, or guarantee of action or quality unless you're sure you can meet it. When you make promises that you can't fulfill, you risk injuring your own reputation when deliveries are late, or costs are higher than expected. If you find yourself forced to make promises when you aren't certain you can meet them, consider taking one of the following actions:

▲ **Hedge:** If forced to make a firm commitment to an action that you're not sure you can meet, hedge your promise as much as possible by building in extra time, staff, money, or other qualifier.

▲ **Buffer time estimates:** If you're forced to make a time commitment that may be unrealistic, buffer the estimate (add extra time to what you think you really need) to give yourself room to maneuver. If your employees deliver early, they'll be heroes.

▲ **Extend deadlines:** As deadlines approach, bring any problems you or your staff encounter—even the most basic ones—to the attention of the person who requested that you do the project. Keeping people informed prevents them from being surprised if you need to extend your deadlines.

12.5.3 Publicizing Success

To get the maximum credit for the efforts of you and your staff, be sure to publicize your department's successes. To ensure that credit is given where credit is due, do the following:

▲ **Advertise your department's successes.** Routinely send copies of successfully completed projects and letters of praise for every member of your staff to your manager and to your manager's boss.

▲ **Use surrogates.** Call on your friends in the organization to help publicize your achievements and those of your employees. Be generous in highlighting your employees' achievements. If you highlight your own achievements at the expense of your hardworking employees, you appear tactless and boastful.

▲ **Be visible.** Make a name for yourself in the organization. The best way to do that is to perform at a level that separates you from the rest of the pack. Work harder, work smarter, and respond better to the needs of the organization and your customers, and you'll be noticed!

SELF-CHECK

1. What is one way you can manage others' expectations of you throughout an important project?
2. Name two ways you can hedge a commitment to a deadline or project?
3. Why is it important to advertise your department's successes?

SUMMARY

Conducting your business relationships in an ethical manner is really only a matter of following the Golden Rule, "treat others as you would want to be treated." In this chapter, you have defined ethics and you have examined a sample code of ethics. In addition, you have learned what sections should be in every code of ethics.

Besides examining ethics, you have assessed what is meant by office politics. You have learned how to identify the key players in your office, how to determine what their relationships are, and how to create an organization chart that truly represents reality. In addition, you have evaluated the hidden meanings behind corporate communications, assessed how to manage your manager and expectations, and learned why it is important to document business transactions.

KEY TERMS

Code of ethics	A document that explicitly states your organization's ethical expectations.
Ethics	Standards of beliefs and values that guide conduct, behavior, and activities.
Mentor	An individual—usually higher up in the organization—who provides advice and helps guide your progress
Office politics	The relationships that you develop with your coworkers—both up and down the chain of command—that allow you to get tasks done, to be informed about the latest goings-on in the business, and to form a personal network of business associates for support throughout your career.

ASSESS YOUR UNDERSTANDING

Go to www.wiley.com/college/nelson to evaluate your knowledge of ethics and office politics.

Measure your learning by comparing pre-test and post-test results.

Summary Questions

1. _____ are usually higher-ups in the organization who can offer advice.

2. If you are forced to make a commitment to a project that you think is unrealistic, the best approach you can take is:

    (a) just nod and agree that it will be done and work all hours to make it happen.

    (b) say that it absolutely cannot be done.

    (c) hedge and say if you have the right amount of time, resources, and money it can be done.

    (d) agree that it will be done, knowing that it is an impossible task that will not be completed.

3. You should always strictly adhere to the company's policy manual. True or false?

4. One way to make policies in regard to sexual discrimination is by addressing the issue in a(n) _____ ____ _____.

5. _____ relish stepping into a potential problem with great fanfare at the last conceivable moment to save a project, client, deadline, or whatever.

6. Those managers who walk the halls tend to be better known than those managers who don't. True or false?

7. If you want credit for a completed project, you should:

    (a) ask your CEO to make an announcement touting your success.

    (b) advertise the success of the department yourself.

    (c) wait until your review and then submit a letter outlining your success to your manager.

    (d) ask your manager to make an announcement touting your success.

8. _____ _____ _____ usually far exceed the boundaries of their office positions.

9. Getting what you want is easier if:

    (a) you buddy up to the CEO.

    (b) you help others get what they want.

    (c) you party with employees and managers after hours.

    (d) you automatically agree to all your manager's requests.

10. When someone asks you to do something unethical, you should _____ it and go to the human resources department.

Applying This Chapter

1. You work for a small marketing group. Every day, one of your employees takes an hour to make personal, long-distance phone calls on the company phone. Do you consider this to be unethical? Why or why not? Would it be ethical for you to listen in on the phone calls? Why or why not?

2. You are the newly appointed director of inside sales for a telephone company. At your last company, a much smaller company, you were able to easily get what you needed by asking. How do you determine how your new company operates?

3. You work in a pharmaceutical company. You just received a memo that the work on the drug you are researching needs to be stopped due to "budget constraints." How can you find out if this is the real reason why your project is being abruptly ended?

4. You are the director of human resources for a hospital that employees one thousand people. You have joined the committee that plans the Christmas party. What do you recommend in terms of serving alcohol?

5. You work in the IT department of a consulting firm and your department has not met its deadlines to finish two important projects in the past. What can you do differently this time to ensure that your manager will not be surprised if your department does not meet the deadlines again?

6. You are a consulting firm and your department just landed three clients that the consulting firm has been pursuing for two years. Write down three ways in which you can advertise your success.

YOU TRY IT

Code of Ethics

You are the CEO of a successful consulting firm. You deal with clients and their private information every day. You also bill clients on an hourly basis, which can sometimes lead to abuse. Think about the ways you can best serve the clients, and how you would treat them in an ethical manner. Write a code of ethics for the consulting firm.

Organization Chart

You are a partner of a small accounting firm with ten employees. You have a CEO, a president, a vice presi-dent, three partners (one is you), three analysts, and a secretary. Create an official organization chart for this company. After you do this, you learn that the secretary is the CEO's daughter and two of the analysts are his sons. In addition, the vice president of the company is the president's wife. Now create an organization chart that reflects this reality.

274

13

WORKING WITH UNIONS
Supervising Union Employees

Starting Point

Go to www.wiley.com/college/nelson to assess your knowledge of working with unions.
Determine where you need to concentrate your effort.

What You'll Learn in This Chapter

▲ How the U.S. government shapes the union-management framework through laws and their interpretation
▲ The typical structures of local unions, national unions, and multiunion organizations
▲ Understand why employees join unions
▲ The steps taken in the union organization process
▲ The management challenges associated with being unionized

After Studying This Chapter, You'll Be Able To

▲ Assess and identify illegal management and union activities as defined by the National Labor Relations Act (NLRA)
▲ Evaluate grievance procedures
▲ Assess the provisions of a union contract
▲ Assess actions that a manager can take to provide a positive work environment

INTRODUCTION

As a supervisor, you may find yourself in an industry that works with unions. A **union** is an organization of workers formed for the purpose of advancing its members' interests with respect to wages, benefits, hours of work, and other conditions of employment.

Although the size and power of the U.S. labor movement has changed in recent years, labor unions remain a powerful political and economic force, particularly in highly industrialized regions and within industries that have a high percentage of unionized workers. The electric utility, manufacturing, trucking, telecommunications, and aerospace industries, and the government are, for example, highly unionized.

It is the supervisors' responsibility to maintain positive employee relations, whether their employees are represented by a union or not. However, if a union exists, managers find that their roles change because both unions and management must comply with the new rules that emerge based on the union–management framework. Some changes are mandated by law, whereas others come from written agreements between the union and management officials. Some businesses try to avoid unions altogether due to the constraints that a unionized workforce puts on an organization.

In this chapter, you'll learn why employees join unions, the laws that govern unions, and how unions are organized. You will also assess the management challenges that come with working with unions and how you can overcome these challenges.

13.1 The Governing Laws of Unions

Unions were established and are governed by different laws. We will discuss the history and implications of each.

13.1.1 The National Labor Relations Act

The **National Labor Relations Act (NLRA),** also known as the Wagner Act, was signed into law by Congress in 1935 during the Great Depression. This law was intended to minimize the disruption of interstate commerce caused by strikes, which at times erupted into violent confrontations as workers trying to form unions fought with the police and the private security forces defending the interests of antiunion companies. Prior to the NLRA becoming law, employers had been free to spy on, interrogate, discipline, discharge, and blacklist union members.

This law gives employees the right to join labor unions without employer interference. It allows employees to form labor organizations and to bargain with management about wages, hours, and other working conditions. Congress also created the **National Labor Relations Board (NLRB)** to enforce this right. The

NLRB ensures that employers don't take part in **unfair labor practices,** such as discouraging or preventing unions, that might discourage employees from organizing or that might prevent workers from negotiating a union contract.

13.1.2 The Taft-Hartley Act

Although most unions did not abuse their power after the NRLA was passed, some did, so Congress passed the Labor Management Relations Act (LMRA) in 1947. This law is more often referred to as the **Taft-Hartley Act,** and it amended the NLRA passed earlier by prohibiting unfair labor practices by unions. The LMRA makes it illegal for unions to force employees to join them, and it outlaws picketing and strikes under certain circumstances.

13.1.3 Right-to-Work Laws

The Taft-Hartley Act also allows the individual states the right to pass **right-to-work laws,** which ensure that new employees are not required to join an already established union as a condition of retaining their jobs. States without such laws are known as **non-right-to-work states,** and employees in these states may be required to join the union and pay union dues if the collective bargaining agreement between the employer and the union requires all new employees to do so. If the collective bargaining agreement does not contain such provisions, a new employee will not be required to be a member of a union or pay it monies as a condition of employment. See Figure 13-1 for a complete breakdown of what states are right-to-work and what states are union. Because state laws often change, you should check the most recent edition of that state's laws.

SELF-CHECK

1. What law was intended to limit disruption caused by strikes?

   (a) Taft-Hartley Act

   (b) Right-to-work law

   (c) Forced unionism law

   (d) National Labor Relations Act (NLRA)

2. The _____ Act allows the individual states the right to pass right-to-work laws.

3. Workers in states without right-to-work laws may be forced to join _____.

Figure 13-1

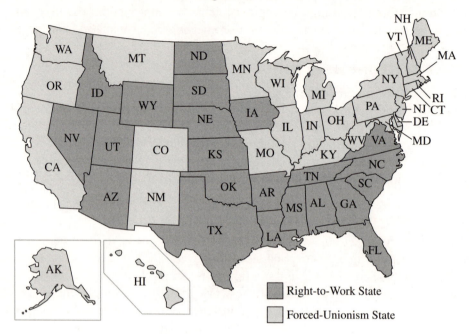

Right-to-Work State

Forced-Unionism State

Right-to-work states and forced unionism states.

13.2 Working with Different Types of Unions

Unions can be categorized into three types; local, national, and multiunion organizations.

13.2.1 Local Unions

For supervisors, **local unions** are probably the most important part of the union structure. They provide the local members, the revenue, and the power behind the entire union movement. The organizational structure of a local union would most likely include a president, a secretary-treasurer, a business agent, a grievance committee, and a bargaining committee. The steward is the first level in the union hierarchy and is normally elected by the workers to help employees present their problems to management. The union steward may also represent the first step in the **grievance process** should an employee or the union feel that some element of the union contract has been violated. Grievance procedures are normally outlined in the union contract, and they may vary from operation to operation, but they often follow a step-by-step procedure such as the following:

Step 1: The employee with the complaint meets with the supervisor and the union steward to discuss the grievance. Most grievances are resolved at this step.

Step 2: If the grievance is not settled, there is a conference between the union steward, the employee, and the supervisor's boss or another manager such as a human resources manager in a larger operation.

Step 3: If the grievance continues to be unsettled, representatives from top management at the operation and top union officials try to settle it.

Step 4: If still unsettled, the grievance is given to a neutral third party such as an **arbitrator** or mediator. A **mediator** listens to both sides and suggests ways to resolve the grievance but has no authority to force either side to accept any of the proposed terms. In arbitration, both parties must agree, in advance of the actual arbitration, that the decision given by the arbitrator will be final and binding.[1]

13.2.2 National Unions

Most local unions are chartered by larger associations called **national unions,** which organize and help the locals. National unions provide their locals with legal assistance and expert advice, and help them with negotiations, training of local officials, and handling grievances. Locals must share their dues with their national union, and they must obey its constitution and bylaws.

FOR EXAMPLE

Unionizing the Hospitality Industry

One of the largest and best-known hospitality industry labor unions is the Hotel Employees and Restaurant Employees International Union (HERE). In 2004, HERE merged with the Union of Needletrades, Textiles, and Industrial Employees (UNITE), and the combined union, now known as UNITE HERE, represents over 440,000 active members throughout the United States and Canada. This labor union represents workers in hotels, casinos, food service operations, airport concessions, and restaurants. For example, UNITE HERE includes employers such as Walt Disney and the Hilton Hotel Corporation. UNITE HERE includes one of the fastest-growing private-sector local unions in the United States—Local 226 in Las Vegas, which has increased its membership from 10,000 members in 1987 to 50,000 members today through an effective organizing program.[2]

13.2.3 Multiunion Associations

Several national unions joined together to form **multiunion associations** as social problems began to affect them. The **American Federation of Labor and Congress of Industrial Organizations (AFL-CIO)** is the most prominent multiunion association; it was formed when the American Federation of Labor and the Congress of Industrial Organizations merged. It is not a union in and of itself; rather, it is an association of unions. Its membership is composed of affiliated national unions. While most major unions in the United States are members of the AFL-CIO, its two biggest and most powerful unions, the International Brotherhood of Teamsters and the Service Employees International Union, chose to break away from the AFL-CIO in 2005 to start their own multiunion association known as the Change to Win Coalition. Five other unions soon followed, including UNITE HERE. Although the AFL-CIO still claims union membership consisting of everyone from airline pilots to letter carriers, from screenwriters to theatrical stage employees, and the organization dwarfs these new start-up multiunion associations, when comparing overall membership numbers, the Change to Win Coalition of unions now represents over 5.4 million members, many of whom are hospitality-industry related.

SELF-CHECK

1. The _____ is the first level in the union hierarchy and is normally elected by the workers to help employees present their problems to management.
2. What is the first step in the **grievance process**?
3. The **AFL-CIO** is the most prominent **multiunion association**. True or false?

13.3 Working with Unions

The first step in working with unions is to understand them. The key to understanding unions is knowing why employees join unions. Once you, as a manager, understand the reasons why employees join unions, then you can easily assess how unions organize, how they work, and the management challenges in dealing with unions.

13.3.1 Why Employees Join Unions

Employees typically join unions because they feel that management is not being responsive to the issues they've raised relating to their job satisfaction. These issues may include wages, benefits, job security, seniority issues, unfair treatment by supervisors, the physical work environment, and whether or not the company offers a career path or upward mobility. In short, most employees within an organization tend to join unions when their concerns about their working conditions are ignored by upper management. Most business owners and managers try to avoid unionization so that they can maintain lower labor costs by paying their employees lower wages and achieve greater management flexibility in the day-to-day operations of their facilities. It is important to note that unions certainly do not mean the end of an organization's success or the end of sound management practices. Although many successful businesses include employees who are members of one or more unions, they continue to perform well financially. Perhaps the key to avoiding the unionization of your business employees is to pay your staff competitive wages and salaries and to provide a positive work climate so they have no reason to join a union.

13.3.2 The Union Organization Process

Unions do not just walk in to your operation and take over; there is a well-established legal process that must take place in order for a union to organize the workers. The steps and guidelines are outlined in the NLRA and overseen by the NLRB to ensure the union adheres to the prescribed guidelines. Your employees may contact a union, or union organizers may contact your employees. Employees who initiate contact with the union will normally be given **union authorization cards** to pass out to coworkers. These cards, when signed by 30 percent of the employees in the organization, authorize the union to represent the employees during negotiations. If and when 30 percent of the employees sign authorization cards, the NLRB has a hearing and will generally set a date for the union election. If the majority of ballots cast are in favor of the union, the union becomes the bargaining agent on behalf of the employees, and management is required by law to bargain in good faith.

The NLRA prohibits employers from retaliating against employees who may be involved in union organization activities.

13.3.3 The Union Contract

Like any other contract, the **collective bargaining agreement,** or union contract, is a legal, binding document. Once both the representatives of the union and the company agree to the proposed terms and conditions, the contract is signed and cannot be changed except during previously agreed-upon renegotiation periods,

FOR EXAMPLE

Employers May Not Retaliate

The NLRB and a federal appeals court recently awarded a Kentucky nurse $400,000 after a six-year battle over her firing from a hospital. The hospital company had contended that she was dismissed because she flushed a heart patient's intravenous line with saline solution without approval from a doctor. The court determined that the hospital illegally fired her because of her union organization activities.[3] The court ordered the hospital company to pay the nurse lost wages and her legal expenses, and it ordered that she be reinstated to her position with full benefits.

usually after three or more years have passed. Management and the union do not necessarily have to agree on each and every term or condition included in the contract, but the law requires that each party bargain in good faith.

Clearly, the union will stress matters it sees as most beneficial to its members, and management will work hard to retain as much control and flexibility over business operations as possible. A union contract typically contains terms and conditions that affect some or all of the following areas:

▲ Wages, salaries, and employee benefits
▲ Holidays and vacations
▲ Overtime pay, sick days, leaves of absence, and personal days
▲ Seniority matters
▲ Training and new employee orientation
▲ Grievance procedures
▲ Disciplinary issues and probationary periods for new hires
▲ Employee performance evaluations, promotions, and transfers
▲ Union dues
▲ Whether new employees are required to join the union and pay dues (in a non-right-to-work state)
▲ Layoffs and other reductions in the workforce

As the union–management relationship matures, each of the points listed is typically defined in greater detail.

13.3.4 Management Challenges When Working with Unions

In addition to the increased labor costs and reduced flexibility in day-to-day decision making brought about by the unionization of their employees, managers and supervisors will often encounter other challenges when their employees belong to a union. Once a union and a collective bargaining agreement are in place at a particular operation, the dynamic in the workplace changes, and routines and procedures that were once commonplace may no longer be allowed. Examples of such challenges include the following:

▲ Promotions, rewards, and who gets overtime may now be based on seniority.
▲ Rewards and recognitions may no longer be based on merit or achievement.
▲ Managers must deal with the union steward instead of directly with the employee on matters outlined in the union contract.
▲ Both management and the union compete for the employee's loyalty.

Effective managers and supervisors realize that most employees in the organization will have no interest in joining a union if the organization pays competitive wages and salaries and if management works hard to provide a positive work environment. Most employees want to feel like the work they do matters and that they contribute to the overall success of the organization. One of the best ways a manager can be responsive to employees' needs is to get to know the employees and understand their likes and dislikes about their jobs and the work environment, as well as what motivates them to do their best. Other steps to take in creating a positive work environment include the following:

▲ Design jobs that are personally satisfying to workers
▲ Develop plans that maximize individual opportunities and minimize the possibility for layoffs
▲ Qualify potential employees and carefully match the right applicant with the right job position
▲ Establish meaningful objective standards to help measure and evaluate individual performance
▲ Train workers and managers to enable them to achieve expected levels of performance
▲ Provide ongoing training for all employees to ensure professional development and growth
▲ Evaluate and reward behavior on the basis of actual job performance

Failure to implement sound management and supervision practices provides the justification and the motivation for workers to be less productive, to seek the help of government regulatory agencies, or to form unions.

SELF-CHECK

1. Employees typically join unions because they believe _____ is not being responsive to the issues they've raised relating to their job satisfaction.

2. Employers cannot _____ against employees who join unions.

3. Unions are authorized when what percentage of employees agree to be unionized?

   (a) 75 percent

   (b) 50 percent

   (c) 30 percent

   (d) 20 percent

4. The union and management must agree on the union contract for it to be put into effect. True or false?

5. Being responsive to management's needs is one way management can prevent employees from organizing. True or false?

SUMMARY

Those who become managers and supervisors in metropolitan areas where unionization is strong will need to understand the do's and don'ts of working with unionized employees. Managers find that their roles change when their employees are unionized because both unions and management must comply with laws and regulations that govern the union–management framework.

Employees often seek union membership because they feel that management is not responsive to their needs. Management should work hard to create a positive work environment as a way of dissuading employees from joining unions. Your job, as a manager, is to create a positive work environment to ensure that employees do not feel the need to join unions.

In this chapter, you assessed why employees join unions, the laws that govern unions, how unions work, and how to overcome management challenges to working with unions.

KEY TERMS

AFL-CIO	The AFL-CIO is the most prominent multi-union association; it was formed when the

	American Federation of Labor and the Congress of Industrial Organizations merged.
Arbitrator	Two parties who have a disagreement may elect to enter into arbitration; the arbitrator's decision in the matter is final.
Collective bargaining agreement	An agreement or a contract that discloses the terms and conditions that shall apply to the union–management relationship within a particular operation.
Grievance process	A process by which an employee will lodge a complaint against management, usually a result of a breach of some term or condition provided for in the collective bargaining agreement between management and the union.
Local union	Usually part of a larger, national organization, the local union provides local members, revenue, and the power of the entire union movement.
Mediator	Two parties who have a disagreement may elect to enter into mediation. The mediator may make only recommendations; the mediator's decision is not final.
Multiunion association	When several national unions join together for a common cause. The AFL-CIO is an example of a multiunion association.
National union	The national labor organization affiliated with the local union.
National Labor Relations Act (NLRA)	A law enacted in 1935 that gives employees the right to join labor organizations or unions free of employer interference.
National Labor Relations Board (NLRB)	A U.S. government agency created to enforce that employers abide by the NLRA.
Non-right-to-work state	A state that has not enacted right-to-work laws.
Right-to-work laws	Laws that have been enacted by individual states to prohibit unions from requiring that new employees join the union and pay union dues. Some state's right-to-work laws may not apply in this matter if a collective bargaining agreement requires new employees to join the union. States that have enacted these laws are known as right-to-work states.

Taft-Hartley Act

Also known as the Labor Management Relations Act. It is a law that prohibits unions from engaging in unfair labor practices.

Unfair labor practices

Certain types of management conduct that might discourage employees from organizing or that might prevent workers from negotiating a union contract. NRLA outlines types of management conduct deemed illegal.

Union

An organization of workers formed for the purpose of advancing its members' interests with respect to their wages, benefits, work hours, and other conditions of employment.

Union authorization card

When a local union is attempting to organize a company, 30 percent of the company's employees must sign a union authorization card, which states that the employee agrees to have the union serve as his or her collective bargaining agent.

ASSESS YOUR UNDERSTANDING

Go to www.wiley.com/college/nelson to evaluate your knowledge of unions. *Measure your learning by comparing pre-test and post-test results.*

Summary Questions

1. A manager may fire any employee who attempts to organize a union. True or false?

2. Employees who are satisfied with their wages and salaries and who feel that management takes an interest in them and their professional future will often have little interest in joining a union. True or false?

3. When a business is unionized, the union is responsible for maintaining positive management–employee relations. True or false?

4. New employees at unionized companies in non-right-to-work states may *not* be required to join a union or pay union dues. True or false?

5. When a dispute goes into arbitration, the arbitrator's decision is:
   (a) binding.
   (b) nonbinding.
   (c) a strong recommendation but cannot be enforced.
   (d) none of the above.

6. Which of the following laws prohibits unfair labor practices by unions?
   (a) The National Labor Relations Board
   (b) The Department of Labor
   (c) The Taft-Hartley Act
   (d) The Wagner Act

7. According to the NLRA, all but which of the following are unfair labor practices?
   (a) Management cannot terminate an employee because he or she joined a union.
   (b) Management may not interfere with employees who desire to join a union.
   (c) Management does not have to bargain with the union if it does not want to do so.
   (d) Management may not discriminate against an employee for joining a union.

8. Which would most likely *not* be a term or condition found in a union contract?

    (a) Conditions applying to wages and salaries

    (b) Conditions applying to promotions

    (c) Conditions applying to meal breaks and rest breaks

    (d) Conditions applying to senior management salaries

Applying This Chapter

1. Assume that you are the manager of a hotel. List and briefly discuss some routine management activities that may not be possible if the establishment's employees were represented by a union. As the manager, how might you overcome these obstacles?

2. List and briefly discuss some of the reasons that employees may seek union representation. Then list and briefly discuss some activities that management can undertake in order to create a positive work climate. Compare and contrast the two lists, and write an action plan that addresses some of the employee concerns.

3. It has been argued that manufacturing companies would prefer to relocate their operations to a right-to-work state so that employees would not be required to join the union. Others have argued that this often has no bearing on a company's decision to relocate its operations from one state to another. What are your thoughts on this issue? Explain your answer in detail.

Interviewing Unionized Employees

If you live in an area with unionized businesses, interview an employee and a manager at one of these establishments, and compare and contrast their views on the reasons for unionization at the property. Do they feel that unionization has helped or hindered the employee–management relations process? If you do not live in an area where businesses are unionized, do some Web research and locate two articles regarding unionization in the industry you have chosen and present two opposing viewpoints. Be prepared to present your findings to the class.

Pros and Cons of Labor Unions

Write a position paper on labor unions in the United States. Are you in favor of labor unions and if so, why? Are you against labor unions? If so, why? Do you feel that labor unions will become more commonplace? What evidence is there to support your assumptions? Be prepared to share your ideas with the rest of the class.

14

BUDGETING AND ACCOUNTING
Working with Numbers

Starting Point

Go to www.wiley.com/college/nelson to assess your knowledge of budgeting and accounting.
Determine where you need to concentrate your effort.

What You'll Learn in This Chapter

▲ The definition and purpose of a budget
▲ How to stay within a budget
▲ The different types of assets and liabilities
▲ How to read common types of financial statements

After Studying This Chapter, You'll Be Able To

▲ Formulate a preliminary budget for your department or company
▲ Use different techniques to stay within a budget
▲ Apply the accounting equation to any company and determine its assets and liabilities
▲ Interpret common types of financial statements

INTRODUCTION

In any organization, money makes the world go around. No matter how great your department is, how exciting your products are, or what a swell bunch of workers you employ, you and your group are in big-time jeopardy if you don't have money. If profits are down and money is increasingly tight in your organization, you'd better take some actions to correct the situation. As a manager, you need to understand the basics of budgeting and accounting.

This chapter covers the importance of budgeting in an organization, as well as putting together a budget by using some of the professional tricks of the budget trade. It then introduces the survival basics of accounting. It isn't going to make you an accountant, but this chapter can help you understand balance sheets and cash flow. And don't forget: Although you may work for a governmental entity or nonprofit organization, and some of these concepts may not directly apply to you, you never know when you may find yourself in a new, private-sector job!

14.1 Exploring Budgets

A **budget** is an itemized forecast of an individual's or company's income and expenses expected for some period in the future. Budgets provide the baseline of expected performance against which managers measure actual performance. Accounting systems that generate reports to compare expected performance against actual performance provide financial information on an organization's actual performance. With this information, managers with budget responsibility act as physicians to assess the current financial health of their businesses.

When you receive the latest accounting report, it says that sales are too low compared to budget. What does that mean? As a responsible manager, you need to figure out why. Are prices too high? Maybe your sales force is having problems getting the product delivered to your customers quickly. Or perhaps your competition developed a product that is taking sales away from your product. Are labor costs exceeding your budget? Perhaps your employees are working too much overtime. Maybe a reduction in production quality has led to an increase in the amount of rework required. Or perhaps employee pay simply is too high.

Because change is highly prevalent in today's business, why should you bother having budgets? You go through all that work and then your budget is out-of-date the day after you finish it, right? Sure, planning becomes more difficult as the world changes all around you, but plan you must. Without a long-term plan and goals, your organization lacks focus and resources are wasted as employees wander aimlessly about. A budget isn't just an educated guess that reflects your long-term plans and allows you to act on them; it's a personal commitment about making a designated future happen. The best budgets are flexible, allowing for changes in different key assumptions, such as revenue results.

Experienced managers already know the importance of budgets. Budgets make plans happen. Through its interaction with lower-level managers during the budgeting process, upper management can have a tremendous impact on the direction that an organization and its employees take. Conversely, lower-level employees can also have a huge impact on the organization during the budgeting process by submitting budget requests to management for approval.

Budgets determine how many people you have on your staff and how much you pay them. Budgets determine the financial resources you have to improve your workplace or to buy necessary office equipment, such as computers and copiers. And budgets determine how much money you have available to support your efforts on projects. Furthermore, budgets allow you to use all that expensive spreadsheet software that the company bought last year.

But budgets also fulfill another important purpose: They provide a baseline against which you can measure your progress toward your goals. For example, if you're 50 percent of the way through your fiscal year but have actually spent 75 percent of your budgeted operating funds, then you have an immediate indication that a potential problem exists if you don't see any significant change in your expenditures. Either you've underbudgeted your expenses for the year, or you're overspending. Whenever budgeted performance and actual performance disagree, or are in **variance,** the job of the responsible manager is to ask why, and to then fix any problems that are found.

14.1.1 Using Different Budgets

Depending on your organization's size, the budgeting process may be quite simple or, alternatively, very complex. Regardless of an organization's size, you can budget most anything in it. Following are some examples:

- ▲ **Sales budget:** The sales budget is an estimate of the total number of products or services that will be sold in a given period. Determine the total revenues by multiplying the number of units by the price per unit.
- ▲ **Labor budget:** Labor budgets consist of the number and name of all the various positions in a company along with the salary or wages budgeted for each position.
- ▲ **Production budget:** The production budget takes the sales budget and its estimate of quantities of units to be sold and translates those figures into the cost of labor, material, and other expenses required to produce them.
- ▲ **Expense budget:** Expense budgets contain all the different expenses that a department may incur during the normal course of operations. You budget travel, training, office supplies, and more as expenses.

▲ **Capital budget:** This budget is a manager's plan to acquire **fixed assets** (anything your organization owns that has a long life) such as furniture, computers, facilities, physical plant, and so forth to support the operations of a business.

14.1.2 Creating a Budget

You have a right and a wrong way to do a budget. The wrong way is simply to make a photocopy of the last budget and submit it as your new budget. The right way is to gather information from as many sources as possible, review and check the information for accuracy, and then use your good judgment to guess what the future may bring. A budget is a **forecast**—a commitment to the future—and is only as good as the data that go into it and the good judgment that you bring to the process.

How do you actually put together a budget? Where does the information come from? With whom should you talk? The possibilities seem endless. However, experienced managers know that when you understand your costs of doing business—and where they come from—the budgeting process is actually quite simple. Review the basic steps in putting together a budget:

Step 1: **Closely review your budgeting documents and instructions.** Take a close look at the budgeting documents that you're working with and read any instructions that your accounting staff provides with them. Although your organization may have done something the same way for years, you never know when that procedure may change.

Step 2: **Meet with staff.** When you're starting the budget process, meet with your staff members to solicit their input. In some cases, you need the specific input of your employees to forecast accurately. For example, you may need to know how many trips your salespeople plan to make next year and where they plan to go. In other cases, you can simply ask for employee suggestions. One employee may ask you to include a pay increase in the next budget. Another may inform you that the current phone system is no longer adequate to meet the needs of employees and customers and that a new one should be budgeted. Whichever the case, your staff can provide you with very useful and important budget information.

Step 3: **Gather data.** Pull copies of previous budgets and accounting reports and then compare budgeted numbers to actual numbers. Were previous budgets overrun or underrun? By how much? If no historical data are available, find other sources of information that can help guide the development of figures for your budget. How much business do you plan to bring in during the next budget period, and what will it cost you to bring it in? Consider whether you need to hire more people, lease new facilities, or buy equipment or supplies. Furthermore, consider the possibility of large increases or decreases in sales or expenses and what effect they would have on your budget.

Step 4: **Apply your judgment.** Hard data and cold facts are very important in the budgeting process; they provide an unbiased, unemotional source of information on which to base your decisions. However, data and facts aren't everything—not by a long shot. Budgeting is part science and part art. Take the data and facts and then apply your own judgment to determine the most likely outcomes. When you're new to management, you have little experience on which to draw, so you have a natural tendency to rely more heavily on data. However, as you become more accomplished in management and budgeting, your personal experience and judgment come to the fore.

Step 5: **Run the numbers.** Depending on how your organization does business, either fill out your budget forms and send them to your budget folks for processing, or enter them in the budget model yourself. The result is a budget draft that you can review and modify before you finalize it. Don't worry if the draft is rough or is missing information. You'll have a chance to fill in the gaps soon enough.

Step 6: **Check results and run the budget again as necessary.** Check over your draft budget and see whether it still makes sense to you. Are you missing any anticipated sources of revenue or expenses? Are the numbers realistic? Do they make sense in a historical perspective? Are they too high or too low? Will you be able to support them when you present them to upper management? The fun part of budgeting is playing with your numbers and trying different scenarios and what-ifs. When you're satisfied with the results, sign off on your budget and turn it in.

14.1.3 Ensuring Your Budget Is Accurate

The accuracy of your budget hinges on two main factors: the quality of the data that you use to develop your budget and the quality of the judgment that you apply to the data you're working with. Although judgment is something that comes with experience, the quality of the data you use depends on where you get them. You can use three basic approaches to develop the data for building a budget:

1. **Build the data from scratch.** In the absence of historical data, when you're starting up a new business unit, or when you just want a fresh view, you want to develop your budgets based strictly on current estimates. In this process, widely known as **zero-based budgeting**, you

build your budget from scratch—determining the people, facilities, travel, advertising, and other resources that are required to support it. You then cost out each need, and the budget is complete. Perhaps not too surprisingly, the answer that comes out of building a budget from scratch is often quite different from one that results from using historical data.

2. **Use historical figures.** One of the easiest ways to develop data for your budget is to use the actual results from the preceding budget period. Although the past is not always an indication of the future—especially when an organization is undergoing significant change—using historical data can be very helpful in relatively stable organizations and it's interesting to see which numbers have gone up, and which have gone down.

3. **Use the combination approach.** Many managers use a combination of both preceding methods for determining which data to include in their budgets. To use this approach, gather historical data and compare the figures to the best estimates of what you think performing a particular function will cost. You then adjust historical data up or down, depending on your view of reality.

SELF-CHECK

1. The process of building a **budget** from scratch is ____ ____ ____.
2. Computers are **fixed assets.** True or false?
3. A **sales budget** includes estimates of costs of labor, materials, and other materials required to produce products. True or false?
4. One of the first things you should do when designing a budget is to meet with ____ and solicit their input.

FOR EXAMPLE

The Make-or-Buy Decision

One of the most common decisions made in business is whether to make—that is, build or perform with in-house staff—or buy goods and services that are necessary for the operation of a business. For example, say you decide that you need to assign a security guard to your reception area to ensure the safety of your clients. Do you hire someone new as an employee, or does

Continued

contracting with a company that specializes in providing security services make more sense?

When you consider such a decision, the first point to consider is the cost of each alternative to your firm. Say that in case A, you hire your security guard as a full-time employee for $6 an hour. In case B, a security services firm provides a guard for $8 an hour. On the surface, hiring a security guard as an employee seems to make the most sense. If the guard works 2000 hours a year, then in case A you spend $12,000 a year for your guard and in case B you spend $16,000 a year. By employing the guard yourself, you stand to save $4,000 a year. Right? Maybe not; here's why.

Case A: Hire in-house security guard
Hourly pay rate $6.00
Fringe benefits rate @ 35% $2.10
Overhead rate @ 50% $<u>3.00</u>
Total effective pay rate $11.10
Hours per year   × <u>2000</u>
Total annual labor cost $22,200
Annual liability insurance increase $4000
Uniforms/cleaning $1000
Miscellaneous equipment $<u>500</u>
Total annual cost $27,700
Case B: Contract with security firm
Hourly pay rate $8.00
Total effective pay rate $8.00
Hours per year   × $<u>2000</u>
Total annual cost $16,000

Instead of saving $4,000 per year by hiring an in-house security guard, you're actually going to spend almost $12,000 more each year because more costs are involved in hiring an in-house employee than just his or her hourly pay. You have to add all the fringe benefits, such as life insurance, medical and dental plans, and more, plus the employee's share of overhead—facilities, electricity, air conditioning, and so forth—to the basic wage rate to get a true picture of the cost of the employee to your organization. Furthermore, you need to purchase additional liability insurance, uniforms, uniform cleaning, and miscellaneous equipment such as a flashlight, Mace, and handcuffs.

On the other hand, when you contract with a security services firm, the firm bears the cost of fringe benefits, overhead, insurance, uniforms, and equipment. You simply pay the hourly fee and forget it. Furthermore, if the guard doesn't work out, you just make a phone call and a replacement is sent immediately. No messy employee terminations or unemployment benefits to worry about.

14.2 Working with Budgets

The budget game is a long-standing tradition in business and government. Managers who discover how to play the game prosper, as do the people who work for them. Managers who fail to find out how to play the game, and the employees who work for them, are doomed to always have to make do with insufficient resources, facilities, pay, and the other niceties of business life. If you're a manager, finding out how the game is played is definitely in your interest.

Generally, the goal of the budget game is to build in enough extra money to actually be able to get the job done. In the worst case, you'll have enough resources available to protect your employees and vital functions when the business goes south. In the best case, you'll have money left over after you pay all your necessary expenses. Either you can turn the money back into accounting with much fanfare and accept the accolades from the powers that be for your expert resource management skills, or you can apply the money to the purchase of some equipment or other department needs. Of course, if you work for the government, your goal is to spend every penny of your budgeted amount so that your budget won't be decreased in the following year.

You can play the budget game up front, when you develop the budget, or during the course of the budget period. The following sections tell you how to develop a solid budget.

14.2.1 Using Up-Front Budgets

Following are some of the games that the pros play when they develop budgets. Although these techniques are most appropriate for new or unstable departments or projects, you can use them when developing any budget.

▲ **Do some selective padding.** Simple, but effective. The idea is to pad your anticipated expenses so that your budget targets are easy to achieve. You end up looking like a hero when you come in underbudget, plus you get some extra money to play with at the end of the year. This situation is known as win-win.

▲ **Tie your budget request to your organization's values.** If you want to beef up your budget in a particular area, just pick one of your organization's values—for example, quality—and tie your request to it.

▲ **Create more requests than you need, and give them up as you have to.** When you draft your budget, build in items that are of relatively low priority to you overall. When your boss puts on the pressure to reduce your budget, give up the stuff you didn't really care so much about anyway. Doing so ensures that you get to keep the items that you really do want.

▲ **Shift the time frame.** Insist that the budget items are an investment in the company's future. The secret is to tie these investments to a big payoff down the road. "If we double our labor budget, we'll be able to attract the talent that we need to expand our operations."

▲ **Be prepared.** The best defense is a good offense. Know your budget numbers cold and be ready to justify each budget item in intimate detail. Don't rely on someone else to prepare for you—it can be your finest hour as a manager.

14.2.2 Staying within Budget

After your new department or project starts up, you need to closely monitor your budget to make sure that you don't exceed it. If your actual expenditures start to exceed your budget, you need to take quick and decisive action. Following are some of the ways that experienced managers make sure they stay on budget:

▲ **Freeze discretionary expenses.** Some expenses, such as labor, benefits, and electricity, are essential to an operation or project and can't be stopped without jeopardizing performance. Others, such as purchasing new carpeting, upgrading computer monitors, or traveling first class, are discretionary and can be postponed without jeopardizing performance. Freezing discretionary expenses is the quickest and least painful way to get your actual expenditures back in line with your budgeted expenditures.

▲ **Freeze hiring.** Although you may have budgeted new hires, you can save money by freezing the hiring of new employees. Not only do you save on the cost of hourly pay or salaries, but you also save on the costs of fringe benefits, such as medical care and overhead expenses like water, electricity, and janitorial services. And because you aren't messing with your current employees' pay or benefits, most everyone will be happy with your decision. Of course, some critical positions in your organization may need to be filled, budget problem notwithstanding. You can determine which positions have to be filled if they become vacant, and which other employees can cover.

▲ **Postpone products and projects.** The development and production phases of new products and projects can burn up a lot of money. By postponing the start-up and rollout of these new products and projects, you can get your budget back on track. Sometimes it only takes a few weeks or months to make a difference.

▲ **Stretch payments to suppliers.** Instead of paying right on time, you can stretch out your payments over a longer period of time. If you're going to go this route, it's generally best to work this out with your suppliers in advance.

▲ **Freeze wages and benefits contributions.** These kinds of savings directly affect your employees, and it's guaranteed that they aren't going

FOR EXAMPLE

General Motors and Ford

In 2006, after years of losing market share in the automobile industry, General Motors and Ford had to take a realistic look at their budgets. Both companies decided that they needed to do everything possible to lower their expenditures. Both companies ended up closing plants, laying off workers, and offering to buy some workers out of their contracts. In addition, they changed the structure of their health insurance plans for retirees.

to like it. Most employees are used to regular wage and benefits increases. Although increases aren't as generous as they were a decade ago, employees still consider them to be essential. However, if you have made cuts and still need to cut more, then you really don't have any choice but to freeze your employees' wages and benefits contributions (medical insurance, 401k matching, and so on) at their current levels.

▲ **Lay off employees and close facilities.** You are in business to make money, not to lose money. When sales aren't sufficient to support your expenses—even after enacting the cost-savings measures just mentioned—you must take drastic action. Action doesn't get much more drastic than laying off employees and closing facilities. However, if your budget is as far off as it must be if you reach this point, then cut you must.

Whether you're responsible for budgeting as a part of your managerial duties or not, you need to have a basic understanding of the process that your business goes through to account for the money it makes and the money it spends. The following section presents all the information that you need to know about accounting to achieve a basic level of comprehension.

SELF-CHECK

1. When possible, you should _____ your budget so you can cover unanticipated expenses.
2. Artwork for the office is an example of a(n) _____ expense.
3. One technique for increasing your budget in one area is to tie your budget request to your organization's values. True or false?
4. Stretching payments to suppliers is never an option when staying within budget. True or false?

14.3 Understanding the Basics of Accounting

The accounting system that takes up gigabytes of storage space on your company's network server is dependent on a few very basic assumptions. These assumptions determine how every dollar and cent that flows into and out of your organization is assigned, reported, and analyzed.

Some managers believe that they can skate by with little or no knowledge of accounting and finance. This attitude is a mistake. As a manager, you must be just as familiar with these accounting basics as are the employees who work in your accounting department. Not only does this knowledge help ensure that you understand and control your organization's financial destiny, but also if you're in command of the financial side of your business as well as the technical side, then you're also much more likely to survive the next round of corporate layoffs.

Daily events affect every business's financial position. A manager spends cash to buy a stapler and is reimbursed out of the petty cash fund. The company taps its bank line of credit to pay vendor invoices. Customers pay bills and those payments are deposited. Employees receive paychecks. Each of these financial transactions and many more has its place in the accounting equation.

The **accounting equation** states that an organization's assets are equal to its liabilities plus its owners' equity. The accounting equation looks like this:

$$\text{Assets} = \text{Liabilities} + \text{Owners' Equity}$$

This simple equation drives the very complex system of accounting that is used to track every financial transaction in a business, provide reports to managers for decision making, and provide financial results to owners, shareholders, lenders, the IRS, and other stakeholders.

So what exactly does each part of the accounting equation represent? Take a look at each part and what it comprises.

14.3.1 Assets

Assets are generally considered to be anything of value—primarily financial and economic resources—that a company owns. The most common forms of assets in a business include the following:

▲ **Cash:** This asset encompasses money in all its forms, including cash, checking accounts, money market funds, and marketable securities, such as stocks and bonds. Every business likes to have lots of cash.

▲ **Accounts receivable:** This asset represents the money that customers who buy goods and services on credit owe to your company. For example, if your business sells a box of floppy disks to another business and then bills the other business for the sale instead of demanding immediate payment in cash, this obligation becomes an account receivable until your customer pays it. Accounts receivable are nice to have unless the companies or individuals that owe you money skip town or decide to delay their payments for six months.

▲ **Inventory:** Inventory is the value of merchandise held by your business for sale, the finished goods that you have manufactured but have not yet sold, as well as the raw materials and work in process that are part of the manufacture of finished goods. Inventory usually becomes cash or an account receivable when sold. Inventory that sits around on a shelf forever isn't the best way to tie up your company's assets. Keeping your inventory moving all the time is much better, because you are generating sales.

▲ **Prepaid expenses:** Prepaid expenses represent goods and services that your firm has already paid for but not yet used. For example, your company may pay its annual liability insurance premium at the beginning of the year, before the insurance policy actually goes into effect. If the policy is canceled during the course of the year, then part of the premium is refunded to your business.

▲ **Equipment:** Equipment is the property—machinery, desks, computers, phones, and similar items—that your organization buys to carry out its operations. For example, if your company sells computer supplies to individuals and other businesses, you need to purchase shelves on which to store your inventory of computer supplies, forklifts to move it around, and phone systems on which to take orders from your customers. As equipment ages, it loses value. You account for this loss through **depreciation,** which spreads the original cost of a piece of equipment across its entire useful lifetime.

▲ **Real estate:** Real estate includes the land, buildings, and facilities that your organization owns or controls. Examples include office buildings, manufacturing plants, warehouses, sales offices, mills, farms, and other forms of real property.

Assets are divided into two major types:

▲ **Current assets** can be converted into cash within one year. Such assets are considered to be liquid. In the preceding list of assets, cash, accounts receivable, inventory, and prepaid expenses are considered current assets. Liquid assets are nice to have around when your business is in trouble and you need to raise cash quickly to make payroll or pay your vendors.

▲ **Fixed assets** require more than one year to convert to cash. In the preceding list of assets, equipment and real estate are classified as fixed assets. If your business gets into trouble and you need cash, fixed assets probably won't do you much good unless you can use them as collateral for a loan.

14.3.2 Liabilities

Liabilities are generally considered to be debts that you owe to others—individuals, other businesses, banks, and so on—outside the company. In essence, liabilities are the claims that outside individuals and organizations have against a business's assets.

The most common forms of business liabilities include the following:

▲ **Accounts payable:** Accounts payable are the obligations that your company owes to the individuals and organizations from which it purchases goods and services. For example, when you visit your local office supply store to buy a couple of pencils and bill the purchase to your company's account, this obligation becomes an account payable. You can conserve your company's cash in times of need by slowing down payments to your vendors and suppliers, although you have to be very careful not to jeopardize your credit in the process.

▲ **Notes payable:** Notes payable are the portion of loans made to your organization by individuals, financial institutions, or other organizations that are due to be paid back within one year. If, for example, your firm takes a ninety-day loan to increase its inventory of compact disks to satisfy a rapid increase in customer demand, the loan is considered a note payable.

▲ **Accrued expenses:** Accrued expenses are miscellaneous expenses that your company incurs but that aren't reimbursed. Examples include obligations for payroll, sick leave due to employees, taxes payable to the government, and interest due to lenders.

▲ **Bonds payable:** Some large companies issue bonds to raise money to finance expansion or achieve other goals. Bonds payable represent the money that a company owes to the individuals and organizations that purchase the bonds as an investment.

▲ **Mortgages payable:** When organizations purchase real estate, they often do so by incurring long-term loans known as mortgages. Mortgages differ from standard loans in that they're usually secured by the real estate that the mortgage finances. For example, if your company defaults in its payments on the mortgage used to purchase your office building, ownership of the office building reverts to the entity that originally issued the mortgage—usually a bank or investment group.

Like assets, liabilities are also divided into two major types:

▲ **Current liabilities** are repaid within one year. In the preceding list of liabilities, accounts payable, notes payable, and accrued expenses are considered current liabilities.

▲ **Long-term liabilities** are repaid in a period greater than one year. In the preceding list of liabilities, bonds payable and mortgages payable are both classified as long-term liabilities.

14.3.3 Owners' Equity

All businesses have owners. In some cases, the owners are a few individuals who founded the company. In other cases, the owners are the many thousands of individuals who buy the company's stock through public offerings. Owners' equity is the owners' share of the assets of a business after all liabilities have been paid.

The most common forms of owners' equity include the following:

▲ **Paid-in capital** is the investment—usually paid in cash—that the owners make in a business. For example, if your firm sells common stock to investors through a public offering, the money that your firm obtains through the sale of the stock is considered paid-in capital.

▲ **Retained earnings** are reinvested by a business and not paid out in dividends to shareholders. A certain amount of earnings are retained in hopes of increasing the firm's overall earnings and also to increase the dividends that are paid to owners.

14.3.4 Knowing Double-Entry Bookkeeping

Double-entry bookkeeping is the standard method of recording financial transactions that forms the basis of modern business accounting. Invented in 1494 by Luca Pacioli, a Franciscan monk, double-entry bookkeeping recognizes that every financial transaction results in a record of a receipt (also known as an asset) and a record of an expense (also known as a liability).

Consider this example: Your company buys $1,000 worth of computer compact discs (CDs) from a manufacturer to resell to your customers. Because your company has established an account with the CD manufacturer, the manufacturer bills you for the $1,000 instead of demanding immediate cash payment. Do you remember the accounting equation that we discuss earlier in this chapter? Here's the double-entry version of the accounting equation illustrating the $1,000 purchase of floppy disks to stock in your inventory:

Assets	=	Liabilities	+	Owners' equity
$1,000	=	$1,000	+	$0
(Inventory)		(Accounts payable)		

In this example, assets (inventory) increase by $1,000—the cost of purchasing the CDs to stock your shelves. At the same time, liabilities (accounts payable) also increase by $1,000. This increase represents the debt that you owe to your supplier of floppy disks. In this way, the accounting equation always stays balanced. Now, imagine the effect of the several hundreds or thousands of financial transactions that hit your accounting system on a daily, weekly, or monthly basis.

FOR EXAMPLE

The Sarbanes-Oxley Act

Numbers can be manipulated and were manipulated by several prominent companies including Enron, WorldCom, and Tyco in a series of accounting scandals that began in 2000. As a result, the U.S. Congress passed the Sarbanes-Oxley Act in 2002. The act consists of eleven provisions including:

▲ The creation of the Public Company Accounting Oversight Board (PCAOB).
▲ A requirement that public companies evaluate and disclose the effectiveness of their internal controls as they relate to financial reporting.
▲ Certification of financial reports by chief executive officers and chief financial officers.
▲ Auditor independence.
▲ Ban on most personal loans to any executive officer or director.
▲ Accelerated reporting of trades by insiders.
▲ Prohibition on insider trades during pension fund blackout periods.
▲ Enhanced penalties for violations of securities laws.
▲ Companies listed on the stock exchange must have fully independent audit committees that oversee the relationship between the company and its auditor.
▲ Additional disclosure.
▲ Employee protections for whistleblowers.

The Sarbanes-Oxley Act is considered to contain some of the most significant changes to United States securities laws since the New Deal in the 1930s.[1]

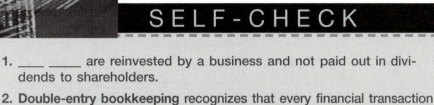

SELF-CHECK

1. _____ _____ are reinvested by a business and not paid out in dividends to shareholders.

2. **Double-entry bookkeeping** recognizes that every financial transaction results in a record of a(n) _____ and a record of a(n) _____.

3. Assets = Liabilities + Owners' Equity is commonly known as:

   (a) a liability equation.

   (b) double-entry bookkeeping.

   (c) an asset equation.

   (d) an accounting equation.

4. Bonds payable represent the money that a company owes to the individuals and organizations that purchase the bonds as an investment. True or false?

5. Mortgages payable are the portion of loans made to your organization by individuals, financial institutions, or other organizations that are due to be paid back within one year. True or false?

14.4 Identifying the Most Common Types of Financial Statements

An accounting system is nice to have, but the system is worthless unless it can produce data that are useful to managers, employees, lenders, vendors, owners, investors, and other individuals and firms that have a financial stake in your business—which means a lot of people.

Does it surprise you to hear that almost everyone wants to know the financial health of your business? Well, they do. Managers want to know so that they can identify and fix problems. Employees want to know because they want to work for a company that's in good financial health and that provides good pay, benefits, and job stability. Lenders and vendors need to know your company's financial health to decide whether to extend credit. And owners and investors want to know because this knowledge helps them determine whether their investment dollars are being used wisely or are instead being frittered away.

Accountants invented financial statements to be able to measure the financial health and performance of a company. **Financial statements** are nothing more than reports—intended for distribution to individuals outside the accounting department—that summarize the amounts of money contained within selected accounts or groups of accounts at a selected point or period of time. Each type of financial statement has a unique value to those people who use them, and different individuals may use some or all of an organization's financial statements during the normal course of business. The following sections review the financial statements that you're most likely to encounter during your career as a manager.

14.4.1 The Balance Sheet

The **balance sheet** is a report that illustrates the value of a company's assets, liabilities, and owners' equity—the company's financial position on a specific date. Think of it as a snapshot of the business. Although it can be prepared at any time, a balance sheet is usually prepared at the end of a definite accounting period—most often a year, quarter, or month. See Figure 14-1 for a sample balance sheet.

As you can see, the balance sheet provides values for every major component of the three parts of the accounting equation. By reviewing each item's value in the balance sheet, managers can identify potential problems and then take action to solve them.

14.4.2 The Income Statement

Many people want to see the bottom line. Did the company make money or lose money? In other words, what was its profit or loss? This job belongs to the income statement.

An **income statement** adds all the sources of a company's revenues and then subtracts all the sources of its expenses to determine its net income or net loss for a particular period of time. Whereas a balance sheet is a snapshot of an organization's financial status, an income statement is more like a movie. See Figure 14-2 for a sample income statement.

Let's look at what each of these terms mean in the sample income statement.

Revenues

Revenue is the value received by a company through the sale of goods, services, and other sources such as interest, rents, royalties, and so forth. To arrive at net sales, total sales of goods and services are offset by returns and allowances.

Expenses

Expenses are all the costs of doing business. For accounting purposes, expenses are divided into two major classifications:

▲ **Cost of goods sold:** For a firm that retails or wholesales merchandise to individuals or other companies, the **cost of goods sold** represents the cost of purchasing merchandise or inventory. By subtracting the cost of goods sold from revenue, you end up with the company's gross margin, also known as **gross profit.**

▲ **Operating expenses: Operating expenses** are all the other costs of doing business not already part of the cost of goods sold. Operating expenses are usually further subdivided into selling expenses, which include marketing,

Figure 14-1

Sample Balance Sheet	
	January 31, 2007
ASSETS	
CURRENT ASSETS	
Cash and cash equivalents	$458,000
Accounts receivable	$11,759,000
Inventory	$154,000
Prepaid expenses and other current assets	$283,000
Refundable income taxes	$165,000
TOTAL CURRENT ASSETS	$12,819,000
EQUIPMENT AND FURNITURE	
Equipment	$4,746,000
Furniture, fixtures, and improvements	$583,000
	$5,329,000
Allowance for depreciation and amortization	($2,760,000)
	$2,569,000
COMPUTER SOFTWARE COSTS, NET	$3,199,000
NET DEPOSITS AND OTHER	$260,000
	$18,847,000
LIABILITIES AND SHAREHOLDERS' EQUITY	
CURRENT LIABILITIES	
Notes payable to bank	$1,155,000
Accounts payable	$2,701,000
Accrued compensation and benefits	$2,065,000
Income taxes payable	$0
Deferred income taxes	$990,000
Current portion of long-term debt	$665,000
TOTAL CURRENT LIABILITIES	$7,576,000
LONG-TERM DEBT, less current portion	$864,000
DEFERRED RENT EXPENSE	$504,000
DEFERRED INCOME TAXES	$932,000
STOCKHOLDERS' EQUITY	
Common stock	$76,000
Additional paid-in capital	$803,000
Retained earnings	$8,092,000
	$8,971,000
	$18,847,000

A typical balance sheet.

Figure 14-2

| | Twelve months ended |
	January 31, 2007
REVENUES	
Gross sales	$58,248,000
Less: Returns	$1,089,000
Net Sales	$57,159,000
COST OF GOODS SOLD	
Beginning inventory	$4,874,000
Purchases	$38,453,000
Less: Purchase discounts	$1,586,000
Net purchases	$36,867,000
Cost of goods available for sale	$41,741,000
Less: Ending inventory	$6,887,000
Cost of Goods Sold	$34,854,000
GROSS PROFIT	$22,305,000
OPERATING EXPENSES	
Total selling expenses	$8,456,000
Total general expenses	$1,845,000
Total operating expenses	$10,301,000
Operating income	$12,004,000
Other income and expenses	
Interest expense (income)	$360,000
Total other income and expenses	$360,000
Income before taxes	$11,644,000
Less: Income taxes	$3,952,000
Net Income	$7,692,000
Average number of shares	$3,500,000
Earnings per share	$2.20

Sample Income Statement

A simple income statement.

advertising, product promotion, and the costs of operating stores, and general and administrative expenses, which are the actual administrative costs of running the business. General and administrative costs typically include salaries for accounting, data processing, and purchasing staff and the cost of corporate facilities including utilities, rent payments, and so on.

Net Income or Loss

The difference between revenues and expenses (after adjustment for interest income or expense and payment of income taxes) is a company's **net income** (profit) or net loss. Also commonly known as a company's bottom line, net income or loss is the cash you have on hand after you've paid all the bills, and it's the one number most often of interest to those people who want to assess the firm's financial health. Many corporate executives and managers have found themselves on the street when their companies' bottom lines dipped too far into the loss side of the equation.

14.4.3 The Cash-Flow Statement

Cash-flow statements show the movement of cash into and out of a business. When more cash is moving out of a business than is moving into the business for a prolonged period of time, the business may be in big trouble.

Cash is sort of like gasoline. Your car requires a plentiful supply of gasoline to run. If you run out of gas, your car is going to stop dead on the highway. One minute, you're going 65 miles an hour, and the next, you're going zero miles an hour. Similarly, if your company runs out of cash, the company is going to stop dead, too. Without cash to pay employees' salaries, vendors' invoices, lenders' loan payments, and so forth, operations quickly cease to exist.

▲ **Simple cash-flow statement:** The simple cash-flow statement arranges all items into one of two categories: cash inflows and cash outflows.

▲ **Operating cash-flow statement:** The operating cash-flow statement limits analysis of cash flows to only those items having to do with the operations of a business, and not its financing.

▲ **Priority cash-flow statement:** The priority cash-flow statement classifies cash inflows and outflows by specific groupings chosen by the manager or other individual who requests preparation of the statement.

USING FINANCIAL RATIOS TO ANALYZE YOUR BUSINESS

If you don't know exactly what you're looking for, analyzing a company's financial records can be quite a daunting task. Fortunately, over a period of many years, expert business financial analysts have developed ways to assess the comparing the ratios of certain key financial indicators to established standards and to other firms in the same industries.

Current ratio: This ratio is the capability of a company to pay its current liabilities out of its current assets. A ratio of 2 or more is generally considered good. Consider this example:

$$\text{Current ratio} = \text{Current assets} \div \text{Current liabilities}$$
$$= \$100 \text{ million} \div \$25 \text{ million}$$
$$= 4.00$$

Quick ratio: The quick ratio (also known as the *acid-test* ratio) is the same as the current ratio with the exception that inventory is subtracted from current assets. This ratio provides a much more rigorous test of a firm's capability to pay its current liabilities quickly than does the current ratio, because inventory can't be liquidated as rapidly as other current assets. A ratio of 1 or better is acceptable.

$$\text{Quick ratio} = (\text{Current assets} - \text{inventory}) \div \text{Current liabilities}$$
$$= (\$100 \text{ million} - \$10 \text{ million}) \div \$25 \text{ million}$$
$$= \$90 \text{ million} \div \$25 \text{ million}$$
$$= 3.60$$

Receivables turnover ratio: This ratio indicates the average time that it takes for a firm to convert its receivables into cash. A higher ratio indicates that customers are paying their bills quickly, which is good. A lower ratio reflects slow collections and a possible problem that management needs to address, which is bad. Your boss isn't going to like it.

$$\text{Receivables turnover ratio} = \text{Net sales} \div \text{Accounts receivable}$$
$$= \$50 \text{ million} \div \$5 \text{ million}$$
$$= 10.00$$

You can gain one more interesting piece of information quickly from the receivables turnover ratio. By dividing 365 days by the receivables turnover ratio, you get the average number of days that it takes your firm to turn over its accounts receivable, which is commonly known as the *average collection period*. The shorter the average collection period, the better the organization's situation is, and the better your job security is.

$$\text{Average collection period} = 365 \text{ days} \div \text{Receivables turnover ratio}$$
$$= 365 \text{ days} \div 10.00$$
$$= 36.5 \text{ days}$$

Debt-to-equity ratio: This ratio measures the extent to which the organization depends on loans from outside creditors versus resources provided by unfavorable because it indicates that the firm may have difficulty repaying its debts. And nobody—especially cranky bankers or vendors—wants to loan money to companies that have problems repaying their debts. A particularly low ratio indicates that management may be able to improve the company's profitability by increasing its debt.

$$\text{Debt-to-equity ratio} = \text{Total liabilities} \div \text{Owners' equity}$$
$$= \$50 \text{ million} \div \$150 \text{ million}$$
$$= 0.33 \text{ or } 33 \text{ percent}$$

Return on investment: Often known by its abbreviation, *ROI,* return on investment measures the capability of a company to earn profits for its owners. Don't forget: Profit is good and loss is bad. Because owners—shareholders and other investors—prefer to make money on their investments, they like an organization's ROI to be as high as possible.

$$\text{Return on investment} = \text{Net income} \div \text{Owners' equity}$$
$$= \$50 \text{ million} \div \$150 \text{ million}$$
$$= 0.33 \text{ or } 33 \text{ percent}$$

SELF-CHECK

1. The **balance sheet** is a report that illustrates the value of a company's assets, liabilities, and _____ _____—the company's financial position on a specific date.

2. An **income statement** adds all the sources of a company's _____ and subtracts all the sources of its expenses to determine its net income.

3. The operating **cash-flow statement** arranges all items into one of two categories: cash inflows and cash outflows. True or false?

4. Which statement classifies cash inflows and outflows by specific groupings chosen by the manager or other individual who requests preparation of the statement?

    (a) Operating cash flow statement

    (b) Income statement

    (c) Simple cash-flow statement

    (d) Priority cash-flow statement

SUMMARY

The corporate budget is often the key to getting the resources you need to perform your job and accomplish your goals. As a manager, you will need to create budgets, be able to understand budgets, and work with others on budgeting. During this chapter, you have assessed how to create a budget and how to use different techniques to stay within a budget. As a manager, you will also need to understand the basics of accounting and need to know how to read common types of financial statements. In this chapter, you have evaluated the accounting equation and how to apply it. In addition, you have read and evaluated different types of financial statements.

KEY TERMS

Accounting equation	Equation that states an organization's assets are equal to its liabilities plus its owners' equity. The accounting equation is commonly expressed as Assets = Liabilities + Owners' Equity.
Assets	Anything of value, primarily financial and economic resources, that a company owns.
Balance sheet	Report that illustrates the value of a company's assets, liabilities, and owners' equity—the company's financial position on a specific date.
Budget	An itemized forecast of an individual's or company's income and expenses expected for some period in the future.
Cash-flow statements	Financial statements that show the movement of cash in and out of a business.
Cost of goods sold	The cost to a business of purchasing merchandise or inventory that is intended for resale.
Current assets	Assets that can be converted into cash within one year.
Current liabilities	Liabilities that are repaid within one year. Examples include accounts payable, notes payable, and accrued expenses.
Depreciation	The process of spreading the original cost of a piece of equipment across its entire useful lifetime.
Double-entry bookkeeping	Standard method of recording financial transactions that forms the basis of modern business accounting.

Expenses	All the costs of doing business.
Financial statements	Reports that summarize the amounts of money contained within selected accounts or groups of accounts at a selected point or period of time.
Fixed asset	Anything a company owns that has a long life, such as furniture, computers, facilities, physical plants, that supports the operations of a business.
Forecast	A prediction of the financial future of a company.
Gross profit	Also known as gross margin; the amount of money a company makes minus the cost of goods sold.
Income statement	Report that adds all the sources of a company's revenues and then subtracts all the sources of its expenses to determine its net income or net loss for a particular period of time.
Liabilities	Debts that the company owes to others outside the company such as other businesses, banks, and individuals.
Long-term liabilities	Liabilities that are repaid in a period greater than one year. Examples include bonds payable and mortgages payable.
Net income	The cash a company has on hand after all bills are paid. This is also known as net loss or the bottom line.
Operating expenses	All costs of doing business with the exception of the cost of goods sold. Examples of operating expenses include property and equipment leasing and salaries.
Paid-in capital	The investment, usually paid in cash, that the owners make in a business.
Retained earnings	Earnings that are reinvested by a business and not paid out in dividends to shareholders.
Revenue	The value received by a company through the sale of goods, services, and other sources.
Variance	The difference between budgeted performance and actual performance.
Zero-based budgeting	The process of building a budget from scratch.

ASSESS YOUR UNDERSTANDING

Go to www.wiley.com/college/nelson to evaluate your knowledge of budgeting and accounting.
Measure your learning by comparing pre-test and post-test results.

Summary Questions

1. _____ occurs when there is a difference between budgeted performance and actual performance.
2. _____ data from previous years can help you create a budget.
3. A budget is a forecast, a commitment to the future. True or false?
4. One technique when budgeting is to create more requests than you need, and give them up as you have to. True or false?
5. Techniques to stay within budget include:
   (a) freezing hiring.
   (b) postponing products and projects.
   (c) freezing discretionary expenses.
   (d) all of the above.
6. This budget is a manager's plan to acquire fixed assets, such as furniture, computers, facilities, physical plant, and so forth to support the operations of a business.
   (a) Sales budget
   (b) Labor budget
   (c) Expense budget
   (d) Capital budget
7. The accounting equation is:
   (a) Revenues − Expenses = Profit.
   (b) Assets = Liabilities + Owners' Equity.
   (c) Assets = Liabilities − Owners' Equity.
   (d) Liabilities = Assets − Owner's Equity.
8. _____ _____ can be converted into cash in one year.
9. _____ _____ are the obligations that your company owes to the individuals and organizations from which it purchases goods and services.
10. A balance sheet adds all the sources of a company's revenues and then subtracts all the sources of its expenses to determine its net income or net loss for a particular period of time. True or false?
11. Salaries are an example of operating expenses. True or false?

Applying This Chapter

1. You are the director of IT for a manufacturing facility and you need to develop a new software program that does a better job of tracking orders. You could hire an IT company for a flat fee of $100,000 or hire an employee for $80,000 and make this his or her primary job. Which is the better solution financially and why?

2. You are the manager in a call center that is understaffed. Your staff works hard, but you receive so many phone calls that you cannot possibly answer them within an appropriate time frame. Fortunately, your boss has asked you to create the budget for your department this year. You put in extra money for a larger staff. How do you justify this to your boss?

3. You own a real estate firm. Unfortunately, the real estate market has had a downturn and the cash flow coming into the company has been severely reduced. You need to act fast to save your company. What are your options to stay within your budget?

4. You are the CEO of a hospital and you receive the income statement from the previous year. After examining it, you learn that your operating expenses were higher than your revenues. What are your options for lowering operating expenses?

5. You own a marketing company and you have two accountants who work for you. What kind of financial reports do you want to see on a regular basis and why?

YOU TRY IT

Creating a Budget

You decide to quit your job and open up a small real estate firm. You find offices to rent for $2,000 per month. You budget $3,000 for computers and office supplies. Think about what other expenses you will have and create a budget for the first year.

Cash-Flow Statement

As in the first example, you decide to quit your job and open a small real estate firm. You find offices to rent for $2,000 per month. You budget $3,000 for computers and office supplies. Think about what other expenses you will have and create a budget for the first year. Using that budget, determine how many sales you need to sell per month (at 7 percent commission) to make $2,000 more than your expenses per month.

Assets and Liabilities

Your school is a business. Think about it in terms of a business and write down a list of assets and liabilities that a typical school would have.

15

USING TECHNOLOGY
Gaining Competitive Advantage and Managing Employees

Starting Point

Go to www.wiley.com/college/nelson to assess your knowledge of using technology.
Determine where you need to concentrate your effort.

What You'll Learn in This Chapter

- ▲ The pros and cons of technology
- ▲ How to network your organization
- ▲ How to manage virtual employees
- ▲ How to manage different shifts of employees with the use of technology

After Studying This Chapter, You'll Be Able To

- ▲ Use technology to gain a competitive advantage in the marketplace
- ▲ Improve efficiency and productivity
- ▲ Write a technology plan
- ▲ Manage remote workers

INTRODUCTION

Technology has infiltrated our lives and made us more productive. Technology has also given us *virtual employees:* employees who spend the majority of their work hours away from established company offices and worksites; employees who are managed from a distance; employees who work a variety of shifts or differing starting and ending times; and employees who telecommute to the office from the comfort of their homes.

Of course, these changes haven't been easy for the managers who are required to implement them. For managers who are used to having employees close by—ready to instantly respond to the needs of customers and clients—managing off-site employees can be a little bit disconcerting.

In this chapter, you will assess this new kind of employee and how best to work with him or her. You will explore strategies for effectively managing far away employees, as well as those employees working differing shifts, and we take a look at the future of telecommuting. You will also evaluate how to harness information technology: technology used to create, store, exchange, and use information in its various forms. You will examine the technology edge, and consider how technology can help or hinder an organization. You will assess how technology can improve efficiency and productivity, and how to get the most out of it. Finally, you will use simple steps to create a technology plan.

15.1 Using Technology to Your Advantage

Computers and telecommunications technology have taken over business. Even the most defiant CEOs are finally taking the plunge and are wireless telephoning and surfing the Web in ever-increasing numbers. Information technology can give you and your business tremendous advantages and, as a manager, you must capitalize on them—before your competition does.

Before you can design and implement information technology in the most effective way, you first have to completely understand how your business works. What work is being done? Who's doing it? What do employees need to get their work done?

One way to know your business is to approach it as an outsider. Pretend you're a customer and see how your company's people and systems handle you. Do the same with your competitors to see how their people and systems handle you. What are the differences? What are the similarities? How can you improve your own organization using information technology as a result of what you've discovered?

15.1.2 Creating a Technology-Competitive Advantage

Few managers understand how technology can become a competitive advantage for their businesses. Although they may have vague notions of potential efficiency gains or increased productivity, they're clueless when dealing with specifics.

Information technology can create real and dramatic competitive advantages over other businesses in your markets, specifically by:

▲ Competing with large companies by marketing on a level playing field (the Internet)

▲ Helping build ongoing, loyal relationships with customers

▲ Connecting with strategic partners to speed up vital processes, such as product development and manufacturing

▲ Linking everyone in the company, as well as with necessary sources of information both inside and outside the organization

▲ Providing real-time information on pricing, products, and so forth to vendors, customers, and original equipment manufacturers (OEMs)

Now is the time to create advantages over your competition. Keep in mind that the company that *has* the most data doesn't win, but the company that *manages* that data best wins.

15.1.2 Developing a Plan

If you're serious about using information technology as an edge, you must have a technology plan. A **technology plan** is a plan for acquiring and deploying information technology. When you design one, remember the following points:

▲ **Don't buy technology just because it's the latest and greatest thing.** You always enjoy shopping for the latest technology. Unfortunately, just because an item is new doesn't mean that it's right for your business. Be sure that whatever technology you include in your plan makes sense for your business.

▲ **Plan for the right period of time.** Different kinds of businesses require different planning horizons: the time periods covered by their plans. If you're in a highly volatile market—wireless communications, for example—then your planning horizon may be only six months or so out. If you're in a stable market—say, a grocery chain—your planning horizon may extend three to five years into the future.

▲ **Make the planning process a team effort.** You're not the only one who's going to be impacted by all this new technology that you bring into your company. Make employees, customers, and vendors a part of your planning team.

▲ **Weigh the costs of upgrading your old system vs. going to a new system.** Every system eventually comes to the end of its useful life. Rather than continuing to patch up a system that's becoming increasingly expensive to maintain, start fresh. Run the numbers and see what alternative makes the most sense for your organization before you finalize your plans.

If you're a fan of technology and pretty knowledgeable in it, that's great—you have a head start on the process. But, if you're not, get help from people who are experts in information technology. Does your company have people who are knowledgeable? Can you hire a technician or technology consultant to fill in the gaps? Whatever you do, don't try it alone. Even if you're a full-fledged techno-geek, enlist others to help.

Many businesses buy bits and pieces of computer hardware, software, and other technology without considering the technology that they already have in place, and without looking very far into the future. Then, when they try to hook everything together, they're surprised that their thrown-together system doesn't work.

Managers who take the time to develop and implement technology plans aren't faced with this problem, and they aren't forced to spend far more money and time fixing the problems with their systems.

What? You've never put together a technology plan before? No problem—here's how the process works:

Step 1: Create the plan.

Step 2: Screen and select the vendors.

Step 3: Implement the plan.

Step 4: Monitor performance.

Technology is no longer an optional expense; technology is a strategic investment that can help push your company ahead of the competition. And every strategic investment requires a plan. In their book *eBusiness Technology Kit for Dummies,*[1] Kathleen Allen and Jon Weisner suggest that you take the following steps in developing your technology plan:

Step 1: Write down your organization's core values.

Step 2: Picture where you see your business ten years from now. Don't limit yourself.

Step 3: Set a major one-year goal for the company that is guided by your vision.

Step 4: List some strategies for achieving the goal.

FOR EXAMPLE

Technology Can Increase Productivity

Implementation of a computerized inventory-management system at Warren, Michigan–based Duramet Corporation—a manufacturer of powdered metal—helped the company double sales over a three-year period without hiring a single new salesperson.

Step 5: Brainstorm some tactics that can help you achieve your strategies.

Step 6: Identify technologies that support your strategies and tactics.

Gather your thoughts—and your employees' thoughts—and write them down. Create a concise document, perhaps no more than five to ten pages, that describes your information technology strategies as simply and exactly as possible. After you create your plan, implement it.

SELF-CHECK

1. What is a **technology plan**?
2. How can information technology give companies a competitive edge in the marketplace?
3. Different kinds of businesses require different _____ _____, the time periods covered by their plans.

15.2 Weighing the Benefits and Drawbacks of Technology

Think for a moment about the incredible progress of information technology just in your lifetime. With so many tools at your fingertips, can you believe that a little more than two decades ago, the personal computer had yet to be introduced commercially? Whereas word processing used to mean a typewriter and a lot of correction fluid or sheets of messy carbon paper, computers have revolutionized the way in which business people can manipulate text, graphics, and other elements in their reports and other documents. Wireless telephones, fax machines, the Internet, and other business technology essentials are all fairly recent innovations.

So, how can technology help your business? Information technology can have a positive impact in two very important ways:

▲ **By automating processes:** Not too many years ago, business processes were manual. For example, your organization's accounting and payroll department may have calculated payroll entirely by hand with the assistance of only a ten-key adding machine. What used to take hours, days, or weeks can now be accomplished in minutes. Other processes that are commonly automated are inventory tracking, customer service, call analysis, purchasing, and more.

▲ **By automating personal management functions:** More managers than ever are taking their calendars and personal planners and moving them onto computers. Although paper-based planners won't die completely, many managers are finding out that computers are much more powerful management tools than their unautomated counterparts. Managers also use computers to schedule meetings, track projects, analyze numbers, manage business contact information, conduct employee performance evaluations, and more.

However, before you run off and automate everything, keep this piece of information in mind: If your manual system is inefficient or ineffective, simply automating the system won't necessarily make your system perform any better. In fact, automating it can make your system perform worse than the manual version. When you automate, review the process in detail. Cut out any unnecessary steps and make sure that your system is optimized for the new, automated environment. The time you take now to improve your processes and functions will pay off when you automate.

But, just as information technology can help a business, it can also hinder it. Here are a few examples of the negative side of information technology:

▲ Widespread worker abuse of Internet access has reduced worker productivity by 10 to 15 percent. According to Forrester Research, 20 percent of employee time on the Internet at work doesn't involve their jobs.

▲ Hackers have sent periodic waves of computer viruses and malicious attacks through the business world, leaving billions of dollars of damage and lost productivity in their wake.

▲ E-mail messages can be unclear and confusing, forcing workers to waste time clarifying their intentions or covering themselves in case of problems.

▲ Employees are forced to wade through an ever-growing quantity of spam and junk e-mail messages.

▲ The slick, animated, and sound-laden computer-based full-color presentations so common today can take longer to prepare than the simple text and graphs that were prevalent a few years ago—especially if you're not technologically savvy.

So, you have to take the bad with the good. But don't take the bad lying down. You can maximize the positives of information technology while minimizing the negatives. You can do this by:

▲ **Staying current on the latest information innovations and news.** Although you don't need to become an expert on how to install a network server or configure your voice-mail system, you do need to become conversant in the technology behind your business systems.

▲ **Hiring experts.** Although you must have a general knowledge of information technology, plan to hire experts to advise you in the design and implementation of critical information technology-based systems.

▲ **Managing by walking around.** Make a habit of dropping in on employees—wherever they're located—and observe how they use your organization's information technology. Solicit their feedback and suggestions for improvement. Research and implement changes as soon as you discover the need.

One point is certain: You can't turn back the clock on technology. To keep up with the competition—and to beat it—you must keep pace with technology and adopt what can make your employees more productive, while improving products and services, customer service, and the bottom line. You really have no other choice.

15.2.1 Improving Efficiency and Productivity

The recent explosion of information technology accompanies the shift in American industry from old-line standards, such as steel mills and petroleum refineries to companies producing semiconductors, computers, and related products. The personal computer industry, which was still in its infancy two decades ago, has quickly grown into a market worth tens of billions of dollars in annual sales.

The idea that business people who best manage information have a competitive advantage in the marketplace seems obvious enough. The sooner you receive information, the sooner you can act on it. The more effectively you handle information, the easier you can access that information when and where you need it. The more efficiently you deal with information, the fewer expenses you incur for managing and maintaining your information.

Management often cites the preceding reasons, and others like them, as justification for spending obscenely huge amounts of corporate resources to buy computers, install e-mail and voice-mail systems, and train employees to use these new tools of the information age. But, have all these expenditures made your workers more productive? Unfortunately, for years, researchers found no evidence to prove that office automation resulted in measurable productivity gains—leading many to label the phenomenon the "productivity paradox."

Author Eliyahu Goldratt defined information as "the answer to a question." Many of today's information systems are great at providing data, but not so hot at providing information (at least within this definition). A manager should first spend a lot of time identifying the "questions" that need an answer. Who needs the answer (customer, supplier, employee, management), how fast do they need the answer (real-time, one minute, one hour, one day), and how frequently do they need the answer (daily, weekly, monthly)? When this becomes clear, you have a rational basis to evaluate alternate technologies based on how well they meet the criteria needed for your "answers." Lots of technology seems to be designed to provide a real-time answer to a question that only needs to be asked once a month.

Information technology—planned and implemented wisely—can improve an organization's efficiency and productivity. More recent studies are beginning to show a relationship between the implementation of information technology and increased productivity. Examples like the following bear out this relationship:

▲ By using information technology to provide employees with real-time information about orders and scheduling that cuts through the traditional walls within the organization, M.A. Hanna, a manufacturer of polymers, reduced its working capital needs by one-third to achieve the same measure of sales. Impressive as this reduction is, Martin D. Walker, CEO of M.A. Hanna, is convinced that his firm can further reduce its working capital by an equal amount simply by communicating with suppliers and customers through computer networks.

▲ At Weirton Steel Corporation—based in Weirton, West Virginia—the company uses only 12 people to run the hot mill that once required 150 people to operate, all because of the technology installed in the production line.

Although evidence is beginning to swing toward productivity gains, studies indicate that merely installing computers and other information technology doesn't automatically lead to gains in employee efficiency. As a manager, you must take the time to improve your work processes before you automate them. If you don't, office automation can actually lead to decreases in employee efficiency and productivity. Instead of the usual lousy results that you get from your manual, unautomated system, you end up with something new: garbage at the speed of light. Don't let your organization make the same mistake!

15.2.2 Getting the Most Out of Information Technology

The personal computer began revolutionizing business a decade ago, shifting the power of computing away from huge mainframes and onto the desks of individual users. Now, computer networks are bringing about a new revolution in business. Although the personal computer is a self-sufficient island of information, when you link these islands together in a network, individual computers have the added benefit of sharing with every computer on the network. Here are the benefits to networking:

▲ **Networks improve communication:** Computer networks allow anyone in an organization to communicate with anyone else quickly and easily. With the click of a button, you can send messages to individuals or groups of employees. You can send replies just as easily. Furthermore, employees on computer networks can access financial, marketing, and product information to do their jobs from throughout the organization.

▲ **Networks save time and money:** In business, time is money. The faster you can get something done, the more tasks you can complete during the course of your business day. Computer e-mail allows you to create messages, memos, and other internal communications, to attach work files, and then to transmit them instantaneously to as many coworkers as you want. And these coworkers can be located across the hall or around the world.

▲ **Networks improve market vision:** Information communicated via computer networks is, by nature, timely and direct. In the old world of business communication, many layers of employees filtered, modified, and slowed the information as it traveled from one part of the organization to another. With direct communication over networks, no one filters, modifies, or slows the original message. What you see is what you get. The sooner you get the information that you need and the higher its quality, the better your market vision.

FOR EXAMPLE

Surfing the Intranet

The big addition in business is the *Intranet*. With few exceptions, America's largest corporations, including Federal Express, AT&T, Levi Strauss, and Ford Motor Company, have built internal versions of the Internet *within* their organizations. For example, employees at DreamWorks SKG, the entertainment conglomerate created by Steven Spielberg, Jeffrey Katzenberg, and David Geffen, use their company's Intranet to produce films and to take care of production details such as tracking animation objects, coordinating scenes, and checking the daily status of projects.

Intranets take the basic tools of the Internet—Web servers, browsers, and Web pages—and bring them inside the organization. Intranets are designed to be accessible strictly by employees and aren't available to outside Internet users. For companies that have already made the investment in Web hardware and software, they're an inexpensive and powerful way to pull together an organization's computers—and its employees.

Not only are Intranets revolutionizing the development of computer networks within organizations, but they're also democratizing them. Where most company computer networks are the sole province of a small staff of computer systems administrators and programmers, Intranets allow novices and experts alike to create Web pages. At Federal Express, for example, employees created many of the company's Web pages.

15.2.3 Using Technology to Support Teamwork

According to a *Fortune* magazine article, the three dominant forces shaping twenty-first-century organizations are the following:

▲ A high-involvement workplace with self-managed teams and other devices for empowering employees.

▲ A new emphasis on managing business processes rather than functional departments.

▲ The evolution of information technology to the point where knowledge, accountability, and results can be distributed rapidly anywhere in the organization.

The integrating ingredient of these three dominant forces is information. Information technology and the way information is handled are increasingly becoming the keys to an organization's success.

But information can be tricky to manage. According to Peter Drucker in *Management: Tasks, Responsibilities, Practices,* "Information activities present a special organizational problem. Unlike most other result-producing activities, they are not concerned with one stage of the process but with the entire process itself. This means that they have to be both centralized and decentralized."[2] Fortunately, information technology has overcome this challenge.

In a team environment, process management information moves precisely to where the team needs it, unfiltered by a hierarchy. Raw numbers go straight to those who need them in their jobs because frontline workers, such as salespeople and machinists, have been trained in how to use that information. By letting information flow wherever the team needs it, a horizontal self-managed company isn't only possible, it's also inevitable. Information technology-enabled team support systems include e-mail, computer conferencing, and videoconferencing that coordinate geographically, as well as across time zones, more easily than ever before. The development and use of computer software to support teams also is growing. An example is the expanding body of software called **groupware**. Groupware consists of computer programs specifically designed to support collaborative work groups and processes.

As organizations make better use of information technology, they don't need middle managers as often to make decisions. The result? The number of management levels and the number of managers can be dramatically reduced. Jobs, careers, and knowledge shift constantly. Typical management career paths are eliminated, and workers advance by learning more skills to be of greater value to the organization.

Those managers who remain need to take on new skills and attitudes to be more of a coach, supporter, and facilitator to the frontline employees. Supervisors and managers no longer have the luxury of spending time trying to control the organization—instead, they change it. Their job is to seek out new customers at the same time as they respond to the latest needs of their established customers. Managers still have considerable authority, but instead of commanding workers, their job is to inspire workers.

SELF-CHECK

1. How can information technology positively impact a business?
2. How can information technology negatively impact a business?
3. What are the three dominant forces shaping organizations today?
4. What is an Intranet and how do companies use them?

15.3 Making Room for a New Kind of Employee

As mentioned at the beginning of this chapter, a new kind of employee is out there—the virtual employee. Exactly what is meant by virtual employee? A **virtual employee** is someone who regularly works at a location other than the brick-and-mortar office that houses a company's business operations. Virtual employees join employees who have accepted (and often clamored for) a variety of alternative working arrangements, including alternate work schedules and flexible work schedules, to name two.

Managing people who aren't physically located near you can be particularly challenging, and you must approach it differently than managing employees who work in the same physical location. Perhaps your employees are located at a different facility or even in a different state (remote employees), or maybe they're telecommuting. Regardless of the reason for the separation, these new distance working relationships make it harder for managers to identify and acknowledge desired behavior and performance. Managers must be more systematic and intentional in determining whether or not employees are fully performing their duties to the same standard as employees housed in a regular office.

With the proliferation of personal computers—both at work and home— and with the availability of fast and inexpensive modems and communications software, the question no longer is, can your employees telecommute? The question is, will you *let* your employees telecommute? The problem that telecommuting presents to managers isn't a problem of technology, but a problem of managing people who aren't working in the office.

In the old-style office, most (if not all) of your employees are just footsteps away from your desk. If you need their help, you can pop your head into their offices to make assignments. Oh, they're away for a break? No problem, you can hunt them down in the breakroom and personally realign their priorities.

Telecommuting has changed all that. When your employees work away from the office, they're no longer at your immediate beck and call. Communication often becomes a long series of voice-mail messages, e-mails, and faxes. Face-to-face communication decreases, as does the feeling of connectedness to the organization.

Regardless, the benefits of telecommuting are many. According to studies, employee productivity can be increased by 30 percent, less time is lost as people sit in cars or mass transit to and from work, workers are more satisfied with their jobs, and society (and our lungs) benefit from fewer cars on the road every rush hour.

Although the idea of virtual employees seems to be catching on in the world of business, you, as a manager, need to consider some pros and cons when your thoughts turn to the idea of telecommuting.

Following are some advantages to telecommuting:

▲ Depending on the job, employees can set their own schedules.

▲ Employees can spend more time with customers.

▲ Employees can conduct more work because everything is there where they need it.

▲ You can save money by downsizing your facilities.

▲ Costs of electricity, water, and other overhead are reduced.

▲ Employee morale is enhanced.

Some of the disadvantages to telecommuting include:

▲ Monitoring employee performance is more difficult.

▲ Scheduling meetings can be problematic.

▲ You may have to pay to set up your employees with the equipment that they need to telecommute.

▲ Employees can lose their feelings of being connected to the organization.

▲ Managers must be more organized in making assignments.

FOR EXAMPLE

Nontraditional Work Arrangements Grow in Popularity

According to a U.S. Labor Department report, approximately one in ten employees today has an alternative work arrangement. These alternative work arrangements can range from something as simple as allowing employees to start and end their workdays at times that are outside the standard, all the way to allowing employees to work full time from their homes.

15.3.1 Preparing to Get Virtual

Is your company ready for virtual employees? Are you ready for virtual employees? The following is a quick-and-easy checklist for determining if your organization is ready.

❑ Your company has established work standards to measure employee performance.

❑ Prospective virtual employees have the equipment they need to properly perform their work off-site.

❑ The work can be performed off-site.

❑ The work can be completed without ongoing interaction with other employees.

❑ Prospective virtual employees have demonstrated that they can work effectively without day-to-day supervision.

❑ Supervisors can manage and monitor employees by their results rather than by direct observation.

❑ Employee worksites have been examined to ensure that they're adequately equipped.

Do most of the boxes have check marks in them, or are most of them empty? If you have several check marks, then your organization is ready, willing, and able to initiate alternative work arrangements with your employees. If you have several empty boxes, you have your work cut out for you before you can reasonably expect virtual employees to be a viable option in your organization.

15.3.2 Understanding Changes to the Office Culture

One of the key concerns for managers when an increasing number of employees become virtual employees is this: What happens to the company's culture (and employee performance) as more and more workers work outside the office? A company's culture, after all, is mostly defined by the day-to-day interactions of employees. For employees who work outside the mainstream of these interactions—and who are therefore not a part of them—they'll probably have no grounding in an organization's culture, and little attachment to other employees, or to the organization's values and goals.

The result is employees who are potentially less productive than regular employees, with lowered teamwork and loyalty. The good news is that you can take a number of steps to help your virtual workers plug into your company's culture, become team players, and gain a stake in the organization's goals in the process.

Consider the following ideas:

▲ Schedule regular meetings that everyone attends—in person, or by conference call or Internet chatroom. Discuss current company events and set aside time for the group to tackle and solve at least one pressing organizational issue, or more, if time permits.

▲ Create communication vehicles that everyone can be a part of. Author Bob Nelson worked with a limousine company that gives all its drivers a monthly cassette tape, which updates them on current company goings on, policies, questions and answers, and more, to listen to in their cars.

▲ Hire a facilitator and schedule periodic team-building sessions with all your employees—virtual and nonvirtual—to build working relationships and trust among employees.

▲ Initiate regular, inexpensive group events that draw out your virtual employees to mingle and get to know regular employees—and each other. Going out to lunch on the company's tab, volunteering to help a local charity, having a potluck at a local park: the possibilities are endless.

But, as a manager, you need to consider something else: Virtual employees face issues that regular employees don't. These issues include:

▲ Virtual employees may find that they're not fairly compensated by their employers for the home resources (office space, computers, electricity, furniture, and so forth) that they contribute to the job.

▲ Virtual employees may feel that their personal privacy is being violated if management efforts are too intrusive. Remember that your employee is not available 24/7. Respect his or her work hours and use work phone numbers and e-mail addresses—not home—when you want to communicate.

▲ Regular employees may become jealous of virtual employees' "special privileges."

▲ Family duties may intrude on work duties much more often for employees who work at home than for employees who work in traditional offices.

These issues don't mean that you just forget about offering your employees alternative working arrangements. Keep these issues in mind and work to ensure that they don't cause problems for your virtual—or regular—employees.

SELF-CHECK

1. A(n) _____ _____ is someone who regularly works at a location other than the brick-and-mortar office that houses a company's business operations.

2. How can you determine if your organization is ready for **virtual employees?**

15.4 Managing from a Distance

With the changing nature of work today, managers have to adapt to new circumstances for managing employees. How can managers keep up with an employee's performance when an employee may not even have physical contact with his or her manager for weeks or months at a time? Some of the answers may lie in a return to the basics of human interaction.

▲ **Make time for people.** Nothing beats face time when it comes to building trusting relationships. Managing is a people job—you need to take time for people. Not only when taking time is convenient, but also whenever employees are available and need to meet.

▲ **Increase communication as you increase distance.** The greater the distance from one's manager, the greater the effort both parties have to make to keep in touch. And, although some employees want to be as autonomous as possible—minimizing their day-to-day contact with you—other employees quickly feel neglected or ignored if you don't make a routine effort to communicate with them. Increase communication by sending regular updates and/or scheduling meetings and visits more frequently. Also, encourage your employees to contact you, and go out of your way to provide the same types of communication meetings with each work shift or arrange meetings that overlap work shifts or duplicate awards for each facility.

▲ **Use technology.** Don't let technology use you. Use technology as a communication vehicle, and not just to distribute data: Promote the exchange of information and encourage questions. Have problem discussion boards or host chatrooms with managers or executives or create an electronic bulletin board to capture the exchange of individual employee and team progress, problems, and solutions.

Today's managers have to work harder to manage distant employees. If you value strong working relationships and clear communication, you need to seek out others to be sure adequate communication is taking place.

15.4.1 Managing Different Shifts

The challenge of managing today's employees is made harder by the fact that the nature of work is changing so dramatically and so quickly. More and more employers have supplemented traditional work schedules with more flexible scheduling options. Managing employees who work differing shifts is a special challenge for today's managers.

Following are some strategies to consider when making the most of working with shift employees.

▲ **Take time to orient shift employees.** All employees need to get their bearings, and shift employees can often be at a disadvantage because they're working outside a company's normal hours. Be sure to let them know what they can expect about the job and the organization, including work policies you expect them to abide by, and make sure they meet all other individuals that they need to know or work with.

▲ **Give them the resources to be productive.** Giving them the resources can range from the right equipment to do the job, to access to others when they have a question. Other resources also include the right training, especially about company products and services, internal procedures, and administrative requirements.

▲ **Make an ongoing effort to communicate.** The importance of communication is almost a cliché, but you can't underestimate its value. Many employees prefer to silently suffer through poor directions rather than risk seeming slow to grasp an assignment—and possibly being labeled as difficult to work with. So, you need to constantly check with shift employees to see if they have any questions or need any help. Make every personal interaction count to find out how the employees are doing and how you can better help them. Some managers schedule meetings at shift change to get two shifts at once.

▲ **Appreciate employees for the job they do.** If the employee is only at work outside the standard work schedule, their need to be recognized for their hard work and accomplishments is as great as any other employee, although their circumstances make it more inconvenient to thank them. Fortunately, a little appreciation can go a long way. Take the time to find out what may motivate extra performance and then deliver such rewards when you receive the desired performance.

▲ **Treat shift employees the way you want them to act.** If you want shift employees to have a long-term perspective, treat them with a long-term perspective. Make them feel a part of the team. Treating shift employees with courtesy and professionalism can help establish your reputation as a desirable employer to work for and thus serve as a draw for additional talent when you need it.

Managing employees who work different shifts is a very achievable task if done with the right effort at the right time. Make the time and the effort and you'll reap the benefits.

15.4.2 Recognizing Employees from a Distance

Every employee needs to be recognized by his or her manager for a job well done. Here are some steps you can take to make sure your virtual employees feel just as appreciated as your regular employees.

▲ Ask virtual team members to keep the leader and other team members apprised of their accomplishments, because they can't be seen as readily.

▲ Keep a recognition log of remote team members so that they don't fall into the cracks—a particularly important consideration for mixed teams (with both traditional and virtual team members).

▲ Make sure that virtual team members are appropriately included in recognition programs (by passing around recognition item catalogs, and by ensuring that remote employees are kept fully in the loop).

▲ Provide some "treat" for virtual team members who can't join in face-to-face socials and celebrations.

▲ Keep a list of recognition activities and items that are appropriate for a mobile workforce, such as thank-you cards and gift certificates.

▲ Become more aware of the recognition capabilities of e-mail, such as virtual flowers or greeting cards.

▲ Involve executives in recognition activities by way of conference calls.

▲ Make a point of employing a variety of team recognition items (such as coffee mugs, T-shirts, jackets, and so forth) when rewarding members of virtual teams. Such items help remind them of the team membership.

SELF-CHECK

1. How can you use technology as a vehicle for employee communication?
2. Name two techniques you can effectively use to manage employees from different shifts.
3. Name two ways you can recognize employees who telecommute.

SUMMARY

Technology has changed the way we live and the way we work. From computers to e-mails to the Internet, technology provides us a way to get information and to communicate more quickly than ever before. In this chapter, you have learned how to use technology to gain a competitive advantage in the marketplace. You have assessed how technology can be used to improve efficiency and productivity. You have evaluated the steps needed in writing a technology plan. You have also assessed a new kind of employee, the virtual employee, and what extra steps you must take when managing virtual employees.

KEY TERMS

Groupware	Computer programs specifically designed to support collaborative work groups and processes.
Technology plan	A plan for acquiring and deploying information technology.
Virtual employee	Someone who regularly works at a location other than the brick-and-mortar office that houses a company's business operations.

ASSESS YOUR UNDERSTANDING

Go to www.wiley.com/college/nelson to evaluate your knowledge of using technology.
Measure your learning by comparing pre-test and post-test results.

Summary Questions

1. Taking manual processes and making them _____ improves productivity.
2. Computer _____ allow anyone in the organization to communicate with anyone else quickly and easily.
3. In developing a technology plan, the first step is to screen and select the vendors. True or false?
4. Computer programs specifically designed to support collaborative work groups and processes are called:
   (a) shareware.
   (b) groupware.
   (c) Intranets.
   (d) networking.
5. Internet abuse is widespread among workers. True or false?
6. Company recognition programs should also include _____ employees.
7. Managers should:
   (a) increase communication as the distance increases.
   (b) decrease communication as the distance increases.
   (c) keep the same level of communication with all employees.
   (d) communicate only through e-mail
8. As organizations make better use of information technology, they don't need _____ _____ as often to make decisions.

Applying This Chapter

1. You own a car dealership. What types of information would you want on a regular basis so you could remain competitive with the other dealerships?
2. You are the manager in a call center for a sales company. You are unhappy with the technology you have, as you cannot get the information you need. What types of issues would you consider before developing a technology plan?

3. You work in a consulting firm. Two consultants have asked you if they can work from home. What advantages and disadvantages do you see in this?

4. You work at a marketing firm and you have some employees who work part time, some that work full time, and some that telecommute. What steps do you take to manage the different shifts?

YOU TRY IT

Technology Plan

You are the manager in a call center for a new company. You do not have any technology available to you. What steps would you take to create a technology plan?

Virtual Employees

You are the manager of a large consulting firm. You have three employees who decide to telecommute rather than come in to the office to work. How do you change your management style to accommodate these employees? What things do you do differently?

16

COMMON MANAGEMENT TRENDS AND MISTAKES
Learning from Others

Starting Point

Go to www.wiley.com/college/nelson to assess your knowledge of common management trends and mistakes.
Determine where you need to concentrate your effort.

What You'll Learn in This Chapter

▲ Common management trends including returning to basics, and flattening an organization
▲ How companies are trying to become learning organizations
▲ How Six Sigma affects the bottom line
▲ Mistakes often made by managers including neglecting employees, failing to accept change, and failing to delegate

After Studying This Chapter, You'll Be Able To

▲ Assess management trends
▲ Avoid common management mistakes

INTRODUCTION

There have been many recent management trends that are designed to improve employee morale, raise the bottom line, or make the workplace into a shining model of productivity and efficiency. Unfortunately, although some of these trends have a lasting impact on the organizations that employ them, others are fads. However, in this lesson you will assess management trends that have staying power.

In addition to management trends, you will examine common management mistakes. By avoiding these mistakes you will be able to avoid pitfalls along the path to building a fantastic team.

16.1 Management Trends

Every management trend has its own unique lifecycle. Most of these trends have value, but unfortunately, few organizations actually make the fundamental process and structural changes required to truly transform the organization. After the program's novelty wears off—often only a few short weeks or months after its introduction—the organization goes back to business as usual. But even the most fleeting management fad has the potential to leave some benefit and positive change within organizations. The secret is to look beyond the "fads" (some of them do have value) and see their place in the never-ending search for success.

We will consider some of the latest management trends, including the return to basics, the learning organization, the flat organization, open-book management, and Six Sigma.

16.1.1 Going Back to Management 101

The new world of business has created all kinds of new opportunities in every industry. But, at the same time, the new world of business has created all kinds of new obstacles for managers and for their employees. How, for example, can managers best direct an employee when he or she may not even have physical contact with the manager for weeks or months at a time?

Answers to questions like this one have led many managers to step out of today's fast-paced, business-at-the-speed-of-light environment and return to the basics of managing others. These basics include:

▲ **Making time for people.** You have no substitute for face time when it comes to building trusting relationships. Managing is a people job, and you need to take time for people.

▲ **Increasing communication as you increase distance.** The greater the distance from one's manager, the greater the effort both parties have to make to keep in touch. But, you can't depend on your employees to take the initiative to keep in touch; you have to keep the channels of communication flowing freely and often.

▲ **Using technology (and not letting it use you).** Technology is obviously great—and it's here to stay—but don't let technology use you. Instead, use technology as a way to leverage your communication with employees, not just as a way to distribute data.

In the new world of business, managers have to work harder to be available to others. If you value strong working relationships and clear communication, you need to return to basics: spending more and higher-quality time with your employees rather than less.

16.1.2 Creating a Learning Organization

A **learning organization** is an organization skilled at creating, acquiring, and transferring knowledge and at modifying its original assumptions, purposes, and behaviors to reflect new knowledge and insights. Ever since Peter Senge's groundbreaking book *The Fifth Discipline*[1] was published more than a decade ago, the question of how to create and lead organizations in which continuous learning occurs has been at the top of many managers' lists of management techniques to consider.

The problem with the old, command-and-control way of doing business is that your organization is built on the premise that the world is predictable. If you can just build a model that is large and complex enough, you can anticipate any eventuality, right? This particular view has a problem: The world isn't predictable. The global world of business is chaotic—what's true today surely is washed away tomorrow as the next wave of change hits. The only constant in today's organizations is change.

The learning organization is designed around the assumption that organizations are going through rapid change and that managers should expect the unexpected. Indeed, managers who work for learning organizations welcome unexpected events that occur within an organization because they consider them to be opportunities, not problems. Instead of static organizations that are strictly hierarchical, learning organizations are flexible. This structure makes managers able to lead change instead of merely reacting to change.

Exactly how do you go about designing a learning organization? Several characteristics are particularly important as you consider turning your organization into a learning organization. The more of each characteristic that your organization exhibits, the closer it is to being a learning organization—one that thrives in times of rapid change.

▲ **Encourage objectivity.** It's inevitable that there are managers who make organizational decisions simply to please someone with power, influence, or an incredible ego. Managers make such subjective decisions, not through a reasoned consideration of the facts, but through emotion. As a manager, you must encourage objectivity in your employees and coworkers and practice objectivity in your own decision making.

▲ **Seek openness.** For an organization to grow, employees have to be willing to tell each other the truth. To make this openness possible, you must create safe environments for your employees to say what is on their minds and to tell you any bad news without fear of retribution. Drive fear out of the organization if you want to build a learning organization.

▲ **Facilitate teamwork.** Deploying employee teams is a very important part in the development of learning organizations. You'd be hard-pressed to name any learning organization that hasn't implemented teams widely throughout the organization. When an organization relies on individuals to respond to changes, one or two individuals may pick up the torch and run with it; however, when an organization relies on teams to respond to change, many more employees are mobilized much more quickly. And this can mean the difference between life and death in the ever-changing global business environment.

▲ **Create useful tools.** Managers in learning organizations need the tools that enable employees to quickly and easily obtain the information that they need to do their jobs. Computer networks, for example, have to be set up with access for all employees, and they have to provide the kinds of financial and other data that decision makers need. The best tools are those that get the right information to the right people at the right time.

▲ **Consider the behavior you're rewarding.** Remember the phrase "you get what you reward." What actions are you rewarding, and what behaviors are you getting in return? If you want to build a learning organization, reward the behaviors that help you create a learning organization. Stop rewarding behaviors that are inconsistent, such as subjectivity and individualism. The sooner you accomplish this mission, the better.

16.1.3 Making a Flat Organization

A **flat organization** is one that has few levels of management. The growing trend exists today to flatten organizations by removing layers of management. When businesses flatten their organizations, they widen the span of control (the number of people directly supervised) of the remaining managers, and push authority farther down the chain of command.

Fewer layers of management, and increased decision making and participation by nonmanagement workers, typically results in the following:

▲ Less bureaucracy

▲ Faster decision making

▲ Organizations that are nimbler and better able to react to changing markets

▲ Increased reliance on self-managing teams

▲ More empowered and happier employees

▲ More satisfied and happier customers

▲ Reduced costs

▲ Increased profits

Instead of focusing on the structures and maintenance of hierarchy—departments, titles, and such—flat organizations:

▲ Focus on their customers, both internal and external

▲ Encourage all employees to become directly responsive to customer needs

▲ Promote decision making by those employees closer to customers

▲ Eliminate bottlenecks in the flow of information

▲ Support open sharing of information

As more and more organizations turn away from the restrictive culture that is a natural byproduct of hierarchy, the flat organization is becoming an obvious choice—and the best opportunity to capitalize on fast-changing markets.

16.1.4 Unlocking Open-Book Management

Until recently, the vast majority of companies treated accounting data—information on sales, revenues, expenses, profits, and more—as secrets that only managers and executives viewed and worked with. Managers used this approach as a way to solidify power at the top of organizations, and to prevent regular workers from providing their own input and suggesting improvements to vital financial processes.

This practice changed when, in a bid to make his company more competitive in a very tough market, Jack Stack, president and CEO of Springfield, Missouri–based engine rebuilder SRC Corporation, provided his employees with company financial reports, unit performance numbers, and production statistics. Thus, he empowered workers by teaching them how to understand and use the reports to help the company make more money—and inviting them to do just that.

The company did. SRC succeeded beyond all expectations, and the open-book management revolution was launched. Today, thousands of businesses are empowering their own employees, and reaping the benefits in the process, by providing them with financial data and then encouraging them to use the data to improve their jobs and their organizations.

According to Stack, three factors must be in place for open-book management to work:

▲ Everyone must know the rules and expectations.

▲ Everyone must have enough information to make the moves and keep score.

▲ Everyone must have a stake in the outcome.

Stack—and the business he created to teach the principles of open-book management, Great Game of Business (a subsidiary of SRC Holdings, Inc.)—has introduced countless business people to the concept of open-book management through books, seminars, videos, and a Web site. Throughout, the emphasis is on creating an environment where employees have major input in the following processes:

▲ Creating the financials
▲ Setting up incentive programs that reward their progress
▲ Discovering how to forecast financial results
▲ Communicating progress to each other
▲ Sharing the rewards of good performance

Do the ends justify the means? Clearly they do. Davenport, Iowa–based staffing company Mid-States Technical saw its sales rise 79 percent in the two years after implementing an open-book management program, while profits tripled. Perhaps managers aren't the only ones who can understand and use company financial data to improve the bottom line after all.

16.1.5 Understanding Six Sigma

If any area of management is particularly subject to trends, it's the area of quality. One of the latest in a long line of such trends is **Six Sigma**, a quality-improvement system originated by electronics manufacturer Motorola some two decades ago, which has gained thousands of dedicated adherents over the past few years.

What exactly is Six Sigma, and what's so special about it?

Six Sigma is a rigorous training program that gives managers highly specialized measurement and statistical analysis tools. They use the tools to reduce defects in products and processes, while cutting business costs and improving customer satisfaction. Key corporate fans include such business giants as General Electric (GE), Citicorp, Johnson & Johnson, and Allied Signal.

Six key concepts are at the heart of Six Sigma:

▲ **Critical to quality.** The attributes most important to the customer.
▲ **Defect.** Failing to deliver what the customer wants.
▲ **Process capability.** What your process can deliver.
▲ **Variation.** What the customer sees and feels.
▲ **Stable operations.** Ensuring consistent, predictable processes to improve what the customer sees and feels.
▲ **Design for Six Sigma.** Designing to meet customer needs and process capability.

According to Dr. Mikel Harry, originator of this management trend, application of Six Sigma principles can result in the following:

▲ Improved customer satisfaction
▲ Reduced cycle times

FOR EXAMPLE

Six Sigma

The numbers seem to support Six Sigma. According to GE, the company saved $500 million in a recent year through the application of Six Sigma. In fact, GE is so excited about Six Sigma that it says in its corporate Six Sigma brochure, "Six Sigma has changed the DNA of GE—it is now the way we work—in everything we do and in every product we design."

▲ Increased productivity

▲ Improved capacity and output

▲ Reduced total defects

▲ Increased product reliability

▲ Decreased work-in-progress (WIP)

▲ Improved process flow

SELF-CHECK

1. What makes an organization a **learning organization**?
2. A **flat organization** has many levels of management. True or false?
3. Managing is a people job, and you must be able to make time for people. True or false?
4. **Six Sigma** reduces business costs. True or false?

16.2 Common Management Mistakes

Managers make mistakes. Mistakes are nature's way of showing you that you're learning. This chapter lists ten traps that new and experienced managers alike can fall victim to.

16.2.1 Not Making the Transition from Worker to Manager

When you're a worker, you have a job and you do it. Although your job likely requires you to join a team or to work closely with other employees, you're ultimately responsible only for yourself. Did you attain your goals? Did you get to work on time? Was your work done correctly? When you become a manager, everything changes. Suddenly, you are responsible for the results of a group of people, not just for yourself. Did your employees attain their goals? Are your employees highly motivated? Did your employees do their work correctly?

Becoming a manager requires the development of a whole new set of business skills—people skills. Some of the most talented employees from a technical perspective become the worst managers because they fail to make the transition from worker to manager.

16.2.2 Not Setting Clear Goals and Expectations

Effective performance starts with clear goals. If you don't set goals with your employees, your organization often has no direction and your employees have few challenges. Therefore, your employees have little motivation to do anything but show up for work and collect their paychecks. Your employees' goals begin with a vision of where they want to be in the future. Meet with your employees to develop realistic, attainable goals that guide them in their efforts to achieve the organization's vision. Don't leave your employees in the dark. Help them to help you, and your organization, by setting goals and then by working with them to achieve those goals.

16.2.3 Failing to Delegate

Some surveys rank "inability to delegate" as the number one reason that managers fail. Despite the ongoing efforts of many managers to prove otherwise, you can't do everything by yourself. And even if you could, doing everything by yourself isn't the most effective use of your time or talent as a manager. You may very well be the best statistician in the world, but when you become the manager of a team of statisticians, your job changes. Your job is no longer to perform statistical analyses, but to manage and develop a group of employees.

When you delegate work to employees, you multiply the amount of work that you can do. A project that seems overwhelming on the surface is suddenly quite manageable when you divide it up among twelve different employees. Furthermore, when you delegate work to employees, you also create opportunities to develop their work and leadership skills. Whenever you take on a new assignment or work on an ongoing job, ask yourself whether one of your employees can do it instead (and if the answer is yes, then delegate it!).

16.2.4 Failing to Communicate

In many organizations, most employees don't have a clue about what's going on. Information is power, and some managers use information—in particular, the control of information—to ensure that they're the most knowledgeable and therefore the most valuable individuals in an organization. Some managers shy away from social situations and naturally avoid communicating with their employees—especially when the communication is negative in some way. Others are just too busy. They simply don't make efforts to communicate information to their employees on an ongoing basis, letting other, more pressing business take precedence by selectively "forgetting" to tell their employees.

The health of today's organizations—especially during times of change—depends on the widespread dissemination of information throughout an organization and the communication that enables this dissemination to happen. Employees must be empowered with information so that they can make the best decisions at the lowest possible level in the organization, quickly and without the approval of higher-ups.

16.2.5 Not Making Time for Employees

To some of your employees, you're a resource. To others, you're a trusted associate. Still others may consider you to be a teacher or mentor, whereas others see you as a coach or parent. However your employees view you, they have one thing in common: All your employees need your time and guidance during the course of their careers. Managing is a people job—you need to make time for people. Some workers may need your time more than others. You must assess your employees' individual needs and address them.

Although some of your employees may be highly experienced and require little supervision, others may need almost constant attention when they're new to a job or task. When an employee needs to talk, make sure that you're available. Put your work aside for a moment, ignore your phone, and give your employee your undivided attention. Not only do you show your employees that they are important, but when you focus on them, you also hear what they have to say.

16.2.6 Not Recognizing Employee Achievements

In these days of constant change, downsizing, and increased worker uncertainty, finding ways to recognize your employees for the good work that they do is more important than ever. The biggest misconception is that managers don't want to recognize employees. Most managers do agree that rewarding employees is important; they just aren't sure how to do so and don't take the time or effort to recognize their employees.

Although raises, bonuses, and promotions have decreased in many organizations as primary motivators, you can take many steps that take little time to accomplish, are easy to implement, and cost little or no money. In fact, the most effective reward—personal and written recognition from one's manager—doesn't cost anything. Don't be so busy that you can't take a minute or two to recognize your employees' achievements. Your employees' morale, performance, and loyalty will surely improve as a result.

16.2.7 Failing to Learn

Most managers are accustomed to success, and they initially learned a lot to make that success happen. Many were plucked from the ranks of workers and

> ### FOR EXAMPLE
>
> #### Management Is a People Job
>
> If you don't like working with people, then you will not like being a manager and you won't be very good at it either. Unfortunately, some people are very good workers and are then promoted to management positions despite the fact that they do not have adequate people skills.
>
> Rich Moore, a senior organization development specialist at AAIM Management Association, says that being an effective manager is all about people. "Good managers get their work done through, with and by developing their people." Managers who are most effective "know their people's talents, and take the time to get to know their people."[2]

promoted into positions as managers for this very reason. Oftentimes, however, they only want things done their way.

Successful managers find the best ways to get tasks done and accomplish their goals, and then they develop processes and policies to institutionalize these effective approaches to doing business. This method is great as long as the organization's business environment doesn't change. However, when the business environment does change, if the manager doesn't adjust—that is, doesn't *learn*—the organization suffers as a result.

This situation can be particularly difficult for a manager who has found success by doing business a certain way. The model of manager as an unchanging rock that stands up to the storm is no longer valid. Today, managers have to be ready to change the way they do business as their environments change around them. They have to constantly learn, experiment, and try new methods.

16.2.8 Resisting Change

The business world changes and you need to concentrate your efforts on taking actions that make a positive difference in your business life. You must discover how to adapt to change and use it to your advantage rather than fight it.

Instead of reacting to changes after the fact, proactively anticipate the changes that are coming your way and make plans to address them before they hit your organization. Ignoring the need to change doesn't make that need go away. The best managers are positive and forward-looking.

16.2.9 Going for the Quick Fix over the Lasting Solution

Every manager loves to solve problems and fix the parts of his or her organization that are broken. The constant challenge of the new and unexpected (and that second-floor, corner office) attracts many people to management in the first place. Unfortunately, in their zeal to fix problems quickly, many managers neglect to take the time necessary to seek out long-term solutions to the problems of their organizations.

Instead of diagnosing cancer and performing major surgery, many managers perform merely what amounts to sticking on a Band-Aid. Although the job isn't as fun as being a firefighter, you have to look at the entire system and find the cause if you really want to solve a problem. After you find the cause of the problem, you can develop real solutions that have lasting effects. Anything less isn't really solving the problem; you're merely treating the symptoms.

16.2.10 Striking a Balance

Yes, business is serious business. Because of the gravity of the responsibilities that managers carry on their shoulders, you must maintain a sense of humor and foster an environment that is fun, both for you and your employees.

When managers retire, they usually aren't remembered for the fantastic job that they did in creating department budgets or disciplining employees. Instead, people remember that someone who didn't take work so seriously and remembered how to have fun brightened their days or made their work more tolerable.

However, you should strike a balance. You want to be friendly to those you manage, but don't feel the need to be their friend. It is very difficult to discipline and coach someone and remain objective about their performance when you're partying with them, shopping with them, or taking fishing trips with them and forming a bond. Employees will take advantage of such a relationship, and you will never be able to regain control over the situation again.

SELF-CHECK

1. You should be your employees' friend. True or false?

2. Managers who do things the way they have always done them can play a role in a learning organization. True or false?

3. Some surveys rank which of the following as the number one reason why managers fail?

   (a) Too friendly with employees

   (b) Failure to set goals

   (c) Failure to delegate

   (d) Failure to communicate

4. Most managers do agree that rewarding employees is important. True or false?

SUMMARY

It is not easy to be a manager. Managers have pressure from their superiors, their staff, and their customers. Businesses are always searching for a management system that can be implemented for success. In this chapter, you evaluated recent management trends including learning organizations, flat organizations, Six Sigma, and returning to the basics. You also assessed and evaluated common management mistakes and how to avoid them.

KEY TERMS

Flat organization	An organization that has few layers of management.
Learning organization	An organization skilled at creating, acquiring, and transferring knowledge and at modifying its original assumptions, purposes, and behaviors to reflect new knowledge and insights.
Six Sigma	A quality-improvement system.

ASSESS YOUR UNDERSTANDING

Go to www.wiley.com/college/nelson to evaluate your knowledge of common management trends and mistakes.
Measure your learning by comparing pre-test and post-test results.

Summary Questions

1. A learning organization is better equipped to cope with _____ than other organizations.
2. Employees are provided with financial data in organizations that:
   (a) are learning organizations.
   (b) use Six Sigma.
   (c) are trying to return to basics.
   (d) use open-book management.
3. Designing a product around the customer is one of the hallmarks of:
   (a) organizations returning to the basics.
   (b) Six Sigma.
   (c) open-book management.
   (d) learning organizations.
4. When managers delegate, they _____ the amount of work they can do.
5. Information is power and some managers do not provide employees with enough information. True or false?
6. The only meaningful way to recognize an employee is through monetary compensation such as a raise. True or false?

Applying This Chapter

1. What similarities exist among flat organizations, learning organizations, Six Sigma, and a return to the basics? What conclusions can you draw from these similarities?
2. You are the president of a medium-sized insurance company that has twenty managers. You have recently learned, from employee surveys, that 70 percent of the employees are dissatisfied with their managers. You decide to hold a management training session. What types of things do you try to teach the managers?

Creating a Budget

You decide to quit your job and begin an Internet start-up company. You receive funding from investors and you can hire forty employees. What type of management structure do you implement and why?

Management Mistakes

You are in charge of a hospital, and you need to hire new managers for the marketing department. Write down a list of qualities you look for and why.

ENDNOTES

Chapter 1

1. Equal Employment Opportunity Commission, "Two Florida Restaurants to Pay $525,000 for Sexual Harassment of Teenagers," January 8, 2004, http://www.eeoc.gov/press/1-8-04-b.html.

Chapter 2

1. Bob Nelson, *1001 Ways to Reward Employees* (New York: Workman, 1994).
2. *Ibid.*
3. *Ibid.*
4. Harvey Seifter and Peter Economy, *Leadership Ensemble: Lessons in Collaborative Management from the World's Only Conductorless Orchestra* (New York: Owl Books, 2002).

Chapter 3

1. Jim Collins, *Good to Great* (New York: HarperBusiness, 2001), 81.
2. *Ibid.*
3. Yale University School of Medicine, "Mission Statement and School Wide Objectives," http://info.med.yale.edu/education/edu/mission.html.
4. David Goodman, "One Step at a Time," *Inc.*, August 1995, http://www.inc.com/magazine/19950801/2367.html.

Chapter 4

1. J. W. Marriott, Jr., and Kathi Ann Brown, *The Spirit to Serve Marriott's Way* (New York: HarperCollins, 1997).

2. Dawn Sagario, "Pssst! Have You Heard That Gossip May Be Damaging to the Workplace?" *Louisville Courier-Journal,* sec. 2D, October 31, 2005.

3. William B. Werther and Keith Davis, *Human Resources and Personnel Management* (New York: McGraw-Hill, 1993).

Chapter 5

1. Jim Collins, *Good to Great* (New York: HarperBusiness, 2001), 81.

2. Bill Clifton, "Disciplining Employees Can Be Tricky," *Macon Telegraph,* September 20, 2006, http://www.macon.com/mld/macon/business/15560009.htm.

Chapter 6

1. Darrell Zahorsky, "Fighting Employee Turnover Costs," http://sbinformation.about.com/od/hiringfiring/a/reduceturnover.htm.

2. Richard Nelson Bolles, *What Color Is Your Parachute? 2007: A Practical Manual for Job-Hunters and Career-Changers* (Berkeley, CA: Ten Speed Press, 2006).

3. Richard D. Walton, "Job Offer Pulled After Degree Revelation," *Indianapolis Star,* September 9, 2006.

Chapter 7

1. Robert B. Nelson and Peter Economy, *Better Business Meetings* (New York: McGraw-Hill, 1995).

2. Gerald Tomlinson, *Speaker's Treasury of Sports Anecdotes, Stories, and Humor* (New York: MJF Books, 1997).

Chapter 8

1. Bob Nelson, *1001 Ways to Reward Employees* (New York: Workman, 1994).

2. *Ibid.*

3. Peter G. Drucker, *Management: Tasks, Responsibilities, Practices* (New York: Collins, 1993).

4. Bob Nelson, *1001 Ways to Reward Employees* (New York: Workman, 1994).

Chapter 9

1. Bob Nelson, *1001 Ways to Reward Employees* (New York: Workman, 1994).

Chapter 10

1. CNN Money, "June Job Cuts Highest Since Jan. '04," July 6, 2005, http://money.cnn.com/2005/07/06/news/economy/job_cuts/.

Chapter 11

1. Marilyn Davidson and Cary L. Cooper, *Shattering the Glass Ceiling: The Woman Manager* (Thousand Oaks, CA: Sage Publications, 1992); Ann M. Morrison, Randall P. White, and Ellen Van Velsor, *Breaking the Glass Ceiling: Can Women Reach the Top of America's Largest Corporations?* (Boston: Addison Wesley, 1994).

Chapter 12

1. Dan Ackman, "While Enron Burned, Wall Street Fiddled," *Forbes,* November 29, 2001, http://www.forbes.com/2001/11/29/1129topnews.html.
2. Ethics Resource Center, "Code Construction and Content," http://www.ethics.org/resources/code-construction.asp.
3. Associated Press, "Ann Baskins Resigns from HP Amid Spying Scandal," September 28, 2006.

Chapter 13

1. Jack Miller, John R. Walker, and Karen Drummond, *Supervision in the Hospitality Industry,* 4th ed. (Hoboken, NJ: Wiley, 2007).
2. Readers desiring additional information about the labor union UNITE HERE are referred to the union's Web site: www.unitehere.org.
3. Patrick Howington, "Norton to Pay Fired Nurse: Union Organizer Won Final Appeal," *Louisville Courier Journal,* sec. 1D, February 8, 2006.

Chapter 14

1. Wikipedia, "Sarbanes-Oxley Act," http://en.wikipedia.org/wiki/Sarbanes-Oxley_Act (accessed 10/3/06).

Chapter 15

1. Kathleen Allen and Jon Weisner, *The eBusiness Technology Kit for Dummies* (Chicago: IDG Books, 2001).

2. Peter G. Drucker, *Management: Tasks, Responsibilities, Practices* (New York: Collins, 1993).

Chapter 16

1. Peter Senge, *The Fifth Discipline: The Art and Practice of the Learning Organization* (New York: Currency, 1994).
2. Kate Lorenz, "Six Tips to Make You a Better Manager," http://www.ccfbest.org/management/sixtipstomakeyoubetter.htm (accessed 10/7/06).

GLOSSARY

80-20 rule Eighty percent of the wealth of most countries is held by only 20 percent of the population; the rule has been applied to many other fields since its discovery.

Accounting equation Equation that states an organization's assets are equal to its liabilities plus its owners' equity. The accounting equation is commonly expressed as Assets = Liabilities + Owners' Equity.

Achievement-oriented culture A culture that confers status according to what people have done.

Actions Individual activities performed between milestones.

Active listening A concentrated effort to focus and to fully understand the message that is being sent.

Ad hoc groups Informal teams of employees assembled to solve a problem with only those who are most likely to contribute invited.

AFL-CIO The AFL-CIO is the most prominent multiunion association; it was formed when the American Federation of Labor and the Congress of Industrial Organizations merged.

Age Discrimination in Employment Act of 1967 This law prohibits discrimination against individuals who are forty years of age and older.

Americans with Disabilities Act (ADA) A federal law that makes it illegal to discriminate against a job applicant or a current employee who is disabled.

Arbitrator Two parties who have a disagreement may elect to enter into arbitration; the arbitrator's decision in the matter is final.

Ascription-oriented culture A culture that rewards people for their position, connections, and even birth.

Assets Anything of value, primarily financial and economic resources, that a company owns.

Balance sheet   Report that illustrates the value of a company's assets, liabilities, and owners' equity—the company's financial position on a specific date.

Bona fide occupational qualification (BFOQ)   A legal loophole, or a legal defense, to job discrimination based on sex, national origin, or religion. There is no BFOQ defense to racial discrimination.

Budget   An itemized forecast of an individual's or company's income and expenses expected for some period in the future.

Cash substitute   Gift with a monetary value that can be redeemed such as gift certificates.

Cash-flow statements   Financial statements that show the movement of cash in and out of a business.

Coaches   Individuals who guide, discuss, and encourage others on their journey.

Code of ethics   A document that explicitly states your organization's ethical expectations.

Collaborative leadership   A leadership style where everyone works together; the leader shares leadership with the employees of the organization.

Collective bargaining agreement   An agreement or a contract that discloses the terms and conditions that shall apply to the union–management relationship within a particular operation.

Communication process   The method by which information is delivered from a sender to a receiver.

Communication systems   Provide formal and informal methods for moving information throughout an organization.

Contingency theory   Belief that there is no single best way to manage others. Under this theory, each manager should use the techniques best suited to each individual situation and to the people involved.

Cost center   Department within a company that provides services to customers or employees that cost the company in terms of salaries, benefits, and equipment, without adding revenue directly to the bottom line.

Cost of goods sold   The cost to a business of purchasing merchandise or inventory that is intended for resale.

Critical path   The longest period of time associated with one task in a project. If it is not completed on time, then it will affect the rest of the project.

Culture   How a group of people or a distinct geographic region operates in terms of laws, mores, and customs.

Current assets   Assets that can be converted into cash within one year.

Current liabilities   Liabilities that are repaid within one year. Examples include accounts payable, notes payable, and accrued expenses.

Depreciation   The process of spreading the original cost of a piece of equipment across its entire useful lifetime.

Development   Teaching employees the kinds of long-term skills that they'll need in the future as they progress in their careers.

Disabled individual   The ADA describes a disabled individual as "any individual who has a physical or mental impairment that substantially limits one or more major life activity, has a record of such impairment, or is regarded as having such impairment."

Discipline   Actions taken with the purpose of correcting problems and improving performance.

Double-entry bookkeeping   Standard method of recording financial transactions that forms the basis of modern business accounting.

Downward communication   Information that flows down the chain of command to set policy, to provide information, and to influence others.

Employee grapevine   Informal communication that arises spontaneously from the social interaction of people in the organization.

Employee suggestion box   A common tool used to seek employee input where employees write suggestions or cost-saving ideas and drop them in a box. Management will later retrieve the suggestions submitted by employees and review them.

Employee turnover   The rate at which a company loses employees.

Empowerment   Transfer of power, responsibility, and authority from higher-level to lower-level employees.

Equal Employment Opportunity Commission (EEOC)   The EEOC is the U.S. government agency charged with overseeing Title VII of the 1964 Civil Rights Act and Title I of the ADA.

Equal Pay Act   The law requires businesses to pay equal wages for equal work without regard to the sex of the employee.

Ethics   Standards of beliefs and values that guide conduct, behavior, and activities.

Expenses   All the costs of doing business.

Financial statements   Reports that summarize the amounts of money contained within selected accounts or groups of accounts at a selected point or period of time.

Fixed asset   Anything a company owns that has a long life, such as furniture, computers, facilities, physical plants, that supports the operations of a business.

Flat organization   An organization that has few layers of management.

Flowcharts   Graphical representations of the sequential flow of projects.

Forecast   A prediction of the financial future of a company.

Formal communication methods   May be written or verbal; examples include memos, reports, employee suggestion boxes, newsletters, and meetings.

Formal teams   Teams chartered by an organization's management and tasked to achieve specific goals.

Gantt charts   Graphical representation of projects using bars, also known as bar charts.

Goal   The specific result of an effort to improve an organization in some way. Goals can be short-term or long-term and should align with the vision of the organization.

Goal statement   Clear directions for employees about what actions are needed for them to improve.

Grievance process   A process by which an employee will lodge a complaint against management, usually a result of a breach of some term or condition provided for in the collective bargaining agreement between management and the union.

Gross profit   Also known as gross margin; the amount of money a company makes minus the cost of goods sold.

Groupware   Computer programs specifically designed to support collaborative work groups and processes.

Headhunter   Someone who specializes in recruiting key employees away from one firm to place in a client's firm.

Horizontal organization   Organization with minimal levels of management.

Hostile work environment   An environment that is hostile can be created when management allows employees to tell off-color jokes, send off-color emails, or put up pictures or photos that someone could deem offensive.

Immigration Reform and Control Act   All workers hired after November 6, 1987, must provide proper documentation and complete the Form I-9 to prove that they have the legal right to work in the United States.

Income statement   Report that adds all the sources of a company's revenues and then subtracts all the sources of its expenses to determine its net income or net loss for a particular period of time.

Informal communication methods   May be written or verbal; examples include open-door policies, the employee grapevine, and MBWA.

Informal teams   Casual associations of employees that spontaneously develop within an organization's formal structure.

Integrity   Adherence to a moral code.

Knowledge power   Authority that comes from the special expertise and knowledge gained during one's career. Also comes from obtaining academic degrees or special training.

Layoffs   When the size of a workforce has to be reduced to external factors such as shrinking profits, duplication of positions resulting from a merger, or a shift in a company's strategy.

Leader   A person who has commanding authority or influence over others and inspires them toward goals.

Learning organization   An organization skilled at creating, acquiring, and transferring knowledge and at modifying its original assumptions, purposes, and behaviors to reflect new knowledge and insights.

Liabilities   Debts that the company owes to others outside the company such as other businesses, banks, and individuals.

Local union   Usually part of a larger, national organization, the local union provides local members, revenue, and the power of the entire union movement.

Long-term liabilities   Liabilities that are repaid in a period greater than one year. Examples include bonds payable and mortgages payable.

Management-by-walking-around (MBWA)   Managers exhibit this method of management when they leave their offices and engage employees one-on-one at their workstations.

Manager   A person who supervises others in an effort to complete tasks or accomplish goals.

Mediator   Two parties who have a disagreement may elect to enter into mediation. The mediator may make only recommendations; the mediator's decision is not final.

Mentor   An individual—usually higher up in the organization—who provides advice and helps guide your progress.

Mentors   Confidential advisers high up in the organization who develop and support employees. They are usually not in the employee's chain of command.

Mergers   When one company buys another one and the two companies form one new company.

Milestones   The checkpoints, events, and markers that show progress toward goals.

Multiunion association   When several national unions join together for a common cause. The AFL-CIO is an example of a multiunion association.

National Labor Relations Act (NLRA)   A law enacted in 1935 that gives employees the right to join labor organizations or unions free of employer interference.

National Labor Relations Board (NLRB)   A U.S. government agency created to enforce that employers abide by the NLRA.

National union   The national labor organization affiliated with the local union.

Negative feedback   Employee feedback that serves to correct behavior that is unacceptable and that does not conform to performance standards. It is essential that negative feedback focus on the employee's behavior rather than on the employee personally.

Net income   The cash a company has on hand after all bills are paid. This is also known as net loss or the bottom line.

Non-right-to-work state   A state that has not enacted right-to-work laws.

Office politics   The relationships that you develop with your coworkers—both up and down the chain of command—that allow you to get tasks done, to be informed about the latest goings-on in the business, and to form a personal network of business associates for support throughout your career.

Open-door policy   A company policy whereby the manager's door is always open to employees who may wish to voice a complaint or state an issue.

Operating expenses   All costs of doing business with the exception of the cost of goods sold. Examples of operating expenses include property and equipment leasing and salaries.

Organizational culture   A reflection of the way an organization operates and a reflection of an organization's core values.

Paid-in capital   The investment, usually paid in cash, that the owners make in a business.

Passive listening   Hearing but not processing the information being sent.

Performance improvement plan (PIP)   Plan designed to improve an employee's job performance. It consists of a goal statement, a schedule of attainment, and a listing of the required resources or training.

Performance standards   Measurements that management and employees agree to use in assessing performance.

Personal power   Authority that comes from within someone's character.

Position power   Authority that comes from rank or title in the organization.

Positive feedback   Employee feedback that seeks to boost morale and to reinforce positive behavior or actions.

Profit center   Department within a company that generates revenue above and beyond the costs of operation. An example of a profit center is the sales department.

Progressive discipline   Selecting the least severe step that results in improved behavior or purpose.

Punishment   Actions taken with the purpose of causing pain or embarrassment to someone in retribution for some perceived error.

Quality circles   Groups of employees who meet regularly to suggest ways to improve the organization.

Quid pro quo   Latin for "this for that."

Readily achievable   This term is associated with the ADA and generally refers to the adjustment of a task or a physical adjustment to the facility that is easily accomplished without great difficulty or expense.

Reasonable accommodation   Under the ADA, an individual who is disabled but otherwise qualified to perform the essential functions of a job may require a reasonable accommodation. This could be a minor adjustment of the individual's work schedule, an adjustment of policy or procedure, or the purchase of a device that would allow the individual to perform the duties of the job.

Relationship power   Authority that comes from close friendships with top executives, partners, or owners; people who owe you favors; and coworkers who provide privileged information and insights.

Relationships   How milestones and actions interact with one another.

Retained earnings   Earnings that are reinvested by a business and not paid out in dividends to shareholders.

Revenue   The value received by a company through the sale of goods, services, and other sources.

Right-to-work laws   Laws that have been enacted by individual states to prohibit unions from requiring that new employees join the union and pay union dues. Some state's right-to-work laws may not apply in this matter if a collective bargaining agreement requires new employees to join the union. States that have enacted these laws are known as right-to-work states.

Schedule   The time it takes to complete a task.

Self-managed teams   Teams that combine the attributes of both formal and informal teams. They usually contain from three to thirty employees whose job is to meet together to find solutions to common worker problems. They are also known as high-performance teams, cross-functional teams, or superteams.

Sexual harassment   A form of sex discrimination according to Title VII of the 1964 Civil Rights Act.

Show-and-tell   Coaching method developed by a post–World War II American industrial society desperate to quickly train new workers.

Six Sigma   A quality-improvement system.

SMART goals   Goals that have the following five characteristics: specific, measurable, attainable, relevant, and time-bound.

Stretch assignments   Assignments that are not too hard or too easy and require some learning.

Stretch goal   Goal that requires you to work beyond your normal level of performance.

Taft-Hartley Act   Also known as the Labor Management Relations Act. It is a law that prohibits unions from engaging in unfair labor practices.

Task power   Authority that comes from the job.

Teams   Two or more people who work together to achieve a common goal.

Technology plan   A plan for acquiring and deploying information technology.

Theory X   A traditional view of motivation that assumes that employees do not want to work and need to be driven to perform.

Theory Y   A view of motivation that assumes that employees actually enjoy work and derive a great deal of satisfaction from work when the proper conditions are met.

Title VII of the 1964 Civil Rights Act   A federal law that makes it illegal to discriminate against job applicants as well as current employees on the basis of sex, race, color, religion, or national origin.

Training   Teaching employees the short-term skills that they need to know to do their jobs.

Undue hardship   A legal defense to the ADA that is generally left up to the interpretation of the courts. It could refer to a financial hardship or a business hardship.

Unfair labor practices   Certain types of management conduct that might discourage employees from organizing or that might prevent workers from negotiating a union contract. NRLA outlines types of management conduct deemed illegal.

Union   An organization of workers formed for the purpose of advancing its members' interests with respect to their wages, benefits, work hours, and other conditions of employment.

Union authorization card   When a local union is attempting to organize a company, 30 percent of the company's employees must sign a union authorization card, which states that the employee agrees to have the union serve as his or her collective bargaining agent.

Upward communication   Information that flows from the lower levels of the organization to the higher levels. This often represents information initiated by employees who seek to inform or influence those who are higher in the corporate hierarchy.

Variance   The difference between budgeted performance and actual performance.

Vertical organization   Organization with many layers of managers and supervisors between top management and frontline workers.

Virtual employee   Someone who regularly works at a location other than the brick-and-mortar office that houses a company's business operations.

Vision   The overall purpose of the organization. A vision is a long-term, broad, strategic direction that will take several years to achieve. The vision is usually set by the CEO, president, or another top-level executive.

Zero-based budgeting   The process of building a budget from scratch.